Literary Glimpses of the Commonwealth

June, 1977

On behalf of the XI Commonwealth Games Foundation (1978), I am delighted to recognize the superb efforts of the Foundation's Education Committee in the production of an anthology of Commonwealth literature. It is the hope of all those involved in the Games that this collection of literary publications will make a substantial contribution to a better understanding of the various cultures throughout the Commonwealth and lead to a greater appreciation of the creative talents around the world.

Dr. Maury Van Vliet
President, XI Commonwealth Games

Senior Editor

James B. Bell
Faculty of Education
University of Alberta

Assistant Editors

Patriciamay McBlane
James MacInnis
Thomas Gee

Literary Glimpses of the Commonwealth

Wiley Publishers of Canada Limited
Toronto

Copyright © 1977 WILEY PUBLISHERS OF
CANADA LIMITED
All rights reserved
No part of this book may be reproduced by any means,
nor transmitted, nor translated into a machine language
without the written permission of the publisher.

Design and Illustrations: Tibor Kovalik
Cover: GLYPHICS
      Division of Kerrigan O'Grady Limited

Canadian Cataloguing in Publication Data

Bell, James B., 1921-
Literary glimpses of the Commonwealth

Bibliography: p.
Includes index.
ISBN   0-471-99861-3 (bd)   ISBN   0-471-99764-1 (pa)

1. English literature.   2. English literature -
Commonwealth of Nations authors.   I. Title.

PR1109.B44   820'.8   C77-001349-X

Printed and bound in Canada

10   9   8   7   6   5   4   3   2   1

Contents

Introduction

Preface

A Glimpse of Britain — 14

Traditional

T'Match	J. B. Priestley	17
The Benefit Concert	Rhys Davis	22
The Fight	Dylan Thomas	34
A Man's a Man for A' That	Robert Burns	39
Highland Graveyard	Kathleen Raine	41

Transitional

A Peasant	R. S. Thomas	43
Lancashire Winter	Tony Connor	44
Digging	Seamus Heaney	45

Contemporary

What Is Our Aim	Winston S. Churchill	47
Cynddylan on a Tractor	R. S. Thomas	51
To Reach the Sea	Monica Dickens	52
Man in Society	Charles P. Snow	56

Further reading — 63

A Glimpse of Canada — 64

Traditional

My Heart Soars	Chief Dan George	67
Grandfather	George Bowering	71

Mr. Portingale	Edward A. McCourt	73
Penny in the Dust	Ernest Buckler	75

Transitional
Lament for the Dorsets	Alfred Purdy	82
Depression Flashback 1937	A. F. Menzies	85
Death of an Outport	Al Pittman	89
The Canadian Personality	Bruce Hutchison	98

Contemporary
Good Old Uncle Albert	Farley Mowat	106
The Sensual City	Peter Desbarats	111
Day of the Butterfly	Alice Munro	117
The Broken Globe	Henry Kreisel	130

Further reading 145

A Glimpse of the West Indies 146

Traditional
Anancy	Andrew Salkey	149
Flame-Heart	Claude McKay	151
Pocomania	P. M. Sherlock	153

Transitional
Poem for My Country	Basil Clare McFarlane	155
Titus Hoyt, I.A.	V. S. Naipaul	157

Contemporary
Calypsonian	Samuel Selvon	173
Jamaican Fragment	A. L. Hendricks	189
Blackout	Roger Mais	192
Jamaica Market	Agnes Maxwell-Hall	198

Further reading ... 199

A Glimpse of Africa — 200

Traditional
Abiku	Wole Soyinka	203
The Rain Came	Grace A. Ogot	205
New Life in Kyerefaso	Efua Theodora Sutherland	217

Transitional
The Gentlemen of the Jungle	Jomo Kenyatta	226
Dead Men's Path	Chinua Achebe	230
And This, At Last	John Nagenda	235
Piano and Drums	G. Okara	243

Contemporary
Telephone Conversation	Wole Soyinka	245
Once upon a Time	Gabriel Okara	246
A Meditation on Man	Kenneth Kaunda	249

Further reading ... 255

A Glimpse of Asia — 256

Traditional
Gitanjali	Rabindranath Tagore	259
Miracle	Kartar Singh Duggal	263
The Cabuliwalah	Rabindranath Tagore	268

Transitional
Street Cries	Sarojini Naidu	277
The Letter	Dhumektu	278

Contemporary

Dasi The Bridegroom	R. K. Narayan	288
On Learning to Be an Indian	Santha Rama Rau	295

Further reading 307

A Glimpse of the South Pacific 308

Traditional
In the Beginning	Kenneth Bain	311
At the River	Patricia Grace	316
The Man Who Caught the Wind	Wolfe Fairbridge	322

Transitional
A Game of Cards	Witi Ihimaera	324
The Crookest Raffle Ever Run	Frank Hardy	332
In Youth Is Pleasure	Maurice Duggan	340
The Pink House in the Town	Albert Wendt	355
To the Woman Selling Handicrafts outside Burns Philp's Doors	Sano Malifa	362

Contemporary
Country Town	Judith Wright	364
The Sunbather	John Thompson	366
Seeing Life in a Suva Bus	Lema Low	367
Suva Market	Sam Simpson	369
Where Are These People Going?	Allain Jaria	371

Further reading 379
List of Selections 380
List of Authors 382

Acknowledgements

Kenneth Bain, "In The Beginning," from THE FRIENDLY ISLANDERS, by Kenneth Bain, published by Hodder & Stoughton Limited. Reprinted by permission of Hodder & Stoughton Limited.

George Bowering, "Grandfather," from SELECTED POEMS OF GEORGE BOWERING, by George Bowering, reprinted by permission of The Canadian Publishers, McClelland and Stewart Limited, Toronto.

Tony Connor, "Lancashire Winter," from LODGERS, by Tony Connor, © Oxford University Press 1965. Reprinted by permission of Oxford University Press.

Rhys Davis, "The Benefit Concert," published by Curtis Brown Ltd. Reprinted by permission of Curtis Brown Ltd.

Dhumektu, "The Letter." Reprinted by permission of Dr. Ghanshyam Gaurishanker Joshi.

K. S. Duggal, "Miracle." Reprinted by permission of Sahitya Akademi.

Maurice Duggan, "In Youth is Pleasure." Reprinted by permission of Barbara Duggan.

Chief Dan George, excerpt from MY HEART SOARS, published by Hancock. Reprinted by permission of Hancock House Publishers Ltd.

Patricia Grace, "At the River," and "A Way of Talking," from WAIARIKI, published by Longman Paul (Pacific Paperbacks). Reprinted by permission of Longman Group Limited.

Seamus Heaney, "Digging," from DEATH OF A NATURALIST, by Seamus Heaney, published by Faber and Faber Ltd. Reprinted by permission of Faber and Faber Ltd.

Bruce Hutchison, "The Canadian Personality," from CBC radio talk show, September 1, 1948. Reprinted by permission of Bruce Hutchison.

Allain Jaria, "Where Are These People Going?" from PAPUA NEW GUINEA WRITING, edited by Roger Boschman, Konedobu, Port Moresby: The Literature Bureau, Department of Information and Extension Services, March, 1972. Reprinted by permission of the author and the publisher.

Kenneth Kaunda, "A Meditation on a Man," from A HUMANIST IN AFRICA, by Kenneth Kaunda, edited by Morris, published by Longmans Green and Co. Ltd. Reprinted by permission of Longman Group Limited.

Jomo Kenyatta, "The Gentlemen of the Jungle," from FACING MOUNT KENYA, by Jomo Kenyatta, published by Martin Secker & Warburg Limited. Reprinted by permission of Martin Secker & Warburg Limited.

Lema Low, "Seeing Life in a Suva Bus." Reprinted by permission of the author and Pacific Publications.

E. A. McCourt, "Mr. Portingale," from SASKATCHEWAN, by E. A. McCourt, reprinted by permission of The Macmillan Company of Canada Limited.

Basil Clare McFarlane, "Poem for my Country," from YOU'D BETTER BELIEVE IT, edited by Paul Breman, published by Penguin Books Ltd. Baltimore, 1973 and published for the first time in JACOB AND THE ANGEL (1952). Reprinted by permission of Arthur J. Seymour.

Claude McKay, "Flame Heart," from SELECTED POEMS OF CLAUDE MCKAY, copyright 1953 by Twayne Publishers, Inc. Reprinted with the permission of Twayne Publishers, A Division of G. K. Hall & Co., Boston.

A. F. Menzies, "Depression Flashback 1937," from TWO DOLLARS PER YEAR, by A. F. Menzies. Reprinted by permission of A. F. Menzies.

Continued on page 384

Preface

The hosting of the XI Commonwealth Games provided a unique opportunity to develop enriched educational programs. It was the hope of the Commonwealth Games Education Committee that such programs would improve the readers' knowledge of people throughout the Commonwealth and, at the same time, increase their enjoyment of the Games.

In September, 1975, eight teachers from the Edmonton Public School System, the Edmonton Separate School System, and the Northern Alberta Institute of Technology were sponsored by the XI Commonwealth Games Foundation to collect material for a unit on Commonwealth literature. As chairman of the Education Committee I wish to thank the eight teachers for their co-operation: Irene Hargreaves (chairman), Jim MacInnis, Pritam Atwal, Gloria Burke, Brian Jones, Maggie Kortes, Shirley Paustian, and Hassan Rushdy.

In September, 1976, the collected materials were turned over to a newly formed committee who were asked to prepare an anthology of Commonwealth literature for use by students and the general public.

I wish to express my thanks to the Editing and Production Committee members: Senior Editor, James Bell, and Assistant Editors, Patriciamay McBlane, James MacInnis, and Thomas Gee.

Audrey Ackroyd, *Chairman*
Commonwealth Games Education Committee

For their assistance in the search for appropriate materials, I am grateful to Dr. J. Forrest and Dr. R. F. Ayling, Department of English, and to Dr. J. Oster, Department of Secondary Education, University of Alberta. I am grateful also to Mrs. Maggie Kortes, Strathcona Academic High School; Mrs. J. Coombs, Salisbury Composite High School; and James H. Bell, student at the University of Alberta, for contributing literary selections and providing background information. For reading and commenting on the African literature, I express thanks to Alfred Ihekoronye, graduate student at the University of Alberta.

I wish to express my indebtedness to those who supplied photos taken in different parts of the Commonwealth: Dr. L. D. Nelson (India), Robert Bell (Australia), Rorri and Patriciamay McBlane (Africa, West Indies, and the South Pacific Islands).

The collection of Commonwealth literature supplied to the Editing and Production Committee by the original committee of eight teachers provided guidelines for developing the anthology and served as a source for many of the selections that appear throughout *Literary Glimpses of the Commonwealth*. On behalf of the members of the Editing and Production Committee, I express sincere thanks to those teachers.

Finally I wish to express my thanks to the members of the Editing and Production Committee: Patriciamay McBlane, who spent many hours in research and writing and who was a constant source of energy and creativity; James MacInnis, who made many unselfish contributions and who served as liaison between the original committee of eight teachers and the Editing and Production Committee; Thomas Gee, who represented the interests of Alberta Education by reading and commenting on all literary materials being considered for inclusion in the anthology.

James B. Bell

Introduction

Literary Glimpses of the Commonwealth is an anthology of short stories, articles, and poetry developed under the auspices of the Commonwealth Games Foundation. The anthology was developed with five guiding purposes in mind:

(1) to provide readers with a glimpse of Commonwealth literature.
(2) to promote awareness of the traditions, customs, beliefs, and ways of life of the Commonwealth people.
(3) to reveal the relationship between the backgrounds and beliefs of people and the literature of a particular time.
(4) to provide a basis for comparing the customs, changes, and current thinking of people in different areas of the Commonwealth.
(5) to present the reader with literature that is both enjoyable and informative.

Literary Glimpses of the Commonwealth is divided into six major geographical divisions:

1. Britain
2. Canada
3. West Indies
4. Africa
5. Asia
6. South Pacific

Each of the six major divisions is divided into three subdivisions:

1. Traditional
2. Transitional
3. Contemporary

Introducing each major division is an overview of literary trends and developments which includes references to several major writers and their works. The subdivisions of literary content in each major area should enable readers to follow the patterns of change and to make comparisons within and beyond each country. A Further Reading list has been provided for those who wish to pursue the literature of any particular area.

It is hoped that the selections in *Literary Glimpses of the Commonwealth* will increase the reader's knowledge of and interest in the literature and the people of the Commonwealth countries.

The Editors

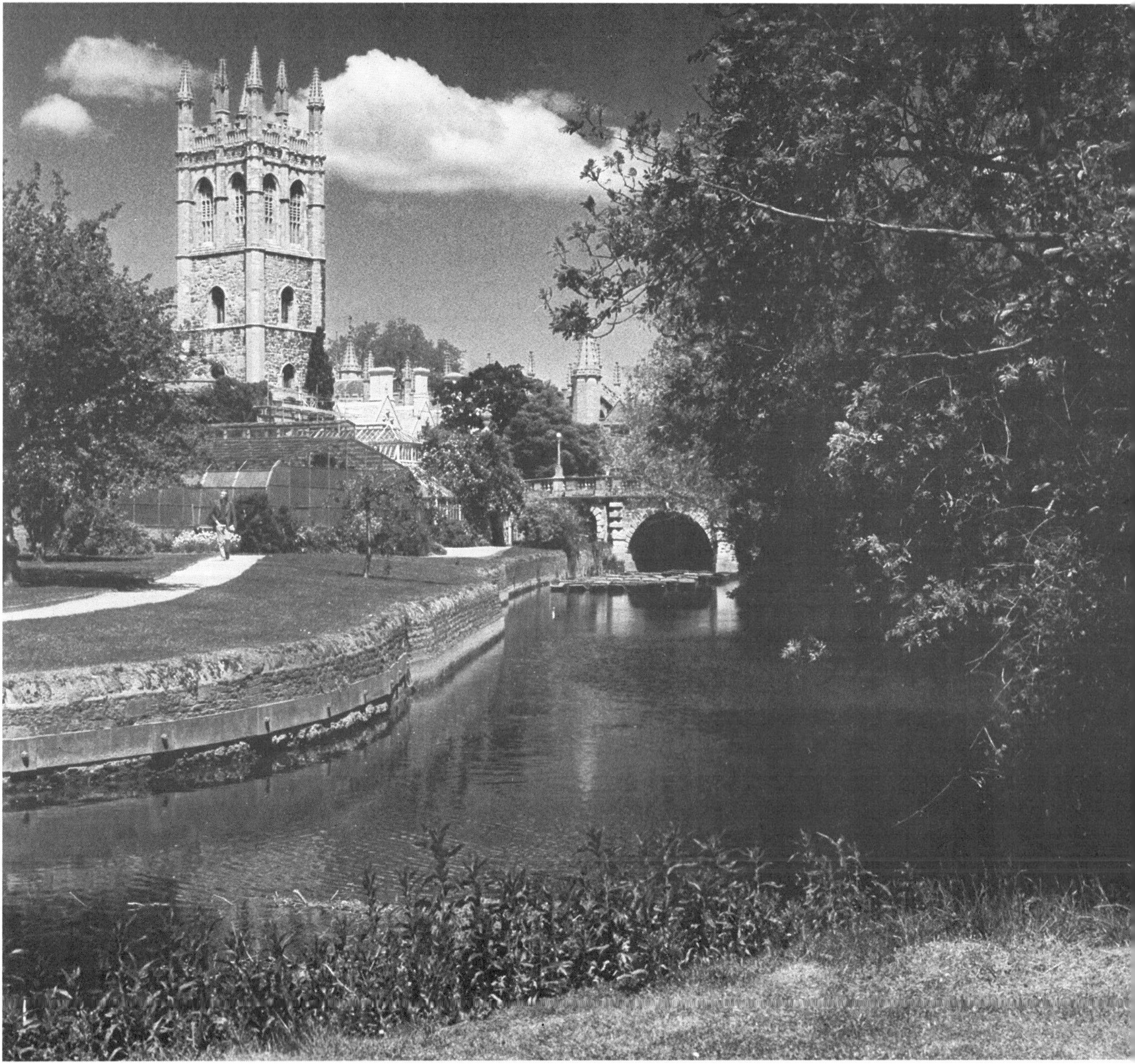

A Glimpse of Britain

sh Information Services

BRITAIN

Britain has a long literary history. A comprehensive survey of British literature would explore the periods now identified as Old English, Middle English, Renaissance, Elizabethan, Jacobean, Restoration, Eighteenth Century, Romantic, Victorian, and Early Twentieth Century.

Modern British writings evolved from social and educational changes of the 1930's. Led by Pound and Eliot and advanced by the critic F. R. Leavis, the new movement asserted that literature should be intelligent and commonsensical, and should illuminate moral or social values.

Dylan Thomas provided an alternative in a new romanticism that exalted life in bold and passionate terms. Scottish literature resurged under the leadership of Hugh MacDiarmid, Edwin Muir, Edwin Morgan, George MacKay Brown, Ian Crichton Smith and Ian Hamilton Finlay. Welsh literature established an identity, through modern thought and indigenous rhetoric, under such writers as T. Gwynn Jones, W. J. Gruffydd, Saunders Lewis, Waldo Williams, Gwynn Thomas, Tegla Davies, and Gwelyn Parry.

In the late 1960's and the 1970's, British literature has shown some tendency to become universal in content, to merge with other disciplines, and to utilize the various media. This is most clearly revealed in the literary writings and broadcasts of Sir Mortimer Wheeler, who integrates archeology and anthropology; Malcolm Muggeridge, who makes philosophy and religion an integral part of life; and Sir Kenneth Clark, who interlaces the arts and the humanities.

During the twentieth century, the emphasis in British literature has shifted from upper-class Victorian concerns about society to psychological and political concerns of the middle and lower classes. Despite attempts by some writers to re-establish old values and literary forms, the trend has been toward specialization and experimentation. Considerable ambiguity and fragmentation has resulted. The only compassions which appear to remain strong within literature are those concerning individuals – their personal life, problems, and solutions.

17   TRADITIONAL

Although the approaches employed by British writers keep changing, the attention given to "typically British" personal characteristics remains constant. "T'Match" reveals the British spirit in football season, while "What Is Our Aim?" represents British attitudes in times of stress. "The Benefit Concert" reflects the exuberant but inherently practical Welsh spirit, whereas "A Man's A Man for A' That" provides a bit of Scottish philosophy. Personalities are explored in "A Peasant" and "The Fight."

T'Match

J. B. Priestley

J. B. Priestley was born in Yorkshire, England, in 1894. After serving in the trenches in World War I, he attended Cambridge and moved into journalism, writing reviews and essays. Novels and then his popular plays followed. Priestley was also an exceptional radio personality; his powerful voice, with its touch of Yorkshire accent, made an interesting contrast with the usual BBC voices.

If you are in Bruddersford on Saturday afternoon, you go to t'match. I was in Bruddersford last Saturday afternoon, and quite automatically set out for t'match. As a matter of fact, there were several football matches, of varying codes, to choose from, and when I marched out of the hotel I had no idea at which particular match I should arrive. I simply followed a grey-green tide of cloth caps, which swept me down streets that grew meaner at every turn, past canals and gas works, until finally we came to the edge of the town. In that part of the West Riding, the Bruddersford district, there is not a very marked difference between town and country. When the last street brings you to a field, you are not aware of any dramatic contrast, simply because the field is not one of your pretty lush meadows, peeping and smiling, but is a dour slab of earth that keeps its grass as short as a wool merchant keeps his hair. This countryside, an angry spur or two of the Pennines, valleys full of black rock, does not regard the local handiwork of man with disfavour. If there must be men about, it says, then let them build factories and railway sidings and gas works: and so all these things seem to flower naturally out of that grim country. There are some parts of the West Riding that do suggest to you that industry is the supreme vandal, that the fair face of Nature has been blackened; but none of these fine thoughts come to you in the neighbourhood of Bruddersford, where it is obvious that town and country are all of a piece and the tall black chimneys seem inevitable if fantastic outcroppings of rock on those steep hillsides. Moors and mills, smoke and stone: I need say no more, because either you know or you don't. (And let us have no talk of the Brontës, who did not live in this particular district, who were not Yorkshire people, and who should be given a close season.) It is a country, whether it expresses itself in fields or streets, moors or mills, that puts man on his mettle. It defies him to live there, and so it has bred a special race that can live there, stocky men with short upper lips and jutting long chins, men who roll a little in their walk and carry their heads stiffly, twelve stone of combative instinct. If you have never seen any of these men, take a look at the Yorkshire cricket team next summer. Or come to t'match.

I paid my shilling and then discovered that it was a rugger match, presumably the Northern Union, the professional, thirteen-a-side, all scrimmage game. I was annoyed to find that the match had started. There were about ten thousand people there, including a thousand little boys all screaming in a special pen, but I was disappointed at the lack of enthusiasm. Nobody apart from the boys seemed to be paying much attention to the game. I noticed too that the players, though sufficiently well-built fellows, were not the giants I expected to find in Northern

Union rugger. It was all very disappointing. "Who are they?" I asked the man on my right. "Nay, ah doan't knaw," he replied. "It's t'lads' match. Under twenty-one." I began to see light. "This isn't the proper match, then?" I remarked to him. He stared at me: "This is nowt," he said, dispassionately. "T'match begins in a minute or two. Bruddersford versus Millsbury." This explained everything: the afternoon had not yet begun.

I cast a complacent eye on t'lads, who very soon cleared off to the sound of an odd cheer or two. Then there was silence. We all waited for Bruddersford and Millsbury to appear. I could feel a difference in the atmosphere. Then they came running on and we all shouted. Bruddersford were in red, and Millsbury were in blue. The forwards on both sides were colossal fellows, fit to engage in a scrum with a few elephants. A minute later t'match had begun. The Bruddersford back immediately performed several miracles, and we all applauded him and called him Joe. "That's right, Joe!" we told him, though I cannot say he took much notice of us. Then Number Eight of Millsbury, who looked like a bull in a blue jersey, grabbed hold of Joe a minute or two after he had rid himself of the ball and threw him several yards. Joe did not seem to care very much, but we were very angry. "Mark him, Joe!" we cried: "Watch Number Eight, Joe!" These tactics, however, could not prevent Bruddersford from scoring. Ginger began it. There is always a red-haired man in every team – or if there is not, then the manager does not know his business – and this one was a little wiry fellow, who played three-quarter. (At least, he was always waiting outside the scrums to pick up the ball, and frequently one saw him emerging from a heap of humanity, looking none the worse for having had about half a ton of bone and muscle piled on him.) Suddenly, then, Ginger went through like a little red shuttle, and we all shouted away as the ball sailed between the tall posts a minute afterwards. Then the game was lost for half an hour in a desert of scrimmages. There are too many scrimmages in this Northern Union game. I got tired of seeing those twelve men pushing and heaving.

The man on my left, whose cap was too small and moustache too large, was disgusted. "Nay, Bruddersford," he kept shouting in my ear, "lake foitball." He was angry, passionate, a man with shattered ideals. He had come to see foitball laked and it was not being laked properly. Bruddersford were winning, but being something more than a mere partisan, being a critic of the art, he was not comforted. "They're not passing, not passing," he told my left ear-drum. "Look at that! Nay, Bruddersford!" he would cry. He appeared to suspect that my left ear-drum entertained views of the game quite different from his own. Just before half-time, a man in front of me but some distance away, a man with a cap at the back of his head, a red muffler, and an angry unshaven face, above which he tilted a beer bottle from time to time, suddenly created a diversion. He was, I think, a Millsbury supporter, one of those men who have no money but yet contrive to follow their football teams wherever they go, and he must have entered into an argument with some Bruddersford enthusiast. I do not know what they were arguing about; all that I do know is that suddenly this man turned round to face us and cried at the top of his voice: "Neck and ankles, that's what I say. Neck and ankles." He seemed to be in a towering rage. Then he turned round again to look at the game, but a moment later, still more furious, he cried to us his mysterious slogan: "Neck and ankles!" Then he added, as an afterthought: "You can't get away from it. Neck and ankles!" He took another long pull at his bottle. "Ger aht wi' yer!" we said to him. This roused him to a frenzy, and putting down his bottle and raising his voice, he yelled: "B——y neck and ankles! B——y neck and b——y ankles!" And he glared defiance at some three thousand of us. "Put a sock in it!" we yelled back to him, and turned our attention to the game.

The two great events of the second half were Nosey's try and the sending off of Millsbury's Number Six. Nosey had done very little up to the time he received that pass, and I had come to the conclusion that he was not a man worth watching. He got the ball, however, well in his own half, and began to race at a prodigious speed down the touchline. Millsbury made a rush at him, but, after he had pushed away one or two and swerved from two or three more, he gathered speed and simply outran all the others, curving in exquisitely at the last to plant the ball neatly between the posts. You should have heard our shouts for Nosey. Even the critic on my left was impressed, and was very satirical at the expense of some unknown detractors of the great Nosey. "And then they say 'e can't run. Can't run!" he sneered. "Beat 'em all. Beat 'em all." He liked this phrase so much that he kept repeating it at odd moments during the next quarter of an hour.

But he was not so repetitious as the little man in the macintosh behind me. It was the sending off of Millsbury's Number Six that set him going. This Number Six had completely lost his temper and made a rush at a Bruddersford man when the ball was far away. The Bruddersford man contrived to throw him down, but the referee determined to make an example of this Number Six – for the play was becoming very rough – and so ordered him off the field. We gave him a boo or two as he left. But the little man in the macintosh was still indignant, and proclaimed, in those flat tones that are sometimes discovered in fanatics, that if he, Number Six, had tried it on with Mulligan (the burliest of all the Bruddersfords) Number Six would not have walked off but would have had to have been carried off. The game began again, and blues and reds charged one another and fell in heaps. "If 'e'd tried it on with Mulligan, 'e'd 'ave been carried off," came the flat voice from behind. Another try for Bruddersford: Ginger again! But Joe couldn't convert it. Hard lines, Joe! "If 'e'd tried it on with Mulligan" – yet once more. The blues are tiring now, and they are bad-tempered, but we are giving them as good as we get. Nearly time, now. Another try? No. Time. We give them a cheer. "If 'e'd tried it on with Mulligan" – but no, we must get out. The little man with the macintosh, we feel, will be the last spectator to leave the ground. He will tell the man who closes the gates what would have happened if Number Six had tried it on with Mulligan. The rest of us are out now, swarming down the narrow road, towards the trams. We are all talkative, amiable, relaxed: our combative instincts put to bed for a little space. We can turn a more gentle regard upon the gloomy hills, the factories and gas works and railway sidings; for the time being they do not trouble us; we have been to t'match.

The Benefit Concert

Rhys Davies

Rhys Davies was born in 1903 in the mining area of the Rhondda Valley, Wales, where he spent his first eighteen years. He moved to London and, later, to Paris and the Riviera, where he came under the influence of D.H. Lawrence and other young artists.

When it was decided to give a Benefit Concert for Jenkin, so that he could buy an artificial leg, no one thought this ordinary event would lead to such strife. But then no one suspected that the loss of his proper leg – it had gone gangrenous through neglect – had turned Jenkin into a megalomaniac. The affair not only divided the valley into bitterly opposed camps, but it nearly caused a strike in the colliery. Imperfect mankind is addicted to warfare, and a false leg is as good a pretext for liberating smouldering passions as greed for a continent.

To begin with, the colliery where Jenkin worked was obliged to give him compensation. He had neglected a wound received in the pit, refusing medical attention, and it was not until some weeks had passed that the leg showed signs of protest. His blood was in bad condition (as the camp later opposed to his side repeated in another sense), and the leg had always been a twitchy one. Though he could have fought his case in the courts, this wasn't done, Jenkin having a horror of courts ever since that time he was accused – unfairly, though none the less he had lost his case – of buying a concertina knowing it had been stolen. Well, now he had lost his leg too, and not a penny in the bank.
He was still convalescent in hospital when his butties in No. 2 pit decided to give

him a benefit. A committee was formed and the valley's Male Voice Choir, ever ready to open their melodious jaws, consented to give a selection from their repertoire, including their famous 'Italian Salad'. This in itself would bring in sufficient money to cover the cost of a leg and the committee decided that two shillings was enough for top-price tickets. They approached the deacons of Horeb chapel for use of this big building; Jenkin, off and on, had been a member of Horeb, though he never had more than one leg – and that the twitchy one – in religion. The deacons, not liking their chapel to be taken out of their hands by a lot of more-or-less outsiders, said they would organize the concert themselves. The rough-and-ready committee readily agreed to this, glad to be rid of the work, and the deacons of Horeb then went into owlish conclave.

'Well, Jenkin bach,' one of his butties said by the hospital bed, 'a present the boys will have ready for you after you come out. Tell that nurse by there to measure you and place the order for it at once.'

Jenkin showed one cunning eye from the bedclothes – for he liked his head covered in this draughty hospital. 'What's that, mun? Coffin is it to be, or a pair of home-made crutches?'

'Wind of it you've got already, I can see, Jenkin. Best quality artificial leg you're going to have, the same as Samson the Fireman's got.' Samson, before wearing it, had proudly exhibited his leg for a week in his front parlour window, so that all passers-by could see the marvel with its silver joints, leather flesh, and delicate screws.

'But what I'm going to do for work I don't know,' Jenkin grunted, however. 'A bacco-shop I'd like to open.'

'The pit's sure to give you a job on top; in the lamp-room p'raps. Don't you worry now. You get well for the concert. On the platform you'll have to sit, and if the leg comes in time it can stand on a table to show everybody.'

Jenkin got better quickly after this and was out of hospital long before the night of the concert. The leg had been ordered, but date of delivery was unknown. But what did become known was that the deacons of Horeb had taken full advantage of this excuse for a concert and done things on a grand scale. They had solicited the charity of four vocalists, and of these four they had persuaded – great triumph – Madame Sarah Watkins to come out of her retirement and shed her lustre gratis on the event.

As soon as it became known that she was to appear all tickets were sold, and as top price for these was five shillings (for the deacons were business men) a sum would be raised far beyond the leg's cost. Sarah Watkins's voice was legendary and a tale told by firesides. Still more enticing, her life had been scandalous, though, of course, her voice covered a multitude of sins. Wife to four men (at different times), a heavy drinker (of whisky), a constant attendant at courts (for debt), notorious for tantrums (in her heyday, that is), a wearer of flashy clothes (all belonging to the era of plush pineapples and whole cygnets on hats), she was an explosion of female vitality to be reckoned with. Though now in her retirement she lived on the coast twenty miles away, Madame Watkins was a native of the valley, where her father had been one of the pioneering miners. And she had always declared, with a heave of her bosom, that she loved dear little Twlldu. Proof of this was now evident. She hadn't sung in public for fifteen years.

'Your leg it is mun,' people said to Jenkin. 'Your leg it is that has given her a push out again.'

What the Jenkin crowd did not know was that it was the honeyed flattery, religious blandishments, and oratorical fervour of one of the Horeb deacons that had worked a spell on Sarah; he had called on her, claiming an acquaintance with her dead father. She didn't care a rap for Jenkin's leg. But, aged now, she had begun to turn an occasional eye to the religious things of her childhood; it was as well to be on the safe side. Yes, she would sing in a chapel, and not for money but for glory; and she had offered the deacon a whisky which he at once declined.

Her name on the posters, with *London, Milan,* and *Twlldu* printed under it, created a sensation. The other three soloists were of local origin too, though, of course, they were not to be compared. But, what with the Choir as well, a huge success was assured. The deacons of Horeb informed the hospital that the bill for Mr. Jenkin Morgans's leg was to be sent to them and same would be paid cash down. It was then that Jenkin began to wake up.

'How much the leg?' he mildly asked the hospital, going up there on crutches, and a sister who had taken a fancy to him promised to find out. 'Like to know I do how much money I am costing,' he explained, 'so that I can give thanks according.'

The day before the concert he called on one of the deacons in his home. 'Sit down by there,' said the deacon kindly, taking the crutches. 'Arrived has the leg in the hospital, then! Fixing it on you they'll be soon, no doubt – '

'Aye', Jenkin blew straight, full of high stomach already because of all the talk about him, 'but what I am wanting to know, Mr. Price-Harris, is what about the extra money?'

'Come now,' purred Mr. Price-Harris, 'your leg you've got.'

'My benefit this concert is,' said Jenkin ominously. 'The talk is that more than a hundred pounds is left over.'

The deacon pronounced, stern at once: 'Work has been done by the deacons of Horeb, and Madame Sarah Watkins is singing out of love for the old chapel of her dead father. On the glory of Horeb the extra money will be spent. Dilapidations there are and a new coat of paint needed, and – '

Jenkin heaved himself up and took his crutches. 'Good day to you now,' he said meekly.

Half an hour before the concert's starting time the chapel was packed with women in all their beads, brooches, and furs; the men in Sunday dark and starch. A wooden platform had been erected under the pulpit; a piano, chairs, and a table stood on it. In the gallery around the pipe organ back of the pulpit the Male Voice Choir assembled in good time. But no one needed to hurry. Madame Watkins wasn't nearly ready. A turmoil was going on in the vestry behind. The diva, like an old war-horse taken out again too near the smell and roar of cannon, was behaving as in her heyday. The deacons were flustered. They couldn't be expected to know that such as Madame Watkins never got the inspiration to sing before they had torn a lion or two into pieces.

The car that had been hired to fetch her was an old decrepit one driven by the fishmonger's lout of a son. And he had taken it into his head to kill two birds on this trip by collecting a small cask of herrings from the coast; it was already beside him on the front seat when he called for Madame Watkins, who brought with her a large suitcase. Secondly, no one had remembered to welcome her arrival with flowers. Thirdly, no one had thought she would need, for changing into a concert dress, somewhere more private than a vestry filled with coming and going persons connected with tonight's affair. The other three soloists, neatly attired but of whom she had never heard, waited open-mouthed.

'Get me screens then,' she bellowed, 'and a full-length mirror, and a dresser . . . Ach,' her body gave a great quake, 'I stink of fish. . . . Violet scent too,' she screamed after people who were running out into the street in search of screens and mirrors. A deacon's wife went into the chapel to scan the tiers of people for someone known to be a dressmaker. Everything was procured in due time, though the mirror was only one taken down from someone's parlour wall. The concert began an hour late.

Yet no one would have guessed the diva's fury when at last she mounted the platform and, amid thunderous applause, gave a superb bow. She advanced like an old ruined queen majestically unaware of new fashions and systems, giving an expert kick to the billowing train of her dragon-coloured but tattered dress. At sight of her, and perhaps the train, a little hiss of awe seemed to come from the goggling women in the audience. The smile issuing from the clumps of fat, the ravines and scarlet meadows of that face, was sweeter than Lucrezia Borgia's. An aigrette leapt from her auburn wig. There was a smell; a fierce perfume could be smelt even all round the gallery. It was as if Madame Watkins, a member of some mythical race, had risen through the parted earth amid the odours of flowers more gloriously ornate than were known above. The slim pianist seemed to wilt over the keys as he waited. Above, the Male Voice Choir, which had already sung an opening chorus, slunk back in abeyance.

'Fancy,' a woman upstairs reminded her companion of the diva's last appearance, 'any Council summonsing her for rates!'

'Oh, there's beautiful she is!' whispered the other in an aghast voice. 'And there's glad I am I've seen her. A pity for him, but if it wasn't for Jenkin's leg – '

But the erstwhile diva was launching into something out of *Carmen*. And soon it became plain that she had already given her performance. In her voice were gaping cracks through which wheezed a ghostly wind. No matter, no matter at all! For they were cracks in a temple of glorious style. A ruined temple far away in the mists of a lonely hill-top, but grander than anything of today.

Everyone felt sorry for the vocalist who followed Madame Watkins; she was still of coltish age, in full possession of her voice, very popular on the wireless, and spick and span to look at as a new button. Madame Watkins refused to give an encore, but she was down to sing 'Home Sweet Home' in the second half. Her exit had even more pomp than her entrance, and the applause (it was said afterwards) brought a rush of soot down the chimney of the house next door up to Horeb.

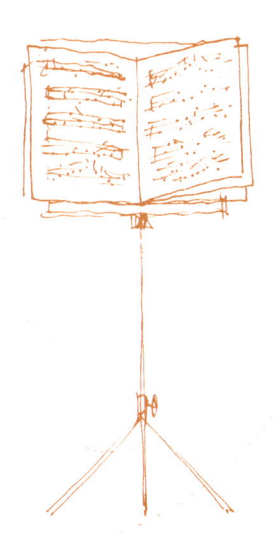

Intermission said the programme, and everyone knew what that meant. Jenkin was going to go on the platform and give a tidy public thanks for his artificial leg. Ah, there he was clumping up on his crutches and followed by a pit butty who carried the leg. Sympathetic applause greeted him. The butty stood shyly holding the limb upright on the table. Those who had missed seeing Fireman Samson's leg in his window now had their opportunity. Necks were craned and approval seemed plain in the air. It was not known then that Jenkin's crutches and his thick-set butty had forced their way to the platform through a wall of hostile deacons.

'No public speaker I am,' began Jenkin in a mild kind of way, 'and not yet properly back from my serious operation under chloroform. But things must be said. The leg by there is come, and very thankful I am for it – and will be more after it is fitted on and got used to my ways.' He ran a cunningly assessing eye round all the chapel and curbed the aggressive note that had crept into his voice – 'But a dispute has arose, sorry to say. For my benefit this concert was made, as my butties in No. 2 pit can prove, and over a hundred pounds is lying in the chapel safe after the leg is paid for. A little bacco-shop I want to open, and the hundred pounds just right! But no – the respected deacons of Horeb say "No". For paint and varnish on Horeb they want the money. Well, permission I am asking to say just now that it is not right!' He nodded his head ominously and finished: 'No more now, then, thanking you one and all, and Mrs. Watkins too, that don't know.' And nodding to the butty, who took the leg under his arm, he began to clump off the platform.

An awkward silence followed him. As far as could be judged, there were those who felt that a concert in a chapel was no place to make such a complaint. But also there were those who, ever ready to suspect ill conduct in high places, followed Jenkin's exit with an approving eye. Then up to the platform walked dignified Mr. J.T. Llewelyn, a deacon of long and admired standing. Sternly he said in the quiet:

'Respecting the matter mentioned just now by Mr. Jenkin Morgans, the benefit that was asked by his friends of the pit is now fulfilled. A leg first-class is given to him. Success of this concert was business of Horeb's deacons, and much interest in the needs of the chapel showed Madame Sarah Watkins when she remembered it was the chapel of her old father. . . . 'Now,' he continued with an air of austere dismissal and looking at a copy of the programme, 'back to the concert! The Choir will open again with a rendering of "Italian Salad". Ladies and gentlemen, "Italian Salad"!' And with this flourish, he swept away.

Whilst Madame Watkins in the vestry – the screens around her – was taking a secret drink of whisky out of a medicine bottle, Mr. J. T. Llewelyn thought it prudent to break into her privacy to mention the leg affair. Infuriated by (a) being caught red-handed drinking an intoxicant in a chapel vestry and (b) the deacon's tale of Jenkin's exhibition on the platform, the diva began to boil again. What, a surgical leg had been displayed on the platform, a few minutes after her appearance! Her sense of style and what was fitting in a concert containing her was outraged. Amateurs, she taunted, bah! The deacon, flustered by this unaccustomed kind of high-mindedness, continued to mumble explanations uselessly. 'Interested in surgical legs I am *not*,' she stormed. 'Ring up that curtain and let me get home.'

'No curtain there is here,' coughed the deacon. 'But a hot supper is waiting for you after the concert, along with the other soloists.'

'What! Who are these persons?' she blew. 'Do they sell cockles and mussels in the daytime?'

And she all but ran out to sing 'Home Sweet Home'. Yet once more the smile that greeted the loving applause was of a piercing and all-embracing sweetness which made few shiver. And the cracked voice gave an added poignancy to the old song. Not many eyes remained quite dry; for was not the celebrated Madame Watkins singing this song in her true birthplace! The concert was considered, and rightly, a red-letter one.

But the matter of Jenkin's leg did not remain there. Many of the men in No. 2 pit took umbrage at the chapel's treatment of their one-time fellow workman. These, in any case, were always critical of chapels and their power over social pleasures. Fierce arguments developed down under, and the ancient question of whether there is an Almighty or not was yet again raised by the opposed forces. Continued in public places on top, the dispute came to some physical combats on Saturday nights. The men's families began to take sides too, and many were the hostilities exchanged over back garden fences by wives pegging out washing, many were the schoolyard tumbles. After three weeks of this a meeting of miners was called in the Workmen's Hall. A strong faction of the men wanted to go on strike if Jenkin did not receive all profits from the concert.

The deacons of Horeb put on their armour. Some of them were officials in the colliery; others hoped to be. They gave an emphatic 'No' to this new blackmail by men whose infamy was worsened by their being of atheistic mind. They sat tight. Out in the valley a complication was added to the affair by Jenkin's decision not to use the artificial leg till his plea had been settled. He went about the place on his pathetic crutches, thus keeping quick his supporters' sympathy.

'No,' he would say, brave, 'all right I am. But set fire to me would that leg if I put it on. Just going down to the barber's I am to read the papers.' Too poor he was to buy them, of course.

Well, the Miners' Federation, getting wind of this unofficial strike, forbade it. Jenkin's supporters became more haughty at this. Hadn't the men of Twlldu downed tools once because an unpopular policeman was carrying on with a married woman! Wasn't this robbery of Jenkin worse? Glittering words were used at a second Workmen's Hall meeting. Finally it was decided to give the deacons another fortnight to hand over the money. There had been no signs of painters and plasterers starting work on the chapel.

'No,' said Bryn Stop Tap, an extremist, 'nor won't be. But fur coats will be seen on the deacons' wives and the ginger-beer van calling every day at their houses.'

Jenkin whimpered with devilish meekness: 'Stop the old fuss. Bad blood I am spreading.' But still he wouldn't use the leg, and his crutches and folded-up trousers were a standing reproach to everybody.

There was a nasty row in the fruit-shop one Friday evening. Mrs. Evans Fruit, a suspected supporter of the deacons' side, was accused by a pro-Jenkin woman of giving her nothing but damaged apples while only healthy ones had just gone into the basket of a customer also suspected to be on the other side. The shop was full of women.

'You get out of my shop, you liar!' shouted Mrs. Evans.

Pointing at the fruiterer, another customer said two words: 'She's Horeb!'

As is known from the conduct of mobs in the French Revolution, a single accusing cry can batter down a palace and spread riot like a tornado. Soon the shop was in a very untidy state and several old insulting scandals had been referred to in the course of the row. Mrs. Evans herself collapsed on to a basket of greengages, but by the time the policeman arrived order had been restored, and everybody felt twice as alive and that the world was worth living in after all. Jenkin heard of course of this battle on his behalf and once more called on the local reporter, trying to incite him to inform his paper. Meanwhile he had also laboured over a long letter to Madame Sarah Watkins, soliciting her opinion. But he received no reply.

'Oh, don't you bother about me,' he whined in the Bracchi ice-cream and coffee shop a week later, as everybody offered him a seat. 'Lean on my crutches I can. Only come in to pass the time I have. If I had my little bacco-shop busy enough I would be.' But it was strange that no one offered him a cigarette that day, or refreshment.

A third Workmen's Hall meeting was held long after the fortnight had gone. The deacons had made no sign. But neither were the painters and ladders about Horeb. At the meeting there was a lot of high talk and everybody had a consoling word for Jenkin; the feeling was that soon as a painter's brush was put to Horeb the bomb would burst. But it was strange that the meeting got on quite soon to New Year fixtures for the Twlldu Fifteen. Jenkin sat with his head on one side like a long-suffering bird.

'Waiting for the spring the deacons are,' someone told Jenkin outside the pub's closed door. 'Horeb will have a spring-cleaning on your money. Better ask for a job on top of the pits, Jenkin.'

One January day Jenkin, giving vent to loud abuse, threw a crutch through a window of Horeb. But all that resulted was a summons, and he had to pay cost of the window. Feeling for and against him was revived for a day or two. Yet it was only talk and argument. Then at the end of February Mrs. Roberts the Washing's house went up in flames. A poor widow who took in washing, her cottage wasn't insured. Though she was out during the fire, and didn't have to be rescued, a long sigh of sorrow for her went right through the valley. It was plain what would have to be done in her aid.

'Ask Madame Sarah Watkins to come again,' several persons said. A committee was formed.

The day after the fire Jenkin's wife took out a long cardboard box from under the bed. She was a quiet little woman who rarely put a foot into the valley's doings. But she had good eyesight and ears clear of wax. Jenkin looked at her sulkily. 'A bit tired I am,' she said, 'of idleness and sloth. Put on your leg, Jenkin, and go up to the pits for work.' On the promise of the Horeb money coming she had been lent cash by her sister. 'Come on, Jenkin bach,' she coaxed. And she said cleverly; 'Put not your trust in princes and the people of this earth.'

Jenkin lifted his head. A religious light shone in his eyes. 'Aye,' he said in grand contempt, 'the bull's eye you said there! Shall a man like me be lowered because all around him are low! Help me with my leg, Maria fach. The hospital said like this – '

In March men placed ladders against Horeb and, carrying cans of primrose paint, they went up them unmolested. But the concert for Mrs. Roberts the Washing's benefit was not held there. And Madame Sarah Watkins did not appear for this; she wrote saying that her retirement was now final unless her health improved. But she was in the papers again before March was out; a firm of licensed victuallers sued her for goods delivered. She told the Court that she had been too good-hearted and lately had sung everywhere for nothing, in aid of this and that charity. After the painters had done the windows of Horeb they varnished the solid pews inside.

The Fight

Dylan Thomas

Dylan Thomas (1914-53) was born in Swansea. He moved to London to do journalistic work, film script writing, and broadcasting. His works, especially his poetry, were powerful and had a strong influence on younger writers.

I was standing at the end of the lower playground and annoying Mr Samuels, who lived in the house just below the high railings. Mr Samuels complained once a week that boys from the school threw apples and stones and balls through his bedroom window. He sat in a deck chair in a small square of trim garden and tried to read the newspaper. I was only a few yards from home. I was staring him out. He pretended not to notice me, but I knew he knew I was standing there rudely and quietly. Every now and then he peeped at me from behind his newspaper, saw me still and serious and alone, with my eyes on his. As soon as he lost his temper I was going to go home. Already I was late for dinner. I had almost beaten him, the newspaper was trembling, he was breathing heavily, when a strange boy, whom I had not heard approach, pushed me down the bank.

I threw a stone at his face. He took off his spectacles, put them in his coat pocket, took off his coat, hung it neatly on the railings, and attacked. Turning round as we wrestled on the top of the bank, I saw that Mr Samuels had folded his newspaper on the deck chair and was standing up to watch us. It was a mistake to turn round. The strange boy rabbit-punched me twice. Mr.Samuels hopped with excitement as I fell against the railings. I was down in the dust, hot and scratched and biting, then up and dancing, and I butted the boy in the belly and we tumbled in a heap. I saw through a closing eye that his nose was bleeding. I hit his nose. He tore at my collar and spun me round by the hair.

'Come on! come on!' I heard Mr Samuels cry.

We both turned towards him. He was shaking his fists and dodging about in the garden. He stopped then, and coughed, and set his panama straight, and avoided our eyes, and turned his back and walked slowly to the deck chair.

We both threw gravel at him.

'I'll give him "Come on!" ' the boy said, as we ran along the playground away from the shouts of Mr Samuels and down the steps on to the hill.

We walked home together. I admired his bloody nose. He said that my eye was like a poached egg, only black.

'I've never seen such a lot of blood,' I said.

He said I had the best black eye in Wales, perhaps it was the best black eye in Europe; he bet Tunney never had a black eye like that.

'And there's blood all over your shirt.'

'Sometimes I bleed in dollops,' he said.

On Walter's Road we passed a group of high school girls, and I cocked my cap and hoped my eye was as big as a bluebag, and he walked with his coat flung open to show the bloodstains.

I was a hooligan all during dinner, and a bully, and as bad as a boy from the Sandbanks, and I should have more respect, and I sat silently, like Tunney, over the sago pudding. That afternoon I went to school with an eyeshade on. If I had had a black silk sling I would have been as gay and desperate as the wounded captain in the book that my sister used to read, and that I read under the bedclothes at night, secretly with a flash-lamp.

On the road, a boy from an inferior school, where the parents did not have to pay anything, called me 'One eye!' in a harsh, adult voice. I took no notice, but walked along whistling, my good eye on the summer clouds sailing, beyond insult, above Terrace Road.

The mathematics master said: 'I see that Mr Thomas at the back of the class has been straining his eyesight. But it isn't over his homework, is it, gentlemen?'

Gilbert Rees, next to me, laughed loudest.

'I'll break your leg after school!' I said.

He'd hobble, howling, up to the head master's study.

A deep hush in the school. A message on a plate brought by the porter. 'The head master's compliments, sir, and will you come at once?' 'How did you happen to break this boy's leg?' 'Oh! damn and bottom, the agony!' cried Gilbert Rees. 'Just a little twist,' I would say. 'I don't know my own strength. I apologize. But there's nothing to worry about. Let me set the leg, sir.' A rapid manipulation, the click of a bone. 'Doctor Thomas, sir, at your service.' Mrs Rees was on her knees. 'How can I thank you?' 'It's nothing at all, dear lady. Wash his ears every morning. Throw away his rulers. Pour his red and green inks down the sink.'

In Mr Trotter's drawing class we drew naked girls inaccurately on sheets of paper under our drawings of a vase and passed them along under the desks. Some of the drawings were detailed strangely, others were tailed off like mermaids. Gilbert Rees drew the vase only.

'Sleep with your wife, sir?'

'What did you say?'

'Lend me a knife, sir?'

'What would you do if you had a million pounds?'

'I'd buy a Bugatti and a Rolls and a Bentley and I'd go two hundred miles an hour on Pendine sands.'

'I'd buy a harem and keep the girls in the gym.'

'I'd buy a house like Mrs Cotmore-Richard's, twice as big as hers, and a cricket field and a football field and a proper garage with mechanics and a lift.'

'And a lavatory as big as, as big as the Melba pavilion, with plush seats and golden chains and . . . .'

'And I'd smoke cigarettes with real gold tips, better than Morris's Blue Book.'

'I'd buy all the railway trains, and only 4A could travel in them.'

'And not Gilbert Rees either.'

'What's the longest you've been?'

'I went to Edinburgh.'

'My father went to Salonika in the War.'

'Where's that, Cyril?'

'Cyril, tell us about Mrs Pussie Edwards in Hanover Street.'

'Well, my brother says he can do anything.'

I drew a wild guess below the waist, and wrote Pussie Edwards in small letters at the foot of the page.

'Cave!'

'Hide your drawings.'

'I bet you a greyhound can go faster than a horse.'

Everybody liked the drawing class, except Mr Trotter.

In the evening, before calling on my new friend, I sat in my bedroom by the boiler and read through my exercise-books full of poems. There were Danger Don'ts on the backs. On my bedroom walls were pictures of Shakespeare, Walter de la Mare torn from my father's Christmas *Bookman*, Robert Browning, Stacy Aumonier, Rupert Brooke, a bearded man who I had discovered was Whittier, Watts's 'Hope', and a Sunday school certificate I was ashamed to want to pull down. A poem I had had printed in the 'Wales Day by Day' column of the *Western Mail* was pasted on the mirror to make me blush, but the shame of the poem had died. Across the poem I had written, with a stolen quill and in flourishes: 'Homer Nods'. I was always waiting for the opportunity to bring someone into my bedroom – 'Come into my den; excuse the untidiness; take a chair. No! not that one, it's broken!' – and force him to see the poem accidentally. 'I put it there to make me blush.' But nobody ever came in except my mother.

A Man's a Man for A' That

Robert Burns

Robert Burns (1759-96), the self-educated "plowman poet" is known for his satirical and philosophical poetry which extoll the Lowland dialect, elevate the common man, and appeal to the brotherhood of all. The tradition established by Burns lay dormant until, in this century, Hugh MacDiarmid began to publish his works.

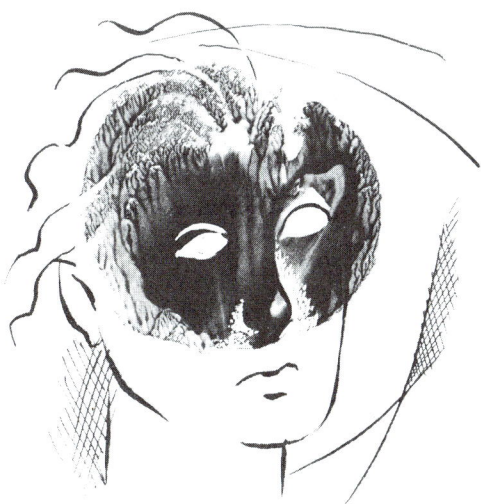

> Is there, for honest poverty,
>   That hings his head, and a' that?
> The coward slave, we pass him by,
>   We dare be poor for a' that!
>   For a' that, an' a' that,
>   Our toils obscure, an' a' that;
>   The rank is but the guinea's stamp;
>   The man's the gowd[1] for a' that.
>
> What tho' on hamely fare we dine,
>   Wear hodden-gray,[2] an' a' that;
> Gie fools their silks, and knaves their wine,
>   A man's a man, for a' that.
>   For a' that, an' a' that,
>   Their tinsel show, an' a' that;
>   The honest man, tho' e'er sae poor,
>   Is king of men for a' that.

[1] gowd - gold
[2] hodden-gray - clothing of coarse, gray cloth.

BRITAIN

Ye see yon birkie,[3] ca'd a lord,
   Wha struts, an' stares, an' a' that;
Tho' hundreds worship at his word,
   He's but a coof[4] for a' that;
     For a' that, an' a' that,
       His riband,[5] star, an' a' that,
     The man o' independent mind,
       He looks and laughs at a' that.

A prince can mak' a belted knight,
   A marquis, duke, an' a' that;
But an honest man's aboon[6] his might,
   Guid faith, he mauna fa'[7] that;
     For a' that, an' a' that,
       Their dignities, an' a' that,
     The pith o' sense, an' pride o' worth,
       Are higher rank than a' that.

Then let us pray that come it may,
   As come it will for a' that,
That sense and worth, o'er all the earth,
   May bear the gree,[8] an' a' that.
     For a' that, an' a' that,
       It's coming yet, for a' that,
     That man to man, the warld o'er
       Shall brothers be for a' that.

---

[3]birkie - a young "sport"
[4]coof - a fool
[5]riband - badges of honour
[6]a boon - above
[7]mauna fa' - mustn't claim
[8]bear the gree - have the prize

Highland Graveyard

Kathleen Raine

Kathleen Raine, born in 1908 and educated at Cambridge, developed her own unique poetic talents which reflected her neo-Platonic vision of life.

Today a fine old face has gone under the soil;
For generations past women hereabouts have borne
Her same name and stamp of feature.
Her brief identity was not her own
But theirs who formed and sent her out
To wear the proud bones of her clan, and live its story,
Who now receive back into the ground
Worn features of ancestral mould.

A dry-stone wall bounds off the dislimned clay
Of many an old face forgotten and young face gone
From boundless nature, sea and sky.
A wind-withered escalonia like a song
Of ancient tenderness lives on
Some woman's living fingers set as shelter for the dead, to tell
In evergreen unwritten leaves,
In scent of leaves in western rain
That one remembered who is herself forgotten.

Many songs they knew who now are silent.
Into their memories the dead are gone
Who haunt the living in an ancient tongue
Sung by old voices to the young,
Telling of sea and isles, of boat and byre and glen;
And from their music the living are reborn
Into a remembered land,
To call ancestral memories home
And all that ancient grief and love our own.

A Peasant

R. S. Thomas

Ronald Stuart Thomas was born in Cardiff, Wales, in 1913 and educated at the colleges of Bangor and Aberystwyth. He was ordained in 1937. His poems express his deep concern for his parishioners.

Iago Prytherch his name, though be it allowed,
Just an ordinary man of the bald Welsh hills,
Who pens a few sheep in a gap of cloud.
Docking mangels, chipping the green skin
From the yellow bones with a half-witted grin
Of satisfaction, or churning the crude earth
To a stiff sea of clods that glint in the wind –
So are his days spent, his spittled mirth
Rarer than the sun that cracks the cheeks
Of the gaunt sky perhaps once in a week.
And then at night see him fixed in his chair
Motionless, except when he leans to gob in the fire.
There is something frightening in the vacancy of his mind.
His clothes, sour with years of sweat
And animal contact, shock the refined,
But affected, sense with their stark naturalness.
Yet this is your prototype, who, season by season
Against siege of rain and the wind's attrition,
Preserves his stock, an impregnable fortress
Not to be stormed even in death's confusion.
Remember him, then, for he, too, is a winner of wars,
Enduring like a tree under the curious stars.

Lancashire Winter

Tony Connor

The town remembers no such plenty,
under the wind from off the moor.
The labour exchange is nearly empty;
stiletto heels on the Palais floor
move between points of patent leather.
Sheepskin coats keep out the weather.

Commerce and Further Education
won't be frozen. Dully free
in snack bars and classrooms sits the patient
centrally heated peasantry,
receiving Wimpies like the Host;
striving to get That Better Post.

Snow on the streets and Mini-Minors
thickens to drifts, and in the square,
from grubby plinths, blind eyes, stone collars,
the fathers of revolution stare,
who, against pikes and burning brands,
built the future with bare hands.

Digging

Seamus Heaney

Between my finger and my thumb
The squat pen rests; snug as a gun.

Under my window, a clean rasping sound
When the spade sinks into gravelly ground:
My father, digging. I look down

Till his straining rump among the flowerbeds
Bends low, comes up twenty years away
Stooping in rhythm through potato drills
Where he was digging.

The coarse boot nestled on the lug, the shaft
Against the inside knee was levered firmly.
He rooted out tall tops, buried the bright edge deep
To scatter new potatoes that we picked
Loving their cool hardness in our hands.

By God, the old man could handle a spade.
Just like his old man.

My grandfather cut more turf in a day
Than any other man on Toner's bog.
Once I carried him milk in a bottle
Corked sloppily with paper. He straightened up
To drink it, then fell to right away

BRITAIN

Nicking and slicing neatly, heaving sods
Over his shoulder, going down and down
For the good turf. Digging.

The cold smell of potato mould, the squelch and slap
Of soggy peat, the curt cuts of an edge
Through living roots awaken in my head,
But I've no spade to follow men like them.

Between my finger and my thumb
The squat pen rests.
I'll dig with it.

What Is Our Aim?

Winston S. Churchill

These extracts are from the speeches of Winston Churchill delivered between 1940 and 1946. On many occasions his words were the inspiration needed by the British people. Even today readers thrill at the power of Winston Churchill's oratory.

Thoughtless, dilettante or purblind worldlings sometimes ask us: "What is it that Britain and France are fighting for?"

To this I answer: "If we left off fighting you would soon find out."

(Broadcast, March 30, 1940.)

I would say to the House, as I said to those who have joined this Government: "I have nothing to offer but blood, toil, tears, and sweat." We have before us an ordeal of the most grievous kind. We have before us many, many long months of struggle and suffering.

You ask: "What is our policy?" I will say: "It is to wage war by sea, land, and air with all our might, and with all the strength that God can give us: to wage war against a monstrous tyranny, never surpassed in the dark lamentable catalogue of human crime." That is our policy.

You ask: "What is our aim?" I can answer in one word: "Victory!" Victory at all costs, victory in spite of all terror, victory however long and hard the road may be; for without victory there is no survival.

(First speech as Prime Minister in the House of Commons, May 13, 1940.)

We shall not flag or fail. We shall go on to the end. We shall fight in France, we shall fight on the seas and oceans, we shall fight with growing confidence and growing strength in the air. We shall defend our island, whatever the cost may be. We shall fight on the beaches, we shall fight on the landing-grounds. We shall fight in the fields and in the streets, we shall fight in the hills. We shall never surrender; and even if, which I do not for a moment believe, this island or a large part of it were subjugated and starving, then our Empire beyond the seas, armed and guarded by the British Fleet, would carry on the struggle, until, in God's good time, the New World, with all its power and might, steps forth to the rescue and liberation of the old.

(Speech in the House of Commons, June 4, 1940.)

If we can stand up to him [Hitler], all Europe may be free and the life of the world may move forward into broad, sunlit uplands. But if we fail, then the whole world, including the United States, including all that we have known and cared for, will sink into the abyss of a new Dark Age made more sinister, and perhaps more protracted, by the lights of perverted science. Let us therefore brace ourselves to our duties, and so bear ourselves that, if the British Empire and its Commonwealth last for a thousand years, men will say: "This was their finest hour."

(Speech in the House of Commons, June 18, 1940 – when France capitulated.)

Here in this strong City of Refuge which enshrines the title-deeds of human progress and is of deep consequence to Christian civilization . . . we await undismayed the impending assault. Perhaps it will come tonight. Perhaps it will never come. We must show ourselves equally capable of meeting a sudden violent shock or (what is perhaps a harder test) a protracted vigil. But be the ordeal sharp, or long, or both, we shall seek no terms, we shall tolerate no parley. We may show mercy – we shall ask for none.

(Broadcast, July 14, 1940.)

Never in the field of human conflict was so much owed by so many to so few.

(Speech in the House of Commons, August 20, 1940.)

When I warned them [the French Government] that Britain would fight on alone whatever they did their Generals told their Prime Minister and his divided Cabinet: "In three weeks England will have her neck wrung like a chicken." Some chicken! Some neck!

(Speech to the Canadian Parliament, December 30, 1941.)

We shall go forward together. The road upward is long. There are upon our journey dark and dangerous valleys through which we have to make and fight our way. But it is sure and certain that if we persevere, and we shall persevere, we shall come through these dark and dangerous valleys into a sunlight broader and more genial and more lasting than mankind has ever known.

(Speech at Leeds, May 16, 1942.)

BRITAIN

A quarter of a century ago . . . the House, when it heard . . . the armistice terms, did not feel inclined for debate or business, but desired to offer thanks to Almighty God, to the Great Power which seems to shape and design the fortunes of nations and the destiny of man; and I therefore . . . move "That the House do now attend at the Church of St. Margaret, Westminster, to give humble and reverent thanks to Almighty God for our deliverance from the threat of German domination." This is the identical motion which was moved in former times.

(Speech in the House of Commons on the German surrender, May 8, 1945.)

God bless you all! This is your victory! . . . Everyone, man or woman, has done their best. Neither the long years nor the dangers, nor the fierce attacks of the enemy, have in any way weakened the independent resolve of the British nation. God bless you all!

(From the balcony in Whitehall, May 8, 1945.)

Neither the sure prevention of war nor the continuous use of world organization will be gained without . . . the fraternal association of the English-speaking peoples. This means a special relationship between the British Commonwealth and Empire and the United States. . . . Eventually there may come principles of common citizenship, but that we may be content to leave to destiny, whose outstretched arm so many of us can clearly see. I feel eventually this will come.

(Speech at Fulton, Missouri, March 3, 1946.)

Cynddylan on a Tractor

R. S. Thomas

Ah, you should see Cynddylan on a tractor.
Gone the old look that yoked him to the soil;
He's a new man now, part of the machine,
His nerves of metal and his blood oil.
The clutch curses, but the gears obey
His least bidding, and lo, he's away
Out of the farmyard, scattering hens.
Riding to work now as a great man should,
He is the knight at arms breaking the fields'
Mirror of silence, emptying the wood
Of foxes and squirrels and bright jays.
The sun comes over the tall trees
Kindling all the hedges, but not for him
Who runs his engine on a different fuel.
And all the birds are singing, bills wide in vain,
As Cynddylan passes proudly up the lane.

To Reach the Sea

Monica Dickens

Monica Dickens, the great-granddaughter of Charles Dickens was born in London, England, in 1915. She is a gifted writer as can be seen in this short story.

It cost $250. When Jane Barlow took courage to question the price, M. Marmaduc, who had made it, said, 'I am an artist, Madame, a very sensitive man. Is Madam trying to say it is not worth it?'

And it was worth it. She wore the wig that evening – blue-black, shining, superb. The party was a little depressing, so when someone said, 'I've been admiring your hair all evening,' she took off the wig, for a joke, and things were gayer. Then she put it on again and presently asked her husband to take her home, because the gaiety had evaporated.

She loved the wig. It sat on a stand like Marie Antoinette's severed head, and when she wore it she saw women look at her as she came into a room, and she could see them wondering: Is it or isn't it? Either way they were envious.

Before long, however, the wig began to worry her. It didn't look right any more; there was too much of it, and her face looked small. She took it back to M. Marmaduc and told him, 'I think it needs redressing. There's something wrong with it.'

'I am an artist, Madame – there can be nothing wrong.' But when she called for it a week later, he admitted, 'I think it is a finished creation, but there was a little too much hair. I have take a soupçon off here, a flick off here – it is now perfect.'

Jane wore it that night, and it was perfect. 'Like living hair,' John said. John was not her husband, but the man she wished she had met first. 'It pales and narrows your face to a kind of tragic beauty.'

Jane laughed, because they must never look as if they were talking seriously in corners; but she did feel a little tragic. They had agreed to be gay and sophisticated about their situation, but tonight it seemed to be closing in on her. Her husband looked at her admiringly across the room, but she felt afraid.

Jane came home after a month's holiday, not caring that her hair was a wreck from the sun and sea, because the wig was waiting. But the very first time she wore it, it seemed wrong again. She set it in pin curls on the severed head, left it for a week, then tried it on late at night after her husband was asleep. She sat in front of her dressing table, staring with dark strange eyes at the white face dwarfed by the glorious mass of black hair.

There was no doubt about it, absolutely no doubt at all.

The wig was growing.

She snatched it off and put it quickly back on the dummy head in the box. It was her imagination. It must be. She left it on the shelf for three weeks; then one night, with a beating heart, she put it on again.

I am going mad, she thought. In a panic, she took scissors and hacked at the hair, gathering up the fallen bits in newspaper and running down to burn them in the furnace.

The wig was unwearable now, lopsidedly chopped. She wept, the uncontrollable sobs shaking her long after she had stuffed the box back on the shelf and gone brokenly to bed.

'Why do you never wear that expensive wig?' her husband asked, and John said, irked by her moodiness when they met in the discreetly shadowed bar, 'Don't let yourself go, Janey. Put on that glorious wig again, and sparkle.'

She went to another hairdresser, not M. Marmaduc, and had her hair deepened in colour and teased into a huge frame for her nervous white face, and asked her husband, 'How does the wig look?' For no one must ever know she could not wear it.

She would not look at it. Every time she opened the closet, her eyes flew to the tall box on the shelf. Her hands went up, impulsively, but she forced them down.

She waited another two months. When her husband was away, she took down the box and opened it.

It was not a shock. It was with a sigh of submissive recognition that she saw that the hair had grown at least two inches – uneven, ragged at the ends, but well below her ears when she put the wig on.

She went out and walked about the streets for half the night, not knowing where she went, knowing only that she was looking for something she would never find.

Many nights in the following months, when her husband was asleep, she would put on the growing wig and slip out of the house to wander through the streets, across the bridges, along the river wall, the long unkempt black hair shrouding her back and shoulders and half veiling her face.

They found her in the river, one cold dawn, her own hair strung like seaweed across her dead face. A boy digging for bait found the wig caught under a jetty, its long hair floating out in the murky water to try to reach the sea . . .

'It will cost Madame two hundred and fifty dollars.'

'All right,' said the customer. 'But where does the hair come from?'

'Northern Italy. I used to get beautiful black hair from Sicily, but I will not buy from that salesman any more. He told me, Madame, about a girl – the young bride of a rich old man. When the old man found her with her lover, he knifed the boy and threw the body from a boat into the sea. Then he cut off all his wife's long black hair, the way they did in the war, for fraternizing.

'The young bride walked out into the sea, crazy with sorrow, looking for her lover. The salesman bought the hair. What a pig. How could I buy any more from such a brute? I am an artist, Madame, a very sensitive man.'

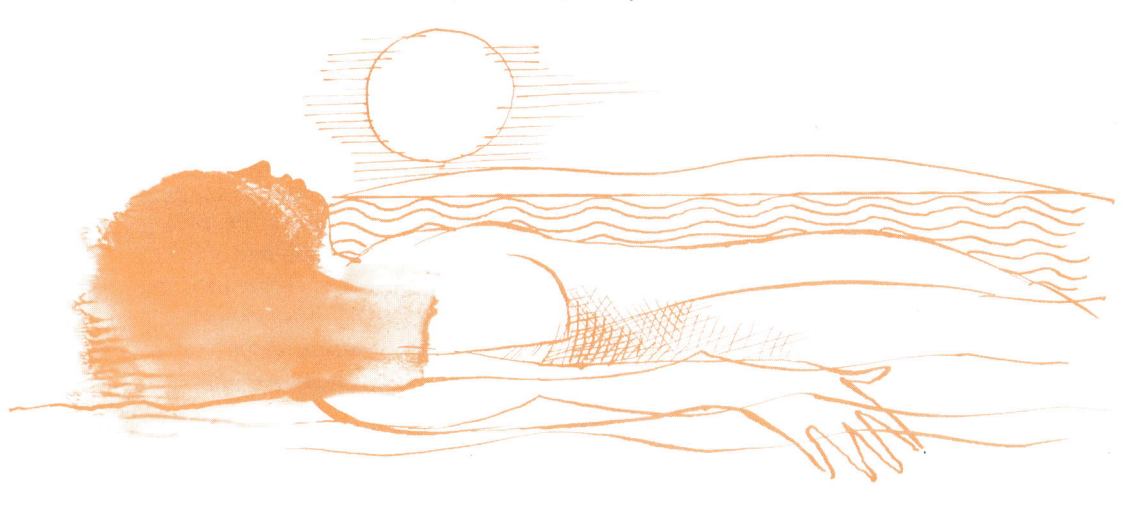

Man in Society

Charles P. Snow

Charles P. Snow was born in Leicester, England in 1905. Trained as a physicist, he went on to become an experienced editor and college teacher and a brilliant novelist. His writing reflects a deep interest in the effect of modern science on our civilization.

Auschwitz and Hiroshima. We have seen all that; in some of it we have acquiesced or helped. No wonder we are morally guilty. Men like ourselves have done such things – and at the same time men like ourselves, sometimes the same men who have taken a hand in the horrors, have been showing more concern for the unlucky round them than has ever been shown by a large society in human history. That is the moral paradox in which we have to live.

It is wrong to try to domesticate the horrors. The mass slaughter of the concentration camps was both the most awful and the most degrading set of actions that men have done so far. This set of actions was ordered and controlled by abnormally wicked men, if you like, but down the line the orders were carried out by thousands of people like the rest of us, civil servants, soldiers, engineers, all brought up in an advanced Western and Christian society. While it was people not like the rest of us but a great deal better, people who for imagination and morality, not to speak of intellect, stand among the finest of our race, people like Einstein, Niels Bohr, and Franck, who got caught up in the tangle of events which led to Hiroshima and Nagasaki. The dropping of those bombs was of a lesser order of wickedness from what was done at Auschwitz. But Western man ought not to forget that he did it; Eastern man certainly won't.

At the same time we ought not to forget what there is to our credit. Some kinds of optimism about man's nature are dangerous – but so are some kinds of pessimism. Think of the care the Swedes and the Danes are taking of their old and poor, or of prisoners, or of social misfits. Nothing like that has been done at any period or in any place until our lifetime. We can congratulate ourselves in this country, too. The Scandinavians have not made anything like a perfect society. In some ways we have not got as near to it as they have. But they and we have made a better shot at it than anyone before us.

This country is a much fairer and a much kinder society than the one I was born into in 1905. It may seem sentimental to have consciences troubled about capital punishment, about removing one life when Western man has recently eliminated twenty million: yet it is a sign of moral sensitivity. So is the attempt, however grudging, to treat women as though they were equal human beings. So is the feeling behind the Wolfenden Report. So is the conviction – so urgent in the United States – that children have a special right to happiness.

Some of these feelings may lead to practical follies (I believe that the American one is making a mess of their education), but that is not the point. They are signs of a development of something very rare in the world up to now, which one might call moral kindness. I have no doubt that in Scandinavia, this country, some, though not all, of the United States, and perhaps three or four other countries in the West, the amount of fairness, tolerance, and effective kindness within the society would seem astonishing to any nineteenth-century man.

It would also seem astonishing to any nineteenth-century man how much we know. There is probably no one now alive as clever as Clerk Maxwell or Gauss; but thousands of people know more than Clerk Maxwell or Gauss, and understand more of those parts of the world that they spent their lives trying to understand. Put those two down, or even greater men, such as Newton and Archimedes, in front of what is now understood – and they would think it wonderful. So it is, and we can take pride and joy in it. It will go on; the search to understand is one of the most human things about us. Compared with our ancestors, there are some trivial physical differences. We are a good deal taller and heavier, we live much longer. But above all, we know more.

All this it would be reasonable to call progress, so long as we don't expect of progress more than it can give. In each of our individual lives there is, of course, something beyond human help. Each of us has to live part of his life alone: and he has to die alone. That part of our experience is right outside of time and history, and progress has no meaning there. In this sense, the individual condition is tragic. But that is no excuse for not doing our best with the social condition.

To think otherwise, to take refuge in facile despair, has been the characteristic intellectual treachery of our day. It is shoddy. We have to face the individual condition: for good and evil, for pettiness and the occasional dash of grandeur, we have to know what men are capable of: and then we can't contract out. For we are part, not only of the privileged North European–British–American *enclave* of progress, but of another progress which is altering the whole world.

I mean something brutally simple. Most people in Asia still haven't enough to eat: but they have a bit more than before. Most people in Asia are still dying before their time (on the average, Indians live less than half as long as Englishmen): but they are living longer than before. Is *that* progress? This is not a subject to be superior or refined or ingenious about, and the answer is: *of course it is*.

It is because Western man has grown too far away from that elemental progress that we can't get on terms with most of the human race. Through luck we got in first with the scientific-industrial revolution; as a result, our lives became, on the average, healthier, longer, more comfortable to an extent that had never been imagined; it doesn't become us to tell our Chinese and Indian friends that that kind of progress is not worth having.

We know what it is like to live among the shops, the cars, the radios, of Leicester, and Orebro, and Des Moines. We know what it is like to ask the point of it all, and to feel the Swedish sadness or the American disappointment or the English Welfare State discontent. But the Chinese and Indians would like the chance of being well-fed enough to ask what is the point of it all. They are in search of what Leicester, Orebro, and Des Moines take for granted, food, extra years of life, modest comforts. When they have got these things, they are willing to put up with a dash of the Swedish sadness or American disappointment. And their determination to get these things is likely in the next thirty years to prove the strongest social force on earth.

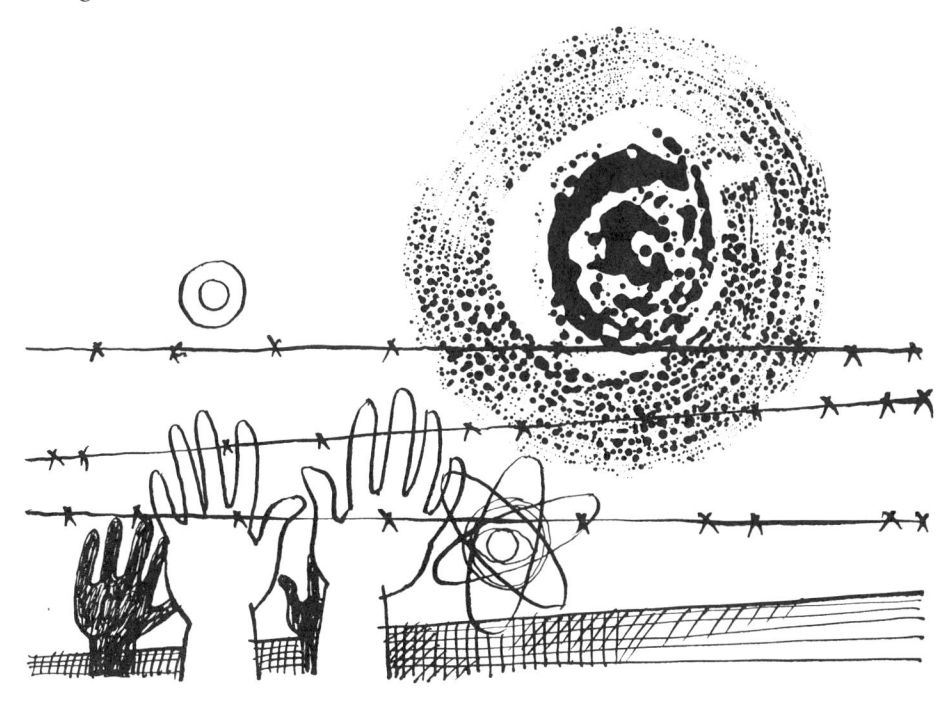

Will they get them? Will the social condition everywhere reach within foreseeable time something like the standard of the privileged Western enclave? There is no technical reason why not. If it does, the level of moral kindness will go up in parallel. These ought to be realistic hopes. There seems only one fatality that might destroy them. That is, it goes without saying, an H-bomb war. That is the only method of committing the final disloyalty to the species, of stopping the hope of progress dead.

No one can pretend that it is not possible. For myself, I think that it won't happen – even though we have seen how good and conscientious men have become responsible for horrors, even though two atomic bombs have been dropped already and by Western man. But I still think, partly as a guess, partly as a calculation, that we shall escape the H-Bomb war – just as I think we shall escape the longer-term danger of Malthusian overpopulation.

It may easily be that I am letting hope run away with me about the H-bomb war. Some of the wisest disagree with me. Let us imagine that they are right and that the H-bombs go off. Is that going to be the end? I find it difficult to believe. In this country a lot of us would be dead, our children with us. A lot of Americans and Russians would also be killed outright. No one knows how many would die afterwards through effects of radiation. But I don't believe that men have at present the resources to destroy the race.

If that is so, and if after an H-bomb war a viable fraction of the world population were left untouched (my own guess is that it would be a very large fraction, at least two-thirds and probably much bigger), then we should all be amazed how soon hope of progress took possession again. The human species is biologically a very tough one, and tough in a sense no animal species can be, through its intelligence, its organisation of knowledge, the capacity of its members not to be totally bound within the rapacious self. After the most hideous H-bomb war, the inhabitants of Africa and India and South America would have the strength of those qualities to build on. The material and scientific gap, left through the devastation of the West and Russia, would be filled up at a speed not flattering to Western or Russian self-esteem. What would the moral scar be?

I think we can already answer that question, for we too have, as I said at the beginning, witnessed horrors and assisted at them. Most of us don't live constantly in the presence of Hiroshima and Auschwitz: the memory doesn't prevent us getting morally concerned about the fate of one murderer or cross because a lonely and impoverished old man doesn't have enough calls from the District Visitor.

It would be just the same if the Northern hemisphere became more or less destroyed. Men elsewhere would not live under that shadow; they would be busy with their own societies. If those societies were less fair and morally sensitive than ours is now, they would soon catch up. Within a bizarrely short interval, after hundreds of millions of people had been incinerated by H-bombs, men in countries unaffected would be passionately debating capital punishment. It sounds mad: but it is the kind of madness which makes human beings as tough as they are, and as capable of behaving better than they have so far behaved.

So there remains a sort of difficult hope. So long as men continue to be men, individual man will perceive the same darkness about his solitary condition as any of us does now. But he will also feel occasional intimations that his own life is not the only one. In the midst of his egotisms, pettinesses, power-seekings, and perhaps the horrors these may cause, he will intermittently stretch a little beyond himself. That little, added to the intelligence and growing knowledge of the species, will be enough to make his societies more decent, to use the social forces for what, in the long sight of history, are good ends.

None of it will be easy. As individuals, each of us is almost untouched by this progress. It is no comfort to remember how short human history is. As individuals, that seems just an irony. But as a race, we have scarcely begun to live.

Further Reading

Cross, E.A., and Daringer, H.F., *Literature: A Series Of Anthologies.* Toronto: The Macmillan Company of Canada Ltd., 1945

Craig, G.A., et al., *English Literature.* Toronto: Ginn and Company, 1964

Jones, G., *Welsh Short Stories.* London: Oxford University Press, 1956

Hendry, J.F., *The Penguin Book of Scottish Short Stories.* Harmondsworth Penguin Books Ltd., 1970

Barrows, M.W., et al., *The English Tradition: Fiction.* New York: Macmillan Publishing Co. Inc., 1968

Inglis, Stauffer, and Larsen, *Adventures in English Literature.* Toronto: W.J. Gage, 1952

Harrison, G.B., *Major British Writers,* Volumes I & II. New York: Harcourt, Brace and Co., 1959

The Oxford Companion to English Literature (4th edition). London: Oxford University Press, 1973

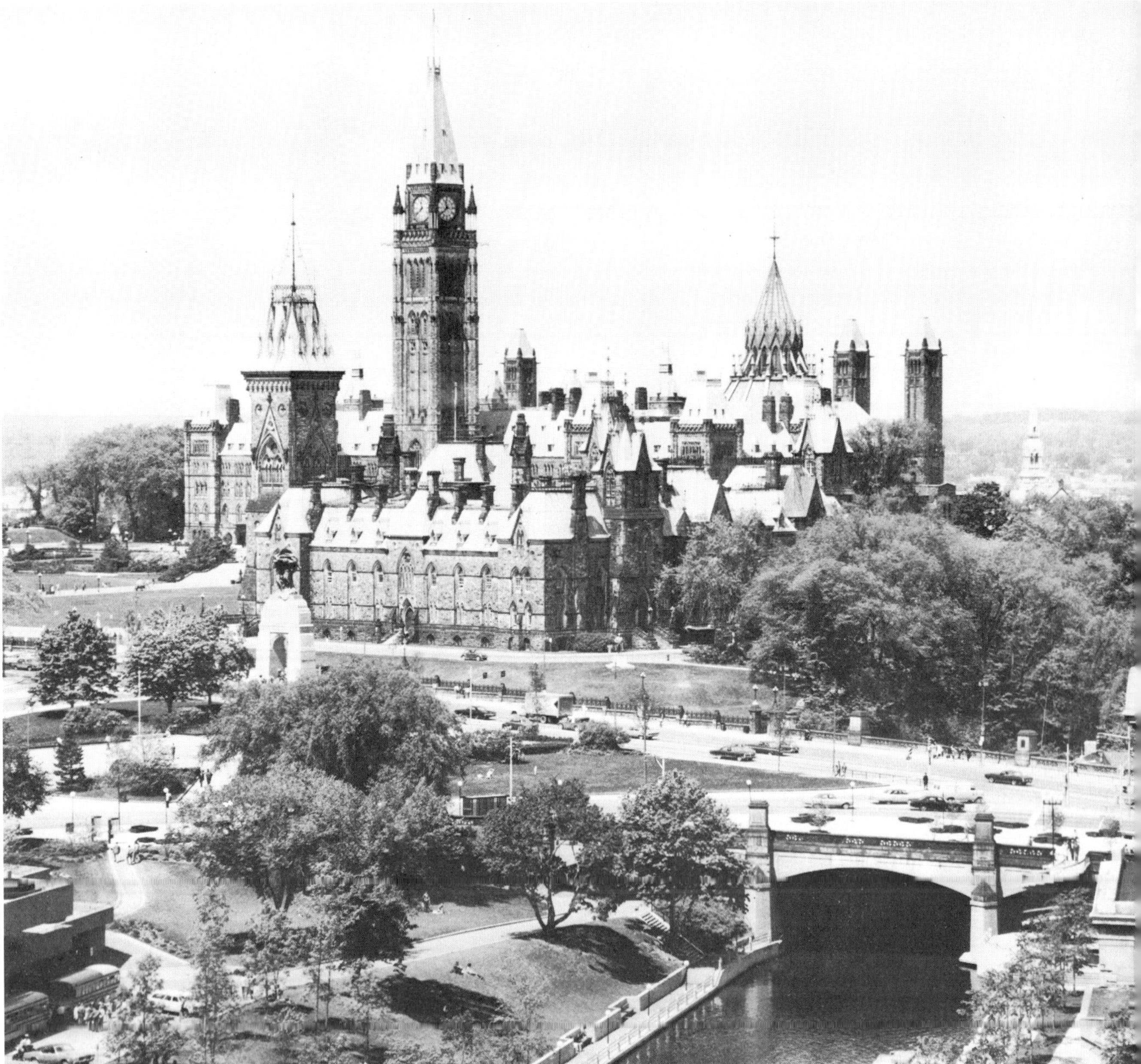

Industry and Tou

A Glimpse of Canada

The first Canadian writer to break from the traditional British literary themes was Thomas Chandler Haliburton (1796-1865), the Supreme Court judge from Nova Scotia who won international fame with his humorous and satirical *Sam Slick*, or *The Clockmaker* series. A Canadian sensibility was maintained by the Confederation poets Archibald Lampman (1861-1899) and Duncan Campbell Scott (1862-1944), and by their contemporaries Charles G.D. Roberts, Wilfred Campbell, Charles Mair, and Bliss Carman.

A bit later in this century the poet-critics A.J.M. Smith, F.R. Scott, and Robert Finch produced poetry relevant to contemporary man with his basic insecurities. A.M. Klein and Leonard Cohen adopted a Jewish sensitivity, while E.J. Pratt, Earl Birney, and A.W. Purdy approached poetry as individualists.
In more recent Canadian fiction, sociological concerns dominate. The many stories of Morley Callaghan reveal lower- and middle-class characters who are locked in a harsh, realistic world. Hugh MacLennan, in his historical novels, presents critical and analytical views of the larger realities of Canadian society. Mordecai Richler turns from an almost vicious splintering of the hypocrisy he found in both Jewish and Gentile traditions to a humorous and germane diagnosis of man. And W.O. Mitchell accepts, with humour and warmth, human imperfections and divisions within society.

Canadian literature has changed. The Colonial, the Romantic, and the Victorian "schools" have gone. Canadian writers have become individualists.

The Canadian section provides a view of the Canadian people and the society in which they live. "My Heart Soars" reveals the pride and concerns of Canada's Indian population. "Lament for the Dorsets" speaks of the Eskimo's struggle for survival. "Good Old Uncle Albert" gives an interesting glimpse of Canadian wildlife. "Grandfather" and "Death of an Outport" portray personal dilemmas in the lives of individual Canadians.

My Heart Soars

Chief Dan George

Chief Dan George, a member of the Co-Salish tribe, was born in 1899 in North Vancouver and reared in the traditional Indian ways. He left school at sixteen to become a logger, married three years later, and worked as a longshoreman until he was injured in 1946. Since then he has become well known as a musician and entertainer, first in television and, later, in motion pictures. He received an Academy Award nomination for his performance in *Little Big Man.* He makes his home on the Burrard Reservation where he was born; he continues to be active in the entertainment field.

I am a native of North America.

In the course of my lifetime I have lived in two distinct cultures. I was born into a culture that lived in communal houses. My grandfather's house was eighty feet long. It was called a smoke house, and it stood down by the beach along the inlet. All my grandfather's sons and their families lived in this large dwelling. Their sleeping apartments were separated by blankets made of bull rush reeds, but one open fire in the middle served the cooking needs of all. In houses like these, throughout the tribe, people learned to live with one another; learned to serve one another; learned to respect the rights of one another. And children shared the thoughts of the adult world and found themselves surrounded by aunts and uncles and cousins who loved them and did not threaten them. My father was born in such a house and learned from infancy how to love people and be at home with them.

And beyond this acceptance of one another there was a deep respect for everything in nature that surrounded them. My father loved the earth and all its creatures. The earth was his second mother. The earth and everything it contained was a gift from See-see-am . . . and the way to thank this great spirit was to use his gifts with respect.

I remember, as a little boy, fishing with him up Indian River and I can still see him as the sun rose above the mountain top in the early morning . . . I can see him standing by the water's edge with his arms raised above his head while he softly moaned . . . "Thank you, thank you". It left a deep impression on my young mind.

And I shall never forget his disappointment when once he caught me gaffing for fish "just for the fun of it". "My Son" he said, "The Great Spirit gave you those fish to be your brothers, to feed you when you are hungry. You must respect them. You must not kill them just for the fun of it." This then was the culture I was born into and for some years the only one I really knew or tasted. This is why I find it hard to accept many of the things I see around me.

I see people living in smoke houses hundreds of times bigger than the one I knew. But the people in one apartment do not even know the people in the next and care less about them.

It is also difficult for me to understand the deep hate that exists among people. It is hard to understand a culture that justifies the killing of millions in past wars, and is at this very moment preparing bombs to kill even greater numbers. It is hard for me to understand a culture that spends more on wars and weapons to kill, than it does on education and welfare to help and develop.

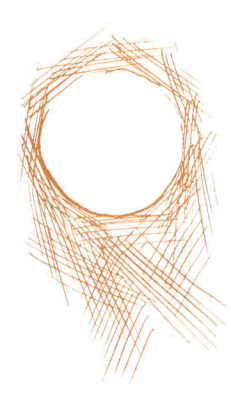

It is hard for me to understand a culture that not only hates and fights his brothers but even attacks nature and abuses her. I see my white brother going about blotting out nature from his cities. I see him strip the hills bare, leaving ugly wounds on the face of mountains. I see him tearing things from the bosom of mother earth as though she were a monster, who refused to share her treasures with him. I see him throw poison in the waters, indifferent to the life he kills there; and he chokes the air with deadly fumes.

My white brother does many things well for he is more clever than my people but I wonder if he knows how to love well. I wonder if he has ever really learned to love at all. Perhaps he only loves the things that are his own but never learned to love the things that are outside and beyond him. And this is, of course, not love at all, for man must love all creation or he will love none of it. Man must love fully or he will become the lowest of the animals. It is the power to love that makes him the greatest of them all . . . for he alone of all animals is capable of love.

Love is something you and I must have. We must have it because our spirit feeds upon it. We must have it because without it we become weak and faint. Without love our self esteem weakens. Without it our courage fails. Without love we can no longer look out confidently at the world. Instead we turn inwardly and begin to feed upon our own personalities and little by little we destroy ourselves.

You and I need the strength and joy that comes from knowing that we are loved. With it we are creative. With it we march tirelessly. With it, and with it alone, we are able to sacrifice for others.

There have been times when we all wanted so desperately to feel a re-assuring hand upon us . . . there have been lonely times when we so wanted a strong arm around us . . . I cannot tell you how deeply I miss my wife's presence when I return from a trip. Her love was my greatest joy, my strength, my greatest blessing.

I am afraid my culture has little to offer yours. But my culture did prize friendship and companionship. It did not look on privacy as a thing to be clung to, for privacy builds up walls and walls promote distrust. My culture lived in big family communities, and from infancy people learned to live with others.

My culture did not prize the hoarding of private possessions, in fact, to hoard was a shameful thing to do among my people. The Indian looked on all things in nature as belonging to him and he expected to share them with others and to take only what he needed.

Everyone likes to give as well as receive. No one wishes only to receive all the time. We have taken much from your culture . . . I wish you had taken something from our culture . . . for there were some beautiful and good things in it.

Soon it will be too late to know my culture, for integration is upon us and soon we will have no values but yours. Already many of our young people have forgotten the old ways. And many have been shamed of their Indian ways by scorn and ridicule. My culture is like a wounded deer that has crawled away into the forest to bleed and die alone.

The only thing that can truly help us is genuine love. You must truly love us, be patient with us and share with us. And we must love you — with a genuine love that forgives and forgets . . . a love like that forgives the terrible sufferings your culture brought ours when it swept over us like a wave crashing along a beach . . . with a love that forgets and lifts up its head and sees in your eyes an answering love of trust and acceptance.

This is brotherhood . . . anything less is not worthy of the name.

I have spoken.

Grandfather

George Bowering

George Bowering was born in Penticton, B.C., in 1935 and educated at the University of British Columbia. He is presently teaching at Simon Fraser University in Vancouver and editing the poetry magazine IMAGO. He has published a number of books of poetry, as well as one novel and several critical essays.

Grandfather
           Jabez Harry Bowering
strode across the Canadian prairie
hacking down trees
           & building churches
delivering personal baptist sermons in them
leading Holy holy holy lord god almighty songs in them
red haired man squared off in the pulpit
reading Saul on the road to Damascus at them

Left home
         big walled Bristol town
at age eight
         to make a living
buried his stubby fingers in root snarled earth
for a suit of clothes & seven hundred gruelly meals a year
taking an anabaptist cane across the back every day
for four years till he was whipt out of England

CANADA

Twelve years old
                     & across the ocean alone
to apocalyptic Canada
                         Ontario of bone bending labor
six years on the road to Damascus till his eyes were blinded
with the blast of Christ & he wandered west
to Brandon among wheat kings & heathen Saturday nights
young red haired Bristol boy shoveling coal
in the basement of Brandon college five in the morning

Then built his first wooden church & married
a sick girl who bore two live children & died
leaving several pitiful letters & the Manitoba night

He moved west with another wife & built children & churches
Saskatchewan Alberta British Columbia Holy holy holy
lord god almighty
                      struck his labored bones with pain
& left him a postmaster prodding grandchildren with crutches
another dead wife & a glass bowl of photographs
& holy books unopened save the bible by the bed

Till he died the day before his eighty fifth birthday
in a Catholic hospital of sheets white as his hair

Mr. Portingale

Edward A. McCourt

Edward A. McCourt was born in Ireland in 1907 and came to Canada with his parents in 1909. He was educated at the University of Alberta and then at Oxford. A Rhodes scholar, he was a professor of English at the University of Saskatchewan when he died. He has published children's literature, fiction, non-fiction, and literary criticism.

In the old homesteading days of more than half a century ago, Mr. Portingale was a near neighbour of ours. He was a scruffy little Englishman born, according to the nomenclature of his time, into the lower middle class. Mr. Portingale was a staunch imperialist and devout church-goer; he knew his place in the scheme of things and until he took to homesteading in the middle of the prairie was content to keep it. A meek little man (but with no hope of inheriting the earth or any part thereof), he never dreamt of calling into question the wisdom and rectitude of either God or the government.

Not, that is, until he had lived – but only barely – through part of a prairie winter. One day in mid January of his first year on the homestead he borrowed my father's team and sleigh and hauled a load of grain to town, thirty miles away. He spent the night in the hotel and next morning, in defiance of warnings from weather-wise old-timers, started for home. Ten miles out, a blizzard met him head on. Fortunately the horses, grizzled old veterans of many a winter storm, took charge of Mr. Portingale and dragged him several hours later into our yard. My father dug him out from under about two feet of snow, unwound him from the horse-blankets he had thoughtfully wrapped himself in, and half-dragged, half-carried him into our kitchen.

Mother superintended the thawing-out operations. She placed one end of Mr. Portingale in a tub of cold water (his feet were badly frost-bitten) and after first clearing a channel through the icicles festooning his scraggy moustache poured into the other end about a gallon of hot tea generously laced with ginger.

Within fifteen minutes Mr. Portingale was thawing out all right and suffering the tortures of the damned. His feet were immersed in a tub of flaming coals and the tea had peeled most of the skin off the roof of his mouth. In the ordinary way Mr. Portingale was the humblest, least aggressive of men, his voice an appropriate piping treble, and the strongest expletive any of us had heard him use – and then only when greatly moved – was 'Gryte Scott!' But now those of us gathered in the kitchen were seeing something vastly more significant than the mere restoration of Mr. Portingale's circulatory system to its more or less normal channels; we were awe-stricken witnesses to a striking spiritual phenomenon peculiar to the prairies. For of a sudden, Mr. Portingale was no longer a humble sheep content to follow the bell-wether of the flock – he was the Stag at Bay. He glared at us out of red-rimmed bloodshot eyes and flung bloated pincushion hands aloft.

'The bloodiest absolutely bloodiest climate on the fice of the bloody earth!' Mr. Portingale bawled. 'And by God something's bloody well got to be done abaat it!'

Saskatchewan teems with Mr. Portingales. Men who, lapped in an enervating cloak of eastern smog or rendered soft and pliable by the eternal West Coast rain, would pass through life in meek unquestioning obedience to those placed in authority over them, develop, after a brief spell of prairie living, affinities with the Mau Mau or the I.R.A. Scorched by sun and battered by wind three months of the year and confined in a deep freeze for six, the prairie dweller is soon afflicted by a kind of nervous irritability which impels him to flail out in all directions. Being, as a rule, a religious man – intimate association with nature at its most awesome inclines to make him so – he hesitates to blame the Almighty for his miseries. The next authority – human, fallible, vulnerable – is the government. And something, by God, has got to be done about it!

Penny in the Dust

Ernest Buckler

Ernest Buckler is a Nova Scotian, born in 1908 and educated at Dalhousie University and the University of Toronto. He has published two novels and is an extensive contributor to periodicals. Since 1936, he has been occupied with farming and writing in Nova Scotia.

My sister and I were walking through the old sun-still fields the evening before the funeral, recalling this or that thing which had happened in this or that place, turning over memories after the fashion of families who gather again in the place where they were born – trying to disclose and identify themselves with the strange children they must have been.

"Do you remember the afternoon we thought you were lost?" my sister said. I did. That was as long ago as the day I was seven.

"We searched everywhere," she said, "up in the meetinghouse, back in the blueberry barrens we even looked in the well. I think it's the only time I ever saw Father really upset. He didn't even stop to tie up the horse's reins. He raced right through the chopping where Tom Reeve was burning brush, looking for you – right through the flames almost. They couldn't do a thing with him. And you up in your bed, sound asleep!

"It was all over losing a penny or something, wasn't it?" she went on, when I didn't answer. It was. She laughed indulgently. "You were a crazy kid, weren't you?"

I was. But there was more to it than that. I had never seen a brand-new penny before. I thought they were all black. This one was bright as gold. And my father had given it to me.

You would have to understand about my father and that is the hard thing to tell. If I say that he worked all day long, but I had never seen him hurry, that would make him sound like a stupid man. If I say that he never held me on his knee and that I never heard him laugh out loud in his life, it would make him sound humorless and severe. If I said that whenever I'd be telling mother some of my fancy plans and he'd come into the kitchen I'd stop, like someone hiding the pages of a foolish book, you'd think that he was distant and that in some kind of way I was afraid of him. None of that would be true.

There's no way you can tell it to make it sound like anything more than an inarticulate man a little at sea with an imaginative child. You'll have to take my word for it that there was more to it than that. It was as if his sure-footed way in the fields forsook him the instant he came near the door of my child's world and that he must wipe off his feet before he stood inside, awkward and conscious of trespass; and that I, sensing that but not understanding it, felt, at the sound of his solid step outside, my world's foolish fragility.

He would fix the small spot where I planted beans and other quick-sprouting seeds before he prepared the big garden, even if the spring was late; but he wouldn't ask me how many rows I wanted and, if he made three tiny rows and I wanted four, I couldn't ask him to change them. If I walked behind the load of hay, longing to ride, and he walked ahead of the oxen, I couldn't ask him to put me up and he wouldn't make any move to do so, until he saw me trying to grasp the binder.

He, my father, had just given me a new penny, bright as gold.

He took it from his pocket several times, pretending to examine the date on it, waiting for me to notice it. He couldn't offer me *anything* until I had shown some sign that the gift would be welcome.

"You can have it if you want it, Dan," he said at last.

I said, "Oh, thanks." Nothing more.

I started with it to the store. For a penny you could buy the magic cylinder of "Long Tom" popcorn, with Heaven knows what colored jewel on the ring inside. But the more I thought of my bright penny disappearing forever into the black drawstring pouch the Assyrian merchant kept his money in, the slower my steps lagged as the store came nearer and nearer. I sat down in the road.

It was that time of magic suspension in an August afternoon. The lifting smells of leaves and cut clover hung still in the sun. The sun drowsed, like a kitten curled upon my shoulder. The deep flour-fine dust in the road puffed about my bare ankles, warm and soft as sleep. A swallow-tailed butterfly clung to the road, its bright-banded wings spreading and converging like the movements of breathing. The sound of the cowbells came sharp and hollow from the cool swamp.

I began to play with the penny, postponing the decision. I would close my eyes and bury it deep in the sand and then, with my eyes still closed, get up and walk around and then come back to search for it, tantalizing myself each time with the thrill of discovering afresh its bright shining edge. I did that again and again. Alas, once too often.

It was almost dark when their excited talking in the room woke me. It was mother who had found me. I suppose when it came dusk she thought of me in the bed other nights and I suppose she looked there without any reasonable hope, but as you do when the search has become desperate, in every place where the thing lost has ever lain before. And now suddenly she was crying.

"Danny!" she cried, with the pointlessness of sudden relief, *"where* have you been!"

"I lost my penny," I said.

"You lost your penny – ? But what made you come up here and hide?"

If my father hadn't been there, I might have told her. But when I looked up at my father, standing there like the shape of everything sound and straight, it was like daylight shredding the memory of a foolish dream. How could I bear the shame of repeating before him the soft twisting visions I had built in my head in the magic August afternoon when almost anything could be made to seem real, as I buried the penny and dug it up again? How could I explain that pit-of-the-stomach sickness which struck through the whole day when I had to believe, at last, that it was really lost? How could I explain that I wasn't really hiding from *them*? How, with the words and the understanding I had then, that the only possible place to run from that awful feeling of loss was the soft, absorbing, dark safeness of bed? That I had cried myself asleep?

"I lost my penny," I said. I looked at father and turned my face into the pillow. "I want to go to sleep."

"Danny," my mother said, "it's almost nine o'clock. You haven't had a bite of supper. Do you know you almost scared the *life* out of us!"

"You better git some supper," my father said. It was the only time he had spoken.

I knew mother would talk about it and talk about it, but I never dreamed of father ever mentioning it again. But the next morning when we had the forks in our hands, ready to toss out the hay, he seemed to hold up the moment of actually leaving for the field. He stuck his fork in the ground and brought in another pail of water, though the kettle was chock-full. He took out the shingle nail that held his broken brace together and put it back in exactly the same hole. He went into the shop to see if the pigs had cleaned up all their breakfast.

"Ain't you got no idea where you lost your penny?" he said suddenly.

"Yes," I said, "I know just about."

"Let's see if we can't find it," he said.

We walked down the road together, stiff with awareness. He didn't hold my hand.

"It's right here somewheres," I said. "I was playin' with it in the dust." He looked at me, questioningly but he didn't ask me what game anyone could possibly play with a penny in the dust.

I might have known he would find it. In making a whistle he could tap alder bark with his jackknife just exactly hard enough so it wouldn't break but so it would twist free from the wood beneath, though I couldn't believe he had ever made a whistle for himself when he was a child. His great fingers could trace loose the hopeless snarl of a fishing line that I could only succeed in tangling tighter and tighter. If I broke the handle of my wheelbarrow ragged beyond sight of any possible repair, he could take it and bring it back to me so you could hardly see the place if you weren't looking for it.

He got down on his knees and drew his fingers carefully through the dust, like a harrow; not clawing it frantically in heaps as I had done, covering even while I uncovered. He found the penny almost at once.

He held it in his hand, as if the moment of passing it to me were a deadline for something he dreaded to say, but must. Something that could not be postponed any longer if it were to be spoken at all.

"Dan," he said, "You needn'ta hid. I wouldn'ta beat you."

"*Beat* me: Oh, Father! You didn't think *that* was the reason – ?" I felt almost sick.

Do you know how I felt then? I felt as if I had beaten *him*. His face looked like I had seen it of an evening when mother wasn't speaking and he would pick up a schoolbook or a paper and follow the lines patiently, though he never read any other time at all. I had to tell him the truth then. Because only the truth, no matter how foolish it was, would have the unmistakable sound of truth, to scatter that awful idea out of his head.

"I wasn't hidin', father," I said, "honest – I was – I was buryin' my penny and makin' out I was diggin' up treasure. I was makin' out I was findin' gold. I didn't know what to *do* when I lost it, I just didn't know where to *go* – " His head was bent forward, like mere listening. I had to make it truer still.

"I made out it was gold," I said desperately, "and I – I was makin' out I bought you a mowin' machine so's you could get your work done early every day so's you and I could go into town in the big automobile I made out I bought and everyone'd turn around and look at us drivin' down the streets – " His head was perfectly still, as if he were only waiting with patience for me to finish.

" – *laughin'* and *talkin'* – " I said, louder, smiling intensely, compelling him, by the absolute conviction of some true particular, to believe me. –

He looked up then. It was the only time I had ever seen tears in his eyes.

I wondered, though, why he hesitated and then put the penny back in his own pocket.

Yesterday I knew. I never found any fortune and we never had a car to ride in together. But I think he knew what that would be like, just the same. I found the penny again yesterday, when we were getting out his good clothes – in an upper vest pocket where no one ever carries change. It was still shining. He must have kept it polished.

I left it there.

Lament for the Dorsets

Alfred Purdy

Alfred Purdy was born near Wooler, Ontario in 1918. Purdy is an accomplished poet who has had several volumes of poetry published.

Animal bones and some mossy tent rings
scrapers and spearheads carved ivory swans
all that remains of the Dorset giants
who drove the Vikings back to their long ships
talked to spirits of earth and water
– a picture of terrifying old men
so large they broke the backs of bears
so small they lurk behind bone rafters
in the brain of modern hunters
among good thoughts and warm things
and come out at night
to spit on the stars

The big men with clever fingers
who had no dogs and hauled their sleds
over the frozen northern oceans
awkward giants
               killers of seal
they couldn't compete with little men
who came from the west with dogs
Or else in a warm climatic cycle
the seals went back to cold waters

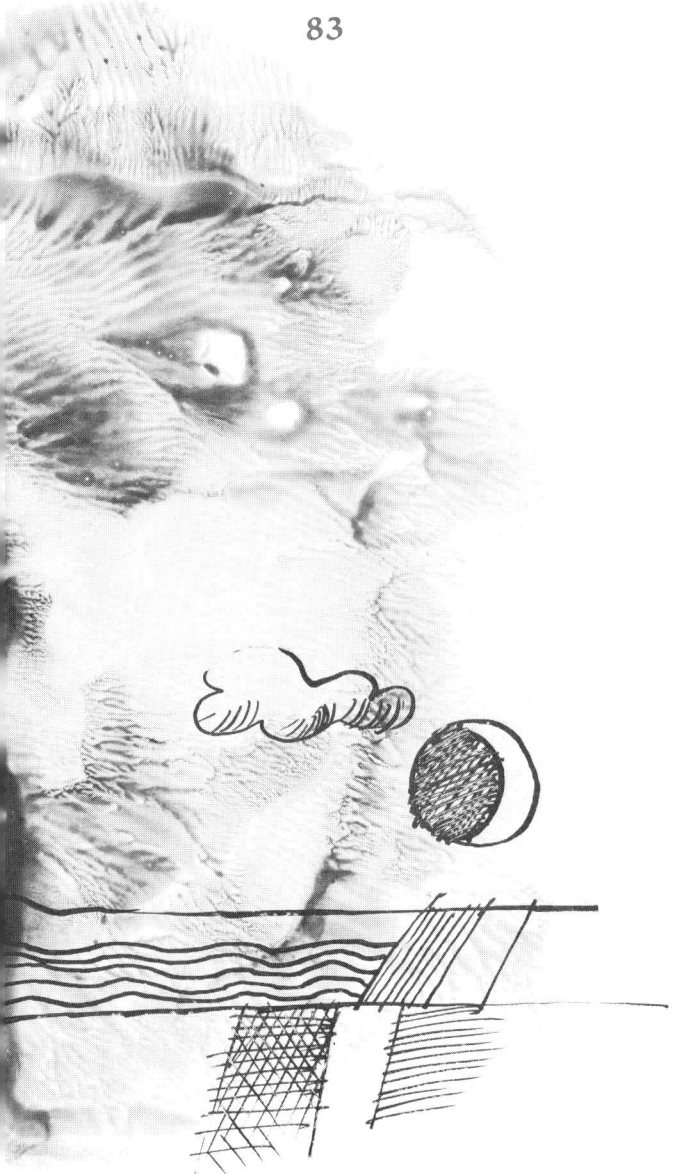

and the puzzled Dorsets scratched their heads
with hairy thumbs around 1350 A.D.
– couldn't figure it out
went around saying to each other
plaintively
            'What's wrong? What happened?
            Where are the seals gone?'
And died

Twentieth century people
apartment dwellers
executives of neon death
warmakers with things that explode
– they have never imagined us in their future
how could we imagine them in the past
squatting among the moving glaciers
six hundred years ago
with glowing lamps?
As remote or nearly
as the trilobites and swamps
when coal became
or the last great reptile hissed
at a mammal the size of a mouse
that squeaked and fled
Did they ever realize at all
what was happening to them?
Some old hunter with one lame leg
a bear had chewed
sitting in a caribou-skin tent
– the last Dorset?
Let's say his name was Kudluk

CANADA

and watch him sitting there
carving 2-inch ivory swans
for a dead grand-daughter
taking them out of his mind
the places in his mind
where pictures are
He selects a sharp stone tool
to gouge a parallel pattern of lines
on both sides of the swan
holding it with his left hand
bearing down and transmitting
his body's weight
from brain to arm and right hand
and one of his thoughts
turns to ivory
The carving is laid aside
in beginning darkness
at the end of hunger
and after a while wind
blows down the tent and snow
begins to cover him
After 600 years
the ivory thought
is still warm

Depression Flashback 1937

A. F. Menzies

A. F. Menzies is a newspaperman who has edited small-town newspapers in Saskatchewan, and, Alberta. He is now retired, living with his wife in Penticton, B. C. His book *Two Dollars per Year* is a collection of his newspaper editorials.

I append the following article for no particular reason except that I sort of like it myself. Driven to desperation by the cruelties of the Great Depression, we had sold our printing business in a Saskatchewan town late in 1936, and had eked out the winter at the Pacific coast as a free-lance writer.

"A Little Place at the Coast" was published in The Western Producer of April 29, 1937. It reflects the general spirit of defeat which existed everywhere following seven years of world depression, during which the standard of living had sunk lower and lower while warehouses were stacked to the ceiling with all the good things of life.

Indeed, the article so well reflected the times that it came near to making me famous. Letters of appreciation poured in from all corners, from people I had never heard of, and in short, "A Little Place at the Coast" was about the only good thing the depression did for me.

A Little Place at the Coast

I have mislaid the statistics, if I ever had them, showing how many people annually forsake the prairies for the Pacific Coast. But the number must be considerable. In fact, it is often said that if you took the prairie people out of Vancouver and its environs, you might just as well close the place up and throw the key into the Fraser river.

During my own thirty years of residence on the prairies most of the people I knew sooner or later left for the Coast. A few left because they could afford to leave; the rest left because they couldn't afford to stay. And, oddly enough, both classes were actuated by the same motive – to get "a little place at the Coast." Three acres of land, a cow, a pig, a stand of bees, two rows of potatoes, three fruit trees and sixty hens.

To those who could afford to retire, the "little place" offered a graceful, even a dignified means of departing this earth in favor of younger people. To the rest it seemed to promise, if not independence, at least a shelter from economic stress until such time as "things would improve."

If you drive along any road on the prairies till you come to a vacant house, and if you hunt up the nearest neighbor and ask him where are the people who used to live in that house, it is an even bet that he will say:

"They moved away a few years ago to the Coast. They expected to get a little place out there – three acres of land, a cow, a pig, a stand of bees, two rows of potatoes, three fruit trees and sixty hens."

Have you ever wondered how they were making out, these people with "little places" at the coast?

Having little to do during the last three months except poke my nose into other people's affairs, I have hunted out a lot of these prairie refugees who have little places out here, and I think that my findings may be of interest, especially to those who may be experiencing a gnawing desire to own three acres of land, a cow, a pig, a stand of bees, two rows of potatoes, three fruit trees and sixty hens on the Pacific Coast.

Mr. A came from – let us say – Quill Lake. He has two acres, all of it under stumps except the portion occupied by the house. The stumps can be taken out at a cost of forty dollars each. Mr. A. has a job firing in a sawmill, though the work does not agree with his back. When he gets steady work he can save enough out of a year's wages to take out one stump. There are 311 stumps on his little place.

Mrs. B. hails from Watrous, and she began life at the Coast with a large drove of hens on Lulu Island. The hens lost money right from the start, and she was hardly sorry when they all died of the roup. Now she has an acre on the mainland, and no hens. She is happier and loses less money than she used to, even when she was farming at Watrous.

Mr. and Mrs. C. arrived from Hanna in 1928 – young, but well fixed. They had clear title to a good section of land at Hanna, a good car, and $5,000 in cash. They rented their farm at Hanna, bought a little place out here for $4,000, and prepared to live the life of Reilly. The Alberta farm hasn't paid them a cent since they left it. They sold their $4,000 place here last year for $1,600, and bought another little place – one with more stumps on it. Every morning Mr. C. goes the rounds of the sawmills, looking for a job, but has had no luck in that direction so far.

Mr. D. is the man who bought Mr. C's place for $1,600. He came from Dauphin. Says he bought a farm there 20 years ago, and got out gravel the same year for the foundation of a new house. Twenty years later they were still living in the old house, and the chickens had eaten all the gravel, so he decided he could not possibly do worse on a little place at the Coast. He and his son also go up to the mills every day to look for work, but so far the mills are managing to struggle along without them. They will have plenty of fruit on their little place, but of course there is the item of sugar.

Mr. E. is from Melville. He has a steady job in a mill, and hopes to have his little place paid for in another three or four years. He denies himself hens and some other luxuries, but he keeps a cow, thereby shouldering a loss which some poor dairy farmer would otherwise have to carry.

Mr. F. has hotel accommodation for 2,000 hens, but he has no hens. He did have hens, then he thought better of it and got a filling station instead. He says there is more fun in the filling station, because there are nineteen other filling stations within a mile to share the total loss with him.

Mr. G. just bought his little place from a Jap. It is well known that Japs work 20 hours a day and require no food. That is what this Jap and his wife did during 17 years. Then the wife got tired of it and died, and the Jap, who had accumulated forty-two dollars, went back to Japan to enjoy his declining years. Such are the roseate prospects of Mr. G.

Down at the mills, of a morning, stand groups of male help who have come to see if they are wanted. They never are – or hardly ever. Once in a blue moon one of them lands a job, but the usual verdict of the boss is "No openings today." But they are courteously treated by the mill owners, for they have a value. Nothing contributes so much to the "contentment" of an industrial worker as to see a crowd of busted farm hands standing outside the gate.

At random, I choose one of the group, and make speech with him.

"Stranger," I say, "what part of Saskatchewan are you from?"

"Hanley," he replies, a bit wistfully. "I farmed there for eighteen years. Now I have a little place out here – three acres. If I could get a job here in the mill for a while, I'd be all right. I figure I could make my living off that little place if I had a cow, a pig, a stand of bees, a few rows of potatoes, two or three fruit trees, and fifty or sixty hens."

Death of an Outport

Al Pittman

Al Pittman is a Newfoundland writer and poet who is presently lecturing at Memorial University, St. John's.

In the summer of 1967 I sat in the kitchen of a fisherman's home on the island of Merasheen in Newfoundland's Placentia Bay. The fisherman, Anthony Wilson, had seen my wife and me walking down the road past his bungalow and, because we were strangers, he had invited us in for a cup of tea.

In Newfoundland "tea" means a fully laid table including linen cloth, the best china in the house, home made bread, a variety of wild berry jams, a platter of luncheon meat, and always a jar of molasses. After we had gorged ourselves on Mrs. Wilson's "tea," Anthony broke out a bottle of rum. He had had the rum come in by mail boat two weeks before and had ever since kept it hidden away in the bedroom only to be opened on the day of the annual garden party three days hence. Anthony, however, decided that having strangers in was excuse enough to break the rule and promptly produced a bottle of black demerara. For an hour we passed the bottle back and forth across the width of the kitchen table and talked of Merasheen.

Merasheen lies about five miles off the west shore of Placentia Bay on Newfoundland's southeast coast. Most of the island's inhabitants live on the island's southern end in the villages of Merasheen, Little Merasheen, and Hickey's Bottom. The villages are located in three adjacent harbours, affording the fishermen of the place a choice of landings when weather conditions prevent them from going in to their usual moorings. Behind the villages lie the barren sheep-dotted hills of Merasheen which give the island its bleak, naked appearance. Beyond the hills, however, there are miles of forest where the men snare rabbits in the fall, and, beyond that, more miles of barrens where caribou roam out of range of the guns of the American big game hunters who come in droves to Newfoundland each autumn. Though the people of Merasheen feast on rabbit stew and caribou steaks in season, their livelihood is harvested out of the dark Atlantic waters that are everywhere around them. The violent rhythm of the sea is the rhythm in which the people of Merasheen have lived since man first set foot on the island's rugged perimeter.

My father was born in Merasheen in 1907 and I was born thirty-three years later in the tiny village of St. Leonard's just across the bay. I had gone there that summer with my wife to put all the stories my father and mother ever told me into their proper setting. I had been taken out of the bay before I was six months old, and though I knew Chapel Pond and the Jawbones, and Soldier's Point, and the Jigging Cove, and St. Kyran's like the palm of my hand I had never seen any of them. So I went that summer to see where my father had come from, where my mother had come from, and where, most of all, I had come from.

"Sounds like a hard way to make a living." I said when Anthony had finished telling of one particularly rough time he'd had in winter fishing.

"Well, I'll tell ye Phonse," he replied, "it's the devil's own handiwork betimes, but once ye leave off on a summer morning, heading out, with the sun just peeping up, the skiff cutting clean in the water, and all that shiny sea stretching out ahead of ye to westward, well Phonse, you go out one morning like that and you can put up with winter fishing the rest of your life."

It wasn't at all the sort of thing I would have expected from the weather-beaten, granite giant of a man sitting across the table from me. Yet, when he said it, it rang so true I felt a sudden surge of sadness sweep over the room, for as we sat talking, we, all of us, knew that this would be the last summer Anthony Wilson or anybody else would head out from Merasheen.

Centralization, Premier Joseph Smallwood's plan to "drag Newfoundland kicking and screaming into the twentieth century," had already taken its toll in Placentia Bay. St. Leonard's, St. Kyran's, Clattice Harbour, St. Anne's, Toslow, and numerous other villages were already being reclaimed by the wilderness into which they had been etched some hundreds of years ago.

The livyers had been paid a subsidy to move to a better life in places like Marystown and Placentia, where, they were promised, there would be jobs galore, and motor cars, and television sets, and better educational facilities for their children.

If such well-timed persuasions as these failed to move the people, the church lent a helping hand. It closed down schools and churches and took away the priests. Inevitably the latter did the trick. The people of Placentia Bay outports could do without cars, and supermarkets, and television sets, but being as religious and as superstitious as they happen to be, they could no more think of living where there was no priest than they could think of living inland. So they moved.

From all the villages of the bay they moved to the government designated "growth centres" where they discovered, too late, that the only growth was the growth in population – the result of their own mass migration. Too often they found the worth of their subsidy not nearly enough to replace the homes they had left behind in the coves and on the islands. Too often they found that the promised jobs were nonexistent. In Placentia, for instance, where so many of them were sent, they found that houses were hard to come by, and jobs even harder. The only sources of employment in the town were the Canadian National coastal boat terminal and the American naval station at Argentia. Due to cutbacks in CN coastal service (now that there were fewer outports to serve) and to cutbacks in U.S. military commitments in Newfoundland there were perhaps fewer employment opportunities than ever before.

And now there was talk of Merasheen.

It seemed there was nothing Anthony Wilson or anyone else could do about it. The government fish plant was closing down, therefore there'd be no market for their fish. They could, as they did for years before the fish plant opened, take their catch to Wareham's in Harbour Buffett. But Wareham's too were curtailing operations.

As well as closing down the fish plant, the government would also halt operation of the dynamos that had, for the past few years, delivered electricity to the islanders' homes. The school had already closed. And the priest was leaving in the fall. So the people of Merasheen would have to move. What else could they do?

Anthony Wilson didn't want to go. He had his own home, and a comfortable and sturdy dwelling it was too. He had a garden out back where his wife grew turnips, potatoes, carrots, beets, cabbage, and a variety of currants and gooseberries. And when I suggested that his fishing take would probably do no more than pay for the gear, he said, "No, Phonse me son, we does a bit better than that."

And when his wife went to the bedroom and returned with the new clothes she had bought by mail order for the children and herself so that they might look "fine" on the day of the garden party, it wasn't hard to tell that the pleasure of the newly acquired finery was in no way diminished by the thought of payments, installments, or "time" as Newfoundlanders refer to credit.

But they would go. There was no other way.

Mike Casey would go too, and his wife Elizabeth, though she kept saying over and over that they would have to drag her away.

Stan Ennis and his son Andrew would go too, though they owned the best boat in the bay and Andrew was as good a fish-killer as his father. And George Wilson would go. Skipper George Wilson, white haired, as tall and dignified as a church spire, skin the texture of rawhide, bread 'n' buttered there some eighty odd years ago, a legend in his time, father to Anthony, village elder, as gentle as the waves lapping the shore below his house, as rough as the rock that threw the sea back upon itself when it erupted with all its fury upon the Jawbones. He would go too. Go leaving his wife's grave to the delinquent sheep. Leaving all he would have passed on to his sons to the wind and the rain and the sea. Would go leaving everything behind with his memory and his old man's heart. But he would go.

"I could see it," Anthony said, passing the bottle, "I could see it maybe if they moved us all into St. Kyran's or anyplace down here in the bay. There's good harbours, the fish is here, the men is here what can catch 'em too. I can see they wants bigger schools. I understands that. We been having hard enough time getting a teacher to come here and they only stays a year at the most. I can see the priest wanting one church to look after 'stead of a whole bunch of 'em. God knows, he has it hard going at it all the time. And a lot of priests don't like it in the bay no more. Well, they isn't fishermen so's I don't know ye could blame 'em any. All the same though, I can't for the life o' me see why they shifts us to

Placentia. Ye knows yourself there's no living to be made there. The base is closing down bit by bit. Where's the men going to work, I asks. A man can't fish outa Placentia, that's for certain and for sure."

I took a long swig on the bottle and regretted that we couldn't stay for the garden party on Sunday. If I had my time back now, I would have stayed no matter what. But at the time the significance of it all passed me by. It didn't strike me as it should have that this garden party would be the last ever to be held in Merasheen. It would be the end of a tradition that went back before my father's father's time. The end of a way of life.

The morning after our visit with Anthony we walked past the parish hall and saw the tarpaulin booths all in a row in the church yard. Sunday they would be ringed by little girls in floral print dresses; by the men of the place, coat pockets bulging with bottles, Sunday tweed caps angled on their heads; by women with babies on their hips, white aprons looking altogether fine in the outdoors; by young girls with the dishes already done and for the first time in three days no rollers in their hair, flirting openly with the Peters and Andrews and Jims of Merasheen; by the boys who made root beer from extract and carried it in bottles, as drunk as their fathers in their fantasies.

Sunday the booths would house ice-cream in heavy canvas khaki bags, wheels of fortune, cabbage-roll dinners, ticket pedlars, bean bags, balloons and darts, sacks for the sack race, ropes for the three-legged race, steaming boilers of good things to eat, coca cola in cases, peanut butter kisses, licorice, and home-knit scarves and caps and socks and mitts to be won as prizes.

But that morning the booths stood empty, their sides flapping noisily in the wind, as they had on that same morning for hundreds of years past.

The Devil was there too, looking very much out of place in the middle of the empty yard. On Sunday every man and boy in Merasheen would take a crack at knocking his head off. How long ago was it that some expert young chucker first knocked the devil's head off, sent it rolling beneath the feet of the crowd, heralding good tidings for the people of Merasheen?

We left the parish ground and went over the hill into Hickey's Bottom. Mike Casey came then and invited us "'ome to 'ave a shave and to meet the missus." As we walked along the beach road, Mike pointed out to me the precise spot where my grandfather's house used to be and the path he used to take "luggin' 'is long tom" going into the barrens to get rabbits.

I could see my father, a little boy, running up the path at dusk to greet him, tall like timber, coming home from a day's hunting on the barrens with his long tom over his shoulder and a brace of rabbits dangling at his side. A vigorous man, still vigorous after a day's trek on the barrens, tossing his young son high into the air and carrying him secure on his shoulder to the house.

"I'm too old to be going anywhere's at my age," Mike said as we sat in his kitchen nipping on his garden party rum. It seemed the invitation to shave was just an excuse to bring strangers home so that he could get at the rum without his wife objecting.

"What the jeesus ye expect a man o' my age to be doing in Placentia, I asks. Lived right here all me born days. Ain't no time to be gallivantin' around at my age."

So he talked on through half the bottle of dark rum, but he would go too. Would go to Placentia or wherever and spend the rest of his days remembering the times back home. What else was there for him to do?

"They's 'll have to drag me," said his Elizabeth with the defiance of a young whippersnapper being sent off to school to repeat a grade.

"They's 'll have to drag me. Without they do, I'll not be going very far. They's 'll have to drag me is all."

She knew in the fall, when the time came, she'd be packing the old clock and her good linen and the quilt her mother gave her for a wedding gift, and she knew in the fall, when the time came, she'd be going too. But she wasn't about to admit it. Not yet. Not until she had to.

In the afternoon we met Stan Ennis. He had heard that Phonse Pittman's son was in and came out to find him. He did find us soon enough and invited us up to his place for a drop o' rum.

"One time," he said, "Phonse was coming over from St. Leonard's to play football, and we was in the same boat together, and I 'ad a bottle o' rum on board, and I passed 'er around to all leaving Phonse out because 'e being the school teacher I didn't know as it'd be right to ask 'im to 'ave a drop, and I been mindin' a long time that it weren't right not offerin' 'im a drop, so I wants ye to come up to the 'ouse and 'ave that drop o' rum that yer father should of 'ad that day."

So we went up to Stan's and had hot toddies – boiling water and sugar laced with black rum, "good for what ails ye whether ye be man or beast."

"Don't know what I'll be doing to 'er," Stan said when I asked him what would become of his boat if he had to move off the island.

"Don't allow as I'll be able to sell 'er. Ain't no one 'll be left to use 'er anyways far as I can see."

The hot toddy was fit for a king.

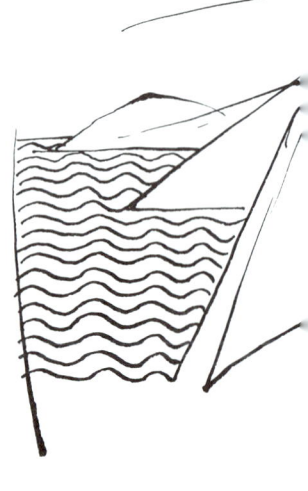

"Always was good fish in the bay, leastwise up 'ere. Man could always make a livin' at the fish. But if they takes the plant, my God, what's the use of catchin' 'em."

So Stan Ennis, the most renowned fish-killer in the bay, would be leaving Merasheen, and his son Andrew would be leaving with him.

"'Ere's to yer father, Phonse, as fine a man as ever broke a cake of the world's bread. Tell 'im I gave 'is son the drop o' rum I owed to 'im."

The next morning, the coastal boat *Petitforte* came in as she was scheduled to, doubling back on the bay run, and we went aboard.

It seemed the whole of Merasheen came to see us off. Men, women and children crowding the small wharf, waving and wishing us well, and saying it was too bad we couldn't stay for the garden party.

Just as the CN boys were pulling in the ropes, preparing to set off, a short stocky man in blue serge, pipe firm in the corner of his mouth, face eroded like a cliff, came over the ramp, walked straight up to me, and, very businesslike, introduced himself.

"I didn't get to have a chat with ye while ye were in which I'm sorry about but I used to know yer father right well when we was young, fished together, first trip for the both of us, didn't want it said that Phonse Pittman's boy was in and I never got to say hello to him."

The whistle blew then and he went back over the ramp as suddenly as he had come. Back on the wharf he merged with all the other pipe smoking blue serge that stood hands in pockets waiting for us to shove off.

The people of Merasheen, as warm as we'd always remember them, stood there and waved us away. They waved us past Soldier's Point and out to the Jawbones where we could see crosses almost everywhere upon the cliffs marking the spots where men of the outports had run foul of the sunkers and gone down in the sea that was at once their sustenance and deprivation, their life and their death.

Baffles of the Wind and Tide, Clyde Rose, ed., Breakwater, 1974.

The Canadian Personality

Bruce Hutchison

Bruce Hutchison was born in Ontario and educated in British Columbia. Hutchison's books, *The Unknown Country: Canada and Her People* (1943), and *Canada – Tomorrow's Giant* (1957) reflect his keen interest in Canada and her relations with other countries. The "Canadian Personality" was first presented as a radio talk by CBC.

Somewhere across this broad land of Canada tonight there is a lost and desperate man trying to find the smallest needle in the largest haystack in the world. He is one of the best American journalists in the business, he has covered important stories in countless countries, but his assignment in Canada has stumped him. His assignment is to discover, analyze, and spread on paper for the American public, the inner meaning of Canadian life.

Well, I did the best I could for the poor fellow. I talked to him all last night but when I had finished he was still pacing my room, aflame with the mystery of his mission and certain other stimulating refreshments I had provided – he was pacing the room at dawn and complaining that I had really told him nothing of Canada. "What I have to find," he cried out in his agony, "is the Canadian character, the Canadian personality, the Canadian dream."

When I last saw him, staggering into the sunrise, he hadn't found what he was looking for. And it suddenly occurred to me that I hadn't found it either, after half a century, that I probably wouldn't find it, that it may be forever undiscoverable. I am not surprised, therefore, when my American friend concludes that there actually is no Canadian character, personality, or dream.

Nevertheless, he was wrong. But he set me thinking. And the more I thought about this thing the more confused I became. Yet he was wrong.

Now, it's true that you can't define the Canadian character, or at least I can't, nor can any of our statesmen, writers, or artists, so far as I have seen. But nothing of importance in life is definable. Once anything yields to definition you can be sure it isn't very important.

So we needn't go on making excuses, as we always do before strangers, because we cannot spell out the life of Canada like a chemical formula. And we shouldn't apologize either because the character of Canada is so divided and complex, holding within itself at least six sub-characters – the proud, grim, and inflexible character of the Maritimes; the gay but hard and practical character of Quebec; the bustling, able, and rather provincial character of Ontario; the character of Toronto, a growth so rare and baffling that I shall not venture, as an outsider, to give it even an adjective; the spacious, generous, and almost naïve character of the prairies; the boyish, ravenous, and self-centred character of British Columbia.

Our national personality is split many ways. So is the personality of every great nation and every great man in history. Britain is commonly supposed to have the most settled and clear-cut character of any country, but set the Scotsman or the Welshman against the Englishman, set the cockney against the north-countryman, and you will observe the startling diversity and contrast of British life.

We Canadians worry too much about our diversity. For it is an illusion, very common with us, to imagine that a nation grows strong by uniformity. Why, in the basic and most essential unit of mankind, in the family itself, diversity is the surest sign of strength and talent, the best guarantee of unity. No man in his senses would try to make his children all alike, and would mercifully extinguish them at birth if he thought they would not resemble him when they grew up. What folly it is, what a will-o'-the-wisp, what a national obsession, to imagine that we shall only achieve a true national character when we have at last turned out a generation as uniform as a package of chewing gum and about as durable.

Nevertheless, as my bewildered American friend told me, it won't do to say that Canadians have strong and varied local characteristics in different parts of the country. That won't prove the existence of a national character. You must be able to prove that throughout the country there are certain dominant, widely shared and fully accepted characteristics, instincts, and deep feelings – certain common denominators by which the intangible thing as a whole can be measured. That is where the argument about our national character always collapses, as I have seen it collapse, over and over again, usually late at night amid a despairing clink of glasses, from Victoria to Halifax.

It's no wonder that it's a difficult thing to clutch in your hand, the character of Canada; wonderful, rather, that there is anything to clutch. Wonderful for this reason: Whereas other nations of the past grew up in a world of watertight compartments, and hardened into individual shape before other nations could touch and dilute them, we began to build a nation here only a few years ago, in a new world, in a violent world revolution, in an age where all nations were being driven together, cheek by jowl, through the new means of transport, information, and propaganda. Our case was peculiarly difficult, much more difficult, for example, than Australia's, because we lived beside a great established nation, the most powerful magnet the world has ever known, and its ideas have washed in on us in a ceaseless tide. We were indeed, and are still today, like a youth starting out on his path, glancing over his shoulder at the ancient glories of his home in Britain or France and, when he looks ahead, dazzled by the glitter of the United States.

Despite everything, however, I think we can begin now to detect some of the special characteristics common to all Canadians, and add them up to something.

First, and most obvious, is our national humility. We are a people bounded on one side by the northern lights and on the other by an inferiority complex just as vivid, a people distracted by the mossy grandeur of the old world from which we came and by the power, wealth, and fury of our American neighbors. We are the last people to realize, and the first to deny, the material achievements of the Canadian nation, which all the rest of the world has already grasped and envied. Self-deprecation is our great national habit.

This is curious, when you come to think of it, because so many of us are of British origin. A few days ago a scholar from India wrote in the London *Times* that the English consider their primary national vice to be hypocrisy, but he said, "I must insist on first things first. The root and beginning is self-admiration, and hypocrisy only its most distinguished product." Now that's an interesting epigram but its reception in England is *more* interesting. In Canada we would resent it, but the English loved it. They have had so much experience, they are so sure of themselves, that they can laugh at the impudence of outsiders. We don't laugh because we lack any self-admiration, and we're not very good at hypocrisy, either. We are hurt by the foreigner's criticism because we have a sneaking suspicion that it must be true, suspicion that would not occur to an Englishman. Never has there been a people in all history which has accomplished so much as the Canadian people and thought so little of it. An Indian scholar won't find self-admiration here. He'll find self-apology written in big black letters across our Canadian map – no, not in big letters. We write everything small if it's Canadian.

This, perhaps, lies close to the root of another national characteristic – we are a conservative and steady people, hardly daring to believe in our own capacity in the more complex affairs of statecraft, afraid to test that capacity too far with new systems and experiments. The Canadian audience at a political meeting (a significant little test, if the glummest), is the most stolid and dead-panned ever known – a collection of dull and sceptical haddock eyes to daunt the boldest politician; and our politicians truly reflect us in their stodgy competence, their unvarying pedestrianism, their high ability, their positive terror of color and flair.

And we are a lonely people, isolated from one another, in a land where the largest city is a frail wink of lights in the darkness of the night.

Lonely, and awed by the immensity of space around us, by the cold sweep of the prairies, by the stark presence of mountains leaning upon us, by the empty sea at our door, and by the fierce northern climate, which colors and toughens the weather of our spirit. And we are closer to the soil still, all of us, even in our cities, than the people of any other great industrial and urban nation.

We are more aware than others of the central physical fact of the earth, of growth, of harvest and decay. This land sense dominates all our national thinking, our politics, our economic system, and our personal habits. It makes our artists instinctively rush out to paint, not the abstractions of other artists, but the hard material of rock and pine tree.

This deep instinct for the land, our constant feeling of struggle against a harsh nature – this and our concentration on the mere task of survival, must be one of the things that makes us an unimaginative people, prosaic, pitifully inarticulate, and singularly lacking in humor. (We haven't even developed the great Canadian joke yet or learned to laugh at ourselves.) It may turn out that we are really filled with fire, poetry, and laughter, which we have repressed, thinking it inferior to other peoples', and perhaps these things will erupt some day, with shattering violence. So far there has been hardly a rumble, nor any tinkle of a national song nor the vague shape of a national myth.

On the evidence so far you might almost say that we have constructed a national character by refusing to construct one. The great void almost becomes a solid thing, the vacuum begins to take on substance, the national silence begins to speak in a clear Canadian voice. We have taken a *nothing* – our pathological horror of expression – and erected a *something* which distinguishes us from all other people. This is not enough to make a character, I admit, but you won't find it anywhere else. And perhaps the refusal to admit achievement is an achievement in itself.

But there is something about us more important and more distinctive than any of these obvious qualities.

We are among the few peoples still in the first throes of collective growth. While older peoples have settled down and accepted certain conventions, conditions, attitudes, and limitations as permanent, we accept nothing, least of all limitations. We live in a constant expectation of change, which we don't particularly relish and rather suspect, but cannot avoid. We have, every one of us, the feeling that we are involved in a process of perpetual expansion, development, and revision, whose end we cannot see.

We have the feeling, not of an old and settled resident in his father's house, but of a young man building a new house for himself, without any clear plan in his head and wondering how large his future family will be.

Ours is the doubt and risk, but the unequalled satisfaction of the man who builds and makes something with his own hands, perhaps the best satisfaction that life offers; and this sense of being only at the beginning of things, this expectation of a greater structure still to be built – this, I think, is the universal and most distinctive feature of the Canadian. We are, above all, a building people, a nation of beavers.

But, my American friend says, all this does not add up to a national character, and hence he concludes there is none. All right, then. We have failed to define that character, as I told you we would. But consider this: We have built here against every obstacle of geography, economics, racial division, and the magnet of our American neighbor – we have built here the greatest nation of its population in all recorded history. How did we do it? Why didn't we break up into inevitable splinters, why didn't we throw in the sponge and join the United States long ago?

No political decision, no economic planning, will explain that. Something much more than politics or economics was at work – the unshakeable will to make a nation, a home, a life of our own, for which no inconvenience was too great, from which no temptation could swerve us – a dim, impalpable, and dumb thing beyond our power to express or even name.

There is the hard, silent, and unyielding core of Canada, the final mystery which, like all the other things that matter in life, like life itself, is forever inexpressible and can only be intimated in myths and parables which, so far, we have been too busy and too reticent to invent. They will come in time, but the thing itself which they will vainly try to voice, is already here, and has been here since Champlain shivered on the rock of Quebec, in that first cruel Canadian winter, and has been carried by every Canadian boy, dumbly in his heart, to the battlefields at the ends of the earth – this dream of high mountains and deep forests and prairie skies, of summer crops and winter snow, and Canadian ways, and all the vast compact of familiar, precious things, making up together the substance of Canada which, through more than three hundred years we have refused to abandon, to sell, or even to mention.

If this is not yet a rounded and settled national character, it is, assuredly, the soil out of which a character is growing as surely as a boy grows into a man. It has grown these last few years faster than we have stopped to realize – of which the best proof, perhaps, is that, as never before, we now pause in our huge labors to ask ourselves what we are and what we hope to be. We cannot answer yet, but we know that we have within us, as our fathers had, one dominant feeling which is so general and unquestioned that we take it for granted. We quarrel about methods, political theories, economic systems, but such things do not make up a national character. Our character is not being built on them but on something much larger, a truly common denominator, the space, the beauty, and the free life of Canada itself.

Well, I wonder what haystack my American friend is searching in tonight for a needle which he could not recognize even if he found it.

Good Old Uncle Albert

Farley Mowat

Farley Mowat was born in Belleville, Ontario, in 1921. He was graduated from the University of Toronto, and began his career as a freelance journalist after spending two years in the Arctic. He has published a number of books, mainly non-fiction, in addition to his extensive contributions to periodicals.

As I grew more completely attuned to their daily round of family life I found it increasingly difficult to maintain an impersonal attitude toward the wolves. No matter how hard I tried to regard them with scientific objectivity, I could not resist the impact of their individual personalities. Because he reminded me irresistibly of a Royal Gentleman for whom I worked as a simple soldier during the war, I found myself calling the father of the family George, even though in my notebooks, he was austerely identified only as Wolf "A."

George was a massive and eminently regal beast whose coat was silver-white. He was about a third larger than his mate, but he hardly needed this extra bulk to emphasize his air of masterful certainty. George had presence. His dignity was unassailable, yet he was by no means aloof. Conscientious to a fault, thoughtful of others, and affectionate within reasonable bounds he was the kind of father whose idealized image appears in many wistful books of human family reminiscences, but whose real prototype has seldom paced the earth upon two legs. George was, in brief, the kind of father every son longs to acknowledge as his own.

His wife was equally memorable. A slim, almost pure-white wolf with a thick ruff around her face, and wide-spaced, slightly slanted eyes, she seemed the picture of a minx. Beautiful, ebullient, passionate to a degree, and devilish when the mood was on her, she hardly looked like the epitome of motherhood; yet there could have been no better mother anywhere. I found myself calling her Angeline, although I have never been able to trace the origin of that name in the murky depths of my own subsconscious. I respected and liked George very much, but I became deeply fond of Angeline, and still live in hopes that I can somewhere find a human female who embodies all her virtues.

Angeline and George seemed as devoted a mated pair as one could hope to find. As far as I could tell they never quarrelled, and the delight with which they greeted each other after even a short absence was obviously unfeigned. They were extremely affectionate with one another, but, alas, the many pages in my notebook which had been hopefully reserved for detailed comments on the sexual behavior and activities of wolves remained obstinately blank as far as George and Angeline were concerned.

Distressing as it was to my expectations, I discovered that physical lovemaking enters into the lives of a pair of mated wolves only during a period of two or three weeks early in the spring, usually in March. Virgin females, (and they are all virginal until their second year) then mate; but unlike dogs, who have adopted many of the habits of their human owners, wolf bitches mate with only a single male, and mate for life.

Whereas the phrase "till death us do part" is one of the more amusing mockeries in the nuptial arrangements of a large proportion of the human race, with wolves it is a simple fact. Wolves are also strict monogamists; and although I do not necessarily consider this an admirable trait, it does make the reputation for unbridled promiscuity which we have bestowed on the wolf somewhat hypocritical.

While it was not possible for me to know with exact certainty how long George and Angeline had been mated, I was later able to discover from Mike that they had been together for at least five years – or the equivalent of thirty years in terms of the relative longevity of wolves and men. Mike and the Eskimos recognized the wolves in their area as familiar individuals, and the Eskimos (but not Mike) held the wolves in such high regard that they would not have thought of killing them or doing them an injury. Thus not only were George, Angeline and other members of the family well known to the Eskimos, but the site of their den had been known for some forty or fifty years, during which time generations of wolves had raised families there.

One factor concerning the organization of the family mystified me very much at first. During my early visit to the den I had seen *three* adult wolves; and during the first few days of observing the den I had again glimpsed the odd-wolf-out several times. He posed a major conundrum, for while I could accept the idea of a contented domestic group consisting of mated male and female and a bevy of pups, I had not yet progressed far enough into the wolf world to be able to explain, or to accept, the apparent existence of an eternal triangle.

Whoever the third wolf was, he was definitely a character. He was smaller than George, not so lithe and vigorous, and with a gray overcast to his otherwise white coat. He became "Uncle Albert" to me after the first time I saw him with the pups.

The sixth morning of my vigil had dawned bright and sunny, and Angeline and the pups took advantage of the good weather. Hardly was the sun risen (at three A.M.) when they all left the den and adjourned to a nearby sandy knoll. Here the pups worked over their mother with an enthusiasm which would certainly have driven any human female into hysterics. They were hungry; but they were also full to the ears with hellery. Two of them did their best to chew off Angeline's tail, worrying it and fighting over it until I thought I could actually see her fur flying like spindrift; while the other two did what they could to remove her ears.

Angeline stood it with noble stoicism for about an hour and then, sadly disheveled, she attempted to protect herself by sitting on her tail and tucking her mauled head down between her legs. This was a fruitless effort. The pups went for her feet, one to each paw, and I was treated to the spectacle of the demon killer of the wilds trying desperately to cover her paws, her tail, and her head at one and the same instant.

Eventually she gave it up. Harassed beyond endurance she leaped away from her brood and raced to the top of a high sand ridge behind the den. The four pups rolled cheerfully off in pursuit, but before they could reach her she gave vent to a most peculiar cry.

The whole question of wolf communications was to intrigue me more and more as time went on, but on this occasion I was still laboring under the delusion that complex communications among animals other than man did not exist. I could make nothing definite of Angeline's high-pitched and yearning whine-cum-howl. I did, however, detect a plaintive quality in it which made my sympathies go out to her.

I was not alone. Within seconds of her *cri-de-coeur*, and before the mob of pups could reach her, a savior appeared.

It was the third wolf. He had been sleeping in a bed hollowed in the sand at the southern end of the esker where it dipped down to disappear beneath the waters of the bay. I had not known he was there until I saw his head come up. He jumped to his feet, shook himself, and trotted straight toward the den – intercepting the pups as they prepared to scale the last slope to reach their mother.

I watched, fascinated, as he used his shoulder to bowl the leading pup over on its back and send it skidding down the lower slope toward the den. Having broken the charge, he then nipped another pup lightly on its fat behind; then he shepherded the lot of them back to what I later came to recognize as the playground area.

I hesitate to put human words into a wolf's mouth, but the effect of what followed was crystal clear. "If it's a workout you kids want," he might have said, "then I'm your wolf!"

And so he was. For the next hour he played with the pups with as much energy as if he were still one himself. The games were varied, but many of them were quite recognizable. Tag was the standby, and Albert was always "it." Leaping, rolling and weaving amongst the pups, he never left the area of the nursery knoll, while at the same time leading the youngsters such a chase that they eventually gave up.

Albert looked them over for a moment and then, after a quick glance toward the crest where Angeline was now lying in a state of peaceful relaxation, he flung himself in among the tired pups, sprawled on his back, and invited mayhem. They were game. One by one they roused and went into battle. They were really roused this time, and no holds were barred – by them, at any rate.

Some of them tried to choke the life out of Albert, although their small teeth, sharp as they were, could never have penetrated his heavy ruff. One of them, in an excess of infantile sadism, turned its back on him and pawed a shower of sand into his face. The others took to leaping as high into the air as their bowed little legs would propel them; coming down with a satisfying thump on Albert's vulnerable belly. In between jumps they tried to chew the life out of whatever vulnerable parts came to tooth.

I began to wonder how much he could stand. Evidently he could stand a lot, for not until the pups were totally exhausted and had collapsed into complete somnolence did he get to his feet, careful not to step on the small, sprawled forms, and disengage himself. Even then he did not return to the comfort of his own bed (which he had undoubtedly earned after a night of hard hunting) but settled himself instead on the edge of the nursery knoll, where he began wolf-napping, taking a quick look at the pups every few minutes to make sure they were still safely near at hand.

His true relationship to the rest of the family was still uncertain; but as far as I was concerned he had become, and would remain, "good old Uncle Albert."

The Sensual City

Peter Desbarats

Peter Desbarats, a bilingual journalist, in this essay approaches the city of Montreal with "subjective passion, rather than with objective analysis." With sardonic wit and effective use of metaphorical comparisons, he paints a vivid picture of his subject.

First of all, a confession: I love this city.

I was born here, in the shadow of the mountain; and I know exactly the few square feet reserved for me in the vault on the same mountain where my ancestors watch, behind wrought-iron gates, the island, the river and the low gray swell of the Laurentians on the northern horizon.

No day passes that I am not consciously grateful to this city and whatever providential quirk cast me upon this island. So don't expect me to describe her in statistics, to measure the depth of her new subway or the height of her latest skyscraper, to punch her population into this essay as if I were a computer, my memory a mere collection of tapes and reels activating the keys of this typewriter. Nor am I an artist portraying an unknown model. I have lived with her for the better part of three decades.

There is no comparison with other Canadian cities. Montreal is sensual. It might have something to do with the contours of the mountain, really two mountains separated by the gentle cleft of Cotes des Neiges; or the St. Lawrence River whose current gives the island shape and movement. Montreal is a river-city like London, Paris, Prague, Vienna. It also can draw an almost physical response from its writers and artists.

I think of the early streetscapes of John Little, the ones that he painted about ten years ago when he lived in a small apartment somewhere near St. Marc street and the only still-life subject he could find was his own toilet bowl, the most eloquent toilet bowl anyone ever painted. Some collector in New York now has it. In most of his paintings, almost always in his paintings of Sherbrooke street before the new buildings spoiled it for him, there was a blonde in a red coat walking away from the viewer toward infinity. She was John Little's spirit of Montreal. I remember, two summers ago, Roussil and Vaillancourt welding and casting their sculptures on top of Mount Royal as if it had been created to pedestal their work. Montrealers have this sense of owning the whole city. I think of the choreography that explodes from the small studio of Les Grands Ballets Canadiens on Stanley street sandwiched in a narrow building between an association of war amputees and a karate salon.

Where is the comparison? Halifax and Quebec City have character. Toronto, recently and strangely, a kind of bounce. Vancouver has the sea and mountains, a kohinoor setting occupied by a chunk of paste. The others are hesitant proposals for cities.

I am not alone. Montreal is a choir of two million voices in a continual hymn of gratitude. They are not heard only in Westmount where the millionnaires live rank upon rank, the poorest of the rich at the bottom of the mountain and the unbelievably wealthy at the narrow top of the pyramid, a diagram of aristocracy by income or birth or both displayed above the city for the edification, emulation and envy of all. No, they are heard also along The Main, in the steamed hot dog parlors (Leonard Cohen returned from Greece the other day and immediately spent a week in these relish and mustard gas chambers seeking native nourishment and inspiration), in the three-feature cinemas and the cheap dance halls where angular Negroes and arrogant French Canadians frug with a fierce escapist intensity. You can hear them in the dark streets of the east end, in summer, when women rock and talk on their iron balconies and every corner seems to have a small store, teen-agers in a patch of light on the sidewalk, the smell of potatoes, hot grease, vinegar and salt.

I know, the *patates frites* imagery is no longer fashionable; nor is one supposed to savor the smell of incense in our streets, the exhaust of a hundred churches hauling at the city like helicopters. One is expected to ignore the nightly radio rosary, the Sorrowful Mysteries a few kilocycles away from beep-beep-zing-a-ling news bulletins, the Top Ten and open-line programs enabling the mute to converse with the deaf. All in glorious bilingualism.

Don't look at: newsstands buried in pulp; crime, perversion, how to improve your personality, astrology, she hungered for the wrong kind of love (with black grease pencil smeared across the right places on the cover), confessions of a sexpot *chanteuse* from Chicoutimi; basement halls filled with white capes and berets, the "original" Créditistes, celebrating the union of the Virgin and Major Douglas; limousines parked illegally before dress shops on Sherbrooke street, their chauffeurs chatting amiably with traffic constables; nuns gliding through office buildings putting the bite on, sweetly, for orphanages in Formosa, still praying for the little adopted ones ransomed years ago from paganism to run things today in Peking.

Even to mention these things, now, is quaint. Perhaps even dangerous for a journalist who wants to appear "with it." It is what we were writing about 20 years ago; the city of churches, vice capital of North America, Westmount barons, outdoor staircases and chips with Pepsi. But they remain, after all the uproar of the "quiet" revolution, the basic ingredients of the city, the mud that has been poured into the mould of the new Montreal.

I know, it is unfashionable to discuss the "patois" spoken by east-end Montrealers. Joual? *B'en why, tabernacle* just because a few uneducated people speak French that sounds like Iroquois to a Parisian, is that any reason to . . . to what? Is it wrong to treasure the patchwork French spoken by many Montrealers? Have not the *chansionniers* themselves worked poetically in this rich vein of popular language? Will not something die in Montreal if the day arrives when every "hot dog steamé" becomes an impeccable *chien chaud?*

I know, it is à la mode today to overlook Catholicism. You can hardly get into the Archbishop's Palace now without a rabbi on one arm and a Jehovah's Witness on the other. But where are those lines of school children going on the first Thursday of every month if not to confession and to cram nine First Friday communions into the school year to guarantee a happy death? Is the crucifix in every Catholic classroom of no more magic than a Greek coin? This remains an intensely Catholic city, from the pre-stressed concrete churches of new French-language parishes to the dark downtown "Irish" churches which still remain closer to the fervent piety of 19th century Kilkenny than the swinging ecumenicism of contemporary Rome.

The modern concept of Montreal as a city with an international rôle is grafted on to the old idea of an "elect" city favored by Heaven. The original "Ville Marie" grew under the Virgin's special care, and still the illuminated steel cross on the east flank of Mount Royal, facing the "French side" of the city, is a symbol of dedication.

Catholicism gave Montreal the gift of sinfulness. Other Canadian cities in other provinces received a Protestant tradition of puritanism. Montreal was blessed with a religion of warmth, color, drama and suffering – a sensual religion which emphasized not the cold virtues of self-denial but the emotional delights of confession and repentance. "There is more joy in Heaven over one sinner who repents...." I am not certain of the quotation, but neither are other Montrealers who joyfully go about the necessary preliminaries. Like Latins, Montrealers draw a kind of suppressed and compressed sensual vitality from their Catholicism, as well as a gift for pageantry. It is no accident that the annual St. Jean Baptiste parade every June is the only major Canadian parade held at night, when illuminated floats and torches create a medieval and almost mystical atmosphere.

There might even be a relationship between this Catholicism and the creativity of the Jewish community in Montreal. This is the only Canadian city where European Jews, particularly those from eastern Europe, were surrounded by a familiar European Catholicism complete, at rare times, with an element of conscious anti-Semitism. Is this why the Jewish writers, poets and artists of Montreal are among the best in Canada, because their fathers did not celebrate Brotherhood Week at the local Rotary Club?

I know, it is anti-revolutionary in the new Montreal to discuss the cultural influence of "les Anglais." French-Canadian historians have carefully noted the slow retreat of the English from Quebec City and the Eastern Townships, have wondered if Westmount is a crumbling citadel, have imagined the fleur-de-lis fluttering over the bird and wildflower sanctuary atop Westmount mountain above the house of Bronfman. In a few more decades, will the French Canadians in Montreal win the final skirmish of the battle that began so badly on the Plains of Abraham more than 200 years ago?

Not likely, for a variety of reasons: the equal birth rate between French and English in Quebec, even before the first French-Canadian housewife crossed herself hastily and gulped down the first pill; the undiminished importance of English-speaking Montrealers in the city's national, international and even local trade; the depth of English-language popular culture in Montreal, including radio, television, newspapers, films and magazines, domestic and imported: and the English-speaking community's tendency to absorb most of the city's new arrivals from Europe and other parts of North America.

The sprawling Victorian heart of McGill University's campus is as dominant a feature of the city as the monumental French-language degree factory that stands on the other side of Mount Royal. The empirical solidity of the Mount Stephen Club, where even the soap in the washrooms is British, is as important to the flavor of the city as the zinc bar and sidewalk tables of the Bistro a block away, where even the oysters are French. And in the Bistro, many of the untidiest writers and artists are descended from the bluest strata of Westmount society, as Westmount in recent years has acquired a class of prosperous French Canadians fonder of stately homes and tree-shaded lawns than the noisy native culture of the outdoor staircase and corner store.

I know, I know, this is not the new Montreal. I am forgetting about the Places des Arts and remembering the Rodeo, the Mocambo, the Centre Grand National, Fawzia's and the more expensive places where the daughters of the daughters who used to flourish on deBullion street ply their trade according to the new rules. I am forgetting about Expo '67 and thinking of bingo in church basements. Why do I dwell on hot dog parlors instead of Café St. Martin, Auberge St. Gabriel, Magnani's, the Continental and the glass gourmets' playpen atop Place Ville Marie?

Because I know that Montreal herself has not forgotten. She, too, is a bit cynical about her new *politique de grandeur*. Maybe that is one reason for her recent success as a "grande dame" of international society. Beneath the mink stole, she still cherishes the old bawdy.

Day of the Butterfly

Alice Munro

Alice Munro was born in a small town in Ontario. Her excellent short stories were collected in *Dance of the Happy Shades,* which won the Governor-General's Award in 1968. A full-length novel, *Lives of Girls and Women,* followed in 1971.

I do not remember when Myra Sayla came to town, though she must have been in our class at school for two or three years. I start remembering her in the last year, when her little brother Jimmy Sayla was in Grade One. Jimmy Sayla was not used to going to the bathroom by himself and he would have to come to the Grade Six door and ask for Myra and she would take him downstairs. Quite often he would not get to Myra in time and there would be a big dark stain on his little button-on cotton pants. Then Myra had to come and ask the teacher: "Please may I take my brother home, he has wet himself?"

That was what she said the first time and everybody in the front seats heard her – though Myra's voice was the lightest singsong – and there was a muted giggling which alerted the rest of the class. Our teacher, a cold gentle girl who wore glasses with thin gold rims and in the stiff solicitude of certain poses resembled a giraffe, wrote something on a piece of paper and showed it to Myra. And Myra recited uncertainly: "My brother has had an accident, please, teacher."

Everybody knew of Jimmy Sayla's shame and at recess (if he was not being kept in, as he often was, for doing something he shouldn't in school) he did not dare go out on the school grounds, where the other little boys, and some bigger ones, were waiting to chase him and corner him against the back fence and thrash him with tree branches. He had to stay with Myra. But at our school there were the two sides, the Boys' Side and the Girls' Side, and it was believed that if you so much as stepped on the side that was not your own you might easily get the strap. Jimmy could not go out on the Girls' Side and Myra could not go out on the Boys' Side, and no one was allowed to stay in the school unless it was raining or snowing. So Myra and Jimmy spent every recess standing in the little back porch between the two sides. Perhaps they watched the baseball games, the tag and skipping and building of leaf houses in the fall and snow forts in the winter; perhaps they did not watch at all. Whenever you happened to look at them their heads were slightly bent, their narrow bodies hunched in, quite still. They had long smooth oval faces, melancholy and discreet – dark, oily, shining hair. The little boy's was long, clipped at home, and Myra's was worn in heavy braids coiled on top of her head so that she looked, from a distance, as if she was wearing a turban too big for her. Over their dark eyes the lids were never fully raised; they had a weary look. But it was more than that. They were like children in a medieval painting, they were like small figures carved of wood, for worship or magic, with faces smooth and aged, and meekly, cryptically uncommunicative.

Most of the teachers at our school had been teaching for a long time and at recess they would disappear into the teachers' room and not bother us. But our own teacher, the young woman of the fragile gold-rimmed glasses, was apt to watch us from a window and sometimes come out, looking brisk and uncomfortable, to stop a fight among the little girls or start a running game among the big ones, who had been huddled together playing Truth or Secrets. One day she came out and called, "Girls in Grade Six, I want to talk to you!" She smiled persuasively, earnestly, and with dreadful unease, showing fine gold rims around her teeth. She said, "There is a girl in Grade Six called Myra Sayla. She is in your grade, isn't she?"

We mumbled. But there was a coo from Gladys Healey. "Yes, Miss Darling!"

"Well, why is she never playing with the rest of you? Every day I see her standing in the back porch, never playing. Do you think she looks very happy standing back there? Do you think you would be very happy, if *you* were left back there?"

Nobody answered; we faced Miss Darling, all respectful, self-possessed, and bored with the unreality of her question. Then Gladys said, "Myra can't come out with us, Miss Darling. Myra has to look after her little brother!"

"Oh," said Miss Darling dubiously. "Well you ought to try to be nicer to her anyway. Don't you think so? Don't you? You will try to be nicer, won't you? I *know* you will." Poor Miss Darling! Her campaigns were soon confused, her persuasions turned to bleating and uncertain pleas.

When she had gone Gladys Healey said softly, "You will try to be nicer, won't you? I *know* you will!" and then drawing her lip back over her big teeth she yelled exuberantly, "I don't care if it rains or freezes." She went through the whole verse and ended it with a spectacular twirl of her Royal Stuart tartan skirt. Mr. Healey ran a Dry Goods and Ladies' Wear, and his daughter's leadership in our class was partly due to her flashing plaid skirts and organdie blouses and velvet jackets with brass buttons, but also to her early-maturing bust and the fine brutal force of her personality. Now we all began to imitate Miss Darling.

We had not paid much attention to Myra before this. But now a game was developed; it started with saying, "Let's be nice to Myra!" Then we would walk up to her in formal groups of three or four and at a signal, say together, "Hel-lo Myra, Hello My-ra!" and follow up with something like, "What do you wash your hair in, Myra, it's so nice and shiny, My-ra." "Oh she washes it in cod-liver oil, don't you Myra, she washes it in cod-liver oil, can't you smell it?"

And to tell the truth there was a smell about Myra, but it was a rotten-sweetish smell as of bad fruit. That was what the Saylas did, kept a little fruit store. Her father sat all day on a stool by the window, with his shirt open over his swelling stomach and tufts of black hair showing around his belly button' he chewed garlic. But if you went into the store it was Mrs. Sayla who came to wait on you, appearing silently between the limp print curtains hung across the back of the store. Her hair was crimped in black waves and she smiled with her full lips held together, stretched as far as they would go; she told you the price in a little rapping voice, daring you to challenge her and, when you did not, handed you the bag of fruit with open mockery in her eyes.

One morning in the winter I was walking up the school hill very early; a neighbour had given me a ride into town. I lived about half a mile out of town, on a farm, and I should not have been going to the town school at all, but to a country school nearby where there were half a dozen pupils and a teacher a little demented since her change of life. But my mother, who was an ambitious woman, had prevailed on the town trustees to accept me and my father to pay the extra tuition, and I went to school in town. I was the only one in the class who carried a lunch pail and ate peanut-butter sandwiches in the high, bare, mustard-coloured cloakroom, the only one who had to wear rubber boots in the spring, when the roads were heavy with mud. I felt a little danger, on account of this; but I could not tell exactly what it was.

I saw Myra and Jimmy ahead of me on the hill; they always went to school very early – sometimes so early that they had to stand outside waiting for the janitor to open the door. They were walking slowly, and now and then Myra half turned around. I had often loitered in that way, wanting to walk with some important girl who was behind me, and not quite daring to stop and wait. Now it occurred to me that Myra might be doing this with me. I did not know what to do. I could not afford to be seen walking with her, and I did not even want to – but, on the other hand, the flattery of those humble, hopeful turnings was not lost on me. A role was shaping for me that I could not resist playing. I felt a great pleasurable rush of self-conscious benevolence; before I thought what I was doing I called, "Myra! Hey, Myra, wait up, I got some Cracker Jack!" and I quickened my pace as she stopped.

Myra waited, but she did not look at me; she waited in the withdrawn and rigid attitude with which she always met us. Perhaps she thought I was playing a trick on her, perhaps she expected me to run past and throw an empty Cracker Jack box in her face. And I opened the box and held it out to her. She took a little. Jimmy ducked behind her coat and would not take any when I offered the box to him.

"He's shy," I said reassuringly. "A lot of little kids are shy like that. He'll probably grow out of it."

"Yes," said Myra.

"I have a brother four," I said. "He's awfully shy." He wasn't. "Have some more Cracker Jack," I said. "I used to eat Cracker Jack all the time but I don't any more. I think it's bad for your complexion."

There was a silence.

"Do you like Art?" said Myra faintly.

"No. I like Social Studies and Spelling and Health."

"I like Art and Arithmetic." Myra could add and multiply in her head faster than anyone else in the class.

"I wish I was as good as you. In Arithmetic," I said, and felt magnanimous.

"But I am no good at Spelling," said Myra. "I make the most mistakes, I'll fail maybe." She did not sound unhappy about this, but pleased to have such a thing to say. She kept her head turned away from me staring at the dirty snowbanks along Victoria Street, and as she talked she made a sound as if she was wetting her lips with her tongue.

"You won't fail," I said. "You are too good in Arithmetic. What are you going to be when you grow up?"

She looked bewildered. "I will help my mother," she said. "And work in the store."

"Well I am going to be an airplane hostess," I said. "But don't mention it to anybody. I haven't told many people."

"No, I won't," said Myra. "Do you read Steve Canyon in the paper?"

"Yes." It was queer to think that Myra, too, read the comics, or that she did anything at all, apart from her role at the school. "Do you read Rip Kirby?"

"Do you read Orphan Annie?"

"Do you read Betsy and the Boys?"

"You haven't had hardly any Cracker Jack," I said. "Have some. Take a whole handful."

Myra looked into the box. "There's a prize in there," she said. She pulled it out. It was a brooch, a little tin butterfly, painted gold with bits of coloured glass stuck onto it to look like jewels. She held it in her brown hand, smiling slightly.

I said, "Do you like that?"

Myra said, "I like them blue stones. Blue stones are sapphires."

"I know. My birthstone is sapphire. What is your birthstone?"

"I don't know."

"When is your birthday?"

"July."

"Then yours is ruby."

"I like sapphire better," said Myra. "I like yours." she handed me the brooch.

"You keep it," I said. "Finders keepers."

Myra kept holding it out, as if she did not know what I meant. "Finders keepers," I said.

"It was your Cracker Jack," said Myra, scared and solemn. "You bought it."

"Well you found it."

"No – " said Myra.

"Go on!" I said. "Here, I'll *give* it to you." I took the brooch from her and pushed it back into her hand.

We were both surprised. We looked at each other; I flushed but Myra did not. I realized the pledge as our fingers touched; I was panicky, but *all right*. I thought, I can come early and walk with her other mornings. I can go and talk to her at recess. Why not? *Why not?*

Myra put the brooch in her pocket. She said, "I can wear it on my good dress. My good dress is blue."

I knew it would be. Myra wore out her good dresses at school. Even in midwinter among the plaid wool skirts and serge tunics, she glimmered sadly in sky-blue taffeta, in dusty turquoise crepe, a grown woman's dress made over, weighted by a big bow at the v of the neck and folding empty over Myra's narrow chest.

And I was glad she had not put it on. If someone asked her where she got it, and she told them, what would I say?

It was the day after this, or the week after, that Myra did not come to school. Often she was kept at home to help. But this time she did not come back. For a week, then two weeks, her desk was empty. Then we had a moving day at school and Myra's books were taken out of her desk and put on a shelf in the closet. Miss Darling said, "We'll find a seat when she comes back." And she stopped calling Myra's name when she took attendance.

Jimmy Sayla did not come to school either, having no one to take him to the bathroom.

In the fourth week, or the fifth, that Myra had been away, Gladys Healey came to school and said, "Do you know what – Myra Sayla is sick in the hospital."

It was true. Gladys Healey had an aunt who was a nurse. Gladys put up her hand in the middle of Spelling and told Miss Darling. "I thought you might like to know," she said. "Oh yes," said Miss Darling. "I do know."

"What has she got?" we said to Gladys.

And Gladys said, "Akemia, or something. And she has blood transfusions." She said to Miss Darling, "My aunt is a nurse."

So Miss Darling had the whole class write Myra a letter, in which everybody said, "Dear Myra, We are all writing you a letter. We hope you will soon be better and be back to school, Yours truly…" And Miss Darling said, "I've thought of something. Who would like to go up to the hospital and visit Myra on the twentieth of March, for a birthday party?"

I said, "Her birthday's in July."

"I know," said Miss Darling. "It's the twentieth of July. So this year she could have it on the twentieth of March, because she's sick."

"But her *birthday* is in July."

"Because she's sick," said Miss Darling, with a warning shrillness. "The cook at the hospital would make a cake and you could all give a little present, twenty-five cents or so. It would have to be between two and four, because that's visiting hours. And we couldn't all go, it'd be too many. So who wants to go and who wants to stay here and do supplementary reading?"

We all put up our hands. Miss Darling got out the spelling records and picked out the first fifteen, twelve girls and three boys. Then the three boys did not want to go so she picked out the next three girls. And I do not know when it was, but I think it was probably at this moment that the birthday party of Myra Sayla became fashionable.

Perhaps it was because Gladys Healey had an aunt who was a nurse, perhaps it was the excitement of sickness and hospitals, or simply the fact that Myra was so entirely, impressively set free of all the rules and conditions of our lives. We began to talk of her as if she were something we owned, and her party became a cause; with womanly heaviness we discussed it at recess, and decided that twenty-five cents was too low.

We all went up to the hospital on a sunny afternoon when the snow was melting, carrying our presents, and a nurse led us upstairs, single file, and down a hall past half-closed doors and dim conversations. She and Miss Darling kept saying, "Sh-sh," but we were going on tiptoe anyway; our hospital demeanor was perfect.

At this small country hospital there was no children's ward, and Myra was not really a child; they had put her in with two grey old women. A nurse was putting screens around them as we came in.

Myra was sitting up in bed, in a bulky stiff hospital gown. Her hair was down, the long braids falling over her shoulders and down the coverlet. But her face was the same, always the same.

She had been told something about the party, Miss Darling said, so the surprise would not upset her; but it seemed she had not believed, or had not understood what it was. She watched us as she used to watch in the school grounds when we played.

"Well, here we are!" said Miss Darling. "Here we are!"

And we said, "Happy birthday, Myra! Hello, Myra, happy birthday!" Myra said, "My birthday is in July." Her voice was lighter than ever, drifting, expressionless.

"Never mind when it is, really," said Miss Darling. "Pretend it's now! How old are you, Myra?"

"Eleven," Myra said. "In July."

Then we all took off our coats and emerged in our party dresses, and laid our presents, in their pale flowery wrappings, on Myra's bed. Some of our mothers had made immense complicated bows of fine satin ribbon, some of them had even taped on little bouquets of imitation roses and lilies of the valley. "Here Myra," we said, "here Myra, happy birthday." Myra did not look at us, but at the ribbons, pink and blue and speckled with silver, and the miniature bouquets; they pleased her, as the butterfly had done. An innocent look came into her face, a partial, private smile.

"Open them, Myra," said Miss Darling. "They're for you!"

Myra gathered the presents around her, fingering them, with this smile, and a cautious realization, an unexpected pride. She said, "Saturday I'm going to London to St. Joseph's Hospital."

"That's where my mother was at," somebody said. "We went and saw her. They've got all nuns there."

"My father's sister is a nun," said Myra calmly.

She began to unwrap the presents, with an air that not even Gladys could have bettered, folding the tissue paper and the ribbons, and drawing out books and puzzles and cutouts as if they were all prizes she had won. Miss Darling said that maybe she should say thank you, and the person's name with every gift she opened, to make sure she knew whom it was from, and so Myra said, "Thank you, Mary Louise, thank you, Carol," and when she came to mine she said, "Thank you Helen." Everyone explained their presents to her and there was talking and excitement and a little gaiety, which Myra presided over, though she was not gay. A cake was brought in with *Happy Birthday Myra* written on it, pink on white, and eleven candles. Miss Darling lit the candles and we all sang Happy Birthday to You, and cried, "Make a wish, Myra, make a wish – " and Myra blew them out. Then we all had cake and strawberry ice cream.

At four o'clock a buzzer sounded and the nurse took out what was left of the cake, and the dirty dishes, and we put on our coats to go home. Everybody said, "Goodbye, Myra," and Myra sat in the bed watching us go, her back straight, not supported by any pillow, her hands resting on the gifts. But at the door I heard her call; she called "Helen!" Only a couple of the others heard; Miss Darling did not hear, she had gone out ahead. I went back to the bed.

Myra said. "I got too many things. You take something."

"What?" I said. "It's for your birthday. You always get a lot at a birthday."

"Well you take something," Myra said. She picked up a leatherette case with a mirror in it, a comb and a nail file and a natural lipstick and a small handkerchief edged with gold thread. I had noticed it before. "You take that," she said.

"Don't you want it?"

"You take it." She put it into my hand. Our fingers touched again.

"When I come back from London," Myra said, "you can come and play at my place after school."

"Okay," I said. Outside the hospital window there was a clear carrying sound of somebody playing in the street, maybe chasing with the last snowballs of the year. This sound made Myra, her triumph and her bounty, and most of all her future in which she had found this place for me, turn shadowy, turn dark. All the presents on the bed, the folded paper and ribbons, those guilt-tinged offerings, had passed into this shadow, they were no longer innocent objects to be touched, exchanged, accepted without danger. I didn't want to take the case now but I could not think how to get out of it, what lie to tell. I'll give it away, I thought, I won't ever play with it. I would let my little brother pull it apart.

The nurse came back, carrying a glass of chocolate milk.

"What's the matter, didn't you hear the buzzer?"

So I was released, set free by the barriers which now closed about Myra, her unknown, exalted, ether-smelling hospital world, and by the treachery of my own heart. "Well, thank you," I said. "Thank you for the thing. Goodbye."

Did Myra ever say goodbye? Not likely. She sat in her high bed, her delicate brown neck rising out of a hospital gown too big for her, her brown carved face immune to treachery, her offering perhaps already forgotten, prepared to be set apart for legendary uses, as she was even in the back porch at school.

The Broken Globe

Henry Kreisel

Henry Kreisel is a successful novelist and short story writer. At present he is a professor in the Department of Comparative Literature, University of Alberta.

Since it was Nick Solchuk who first told me about the opening in my field at the University of Alberta, I went up to see him as soon as I received word that I had been appointed. He lived in one of those old mansions in Pimlico that had once served as town houses for wealthy merchants and aristocrats, but now housed a less moneyed group of people – stenographers, students, and intellectuals of various kinds. He had studied at Cambridge and got his doctorate there and was now doing research at the Imperial College and rapidly establishing a reputation among the younger men for his work on problems which had to do with the curvature of the earth.

His room was on the third floor, and it was very cramped, but he refused to move because he could look out from his window and see the Thames and the steady flow of boats, and that gave him a sense of distance and of space also. Space, he said, was what he missed most in the crowded city. He referred to himself, nostalgically, as a prairie boy, and when he wanted to demonstrate what he meant by space he used to say that when a man stood and looked out across the open prairie, it was possible for him to believe that the earth was flat.

"So," he said, after I had told him my news, "you are going to teach French to prairie boys and girls. I congratulate you." Then he cocked his head to one side, and looked me over and said: "How are your ears?"

"My ears?" I said. "They're all right. Why?"

"Prepare yourself," he said. "Prairie voices trying to speak French – that will be a great experience for you. I speak from experience. I learned my French pronunciation in a little one-room school in a prairie village. From an extraordinary girl, mind you, but her mind ran to science. Joan McKenzie – that was her name. A wiry little thing, sharp-nosed, and she always wore brown dresses. She was particularly fascinated by earthquakes. 'In 1755 the city of Lisbon, Portugal, was devastated. 60,000 persons died; the shock was felt in Southern France and North Africa; and inland waters of Great Britain and Scandinavia were agitated.' You see, I still remember that, and I can hear her voice too. Listen: 'In common with the entire solar system, the earth is moving through space at the rate of approximately 45,000 miles per hour, toward the constellation of Hercules. Think of that, boys and girls.' Well, I thought about it. It was a lot to think about. Maybe that's why I became a geophysicist. Her enthusiasm was infectious. I knew her at her peak. After a while she got tired and married a solid farmer and had eight children."

"But her French, I take it, was not so good," I said.

"No," he said. "Language gave no scope to her imagination. Mind you, I took French seriously enough. I was a very serious student. For a while I even practised French pronunciation at home. But I stopped it because it bothered my father. My mother begged me to stop. For the sake of peace."

"Your father's ears were offended," I said.

"Oh, no," Nick said, "not his ears. His soul. He was sure that I was learning French so I could run off and marry a French girl. . . . Don't laugh. It's true. When once my father believed something, it was very hard to shake him."

"But why should he have objected to your marrying a French girl anyway?"

"Because," said Nick, and pointed a stern finger at me, "because when he came to Canada he sailed from some French port, and he was robbed of all his money while he slept. He held all Frenchmen responsible. He never forgot and he never forgave. And, by God, he wasn't going to have that cursed language spoken in his house. He wasn't going to have any nonsense about science talked in his house either." Nick was silent for a moment, and then he said, speaking very quietly. "Curious man, my father. He had strange ideas, but a strange kind of imagination, too. I couldn't understand him when I was going to school or to the university. But then a year or two ago, I suddenly realized that the shape of the world he lived in had been forever fixed for him by some medieval priest in the small Ukrainian village where he was born and where he received an education of sorts when he was a boy. And I suddenly realized that he wasn't mad, but that he lived in the universe of the medieval church. The earth for him was the centre of the universe, and the centre was still. It didn't move. The sun rose in the East and it set in the West, and it moved perpetually around a still earth. God had made this earth especially for man, and man's function was to perpetuate himself and to worship God. My father never said all that in so many words, mind you, but that is what he believed. Everything else was heresy."

He fell silent.

"How extraordinary," I said.

He did not answer at once, and after a while he said, in a tone of voice which seemed to indicate that he did not want to pursue the matter further, "Well, when you are in the middle of the Canadian West, I'll be in Rome. I've been asked to give a paper to the International Congress of Geophysicists which meets there in October."

"So I heard," I said. "Wilcocks told me the other day. He said it was going to be a paper of some importance. In fact, he said it would create a stir."

"Did Wilcocks really say that?" he asked eagerly, his face reddening, and he seemed very pleased. We talked for a while longer, and then I rose to go.

He saw me to the door and was about to open it for me, but stopped suddenly, as if he were turning something over in his mind, and then said quickly, "Tell me – would you do something for me?"

"Of course," I said. "If I can."

He motioned me back to my chair and I sat down again. "When you are in Alberta," he said, "and if it is convenient for you, would you – would you go to see my father?"

"Why, yes," I stammered, "why, of course. I – I didn't realize he was still. . . ."

"Oh, yes," he said, "he's still alive, still working. He lives on his farm, in a place called Three Bear Hills, about sixty or seventy miles out of Edmonton. He lives alone. My mother is dead. I have a sister who is married and lives in Calgary. There were only the two of us. My mother could have no more children. It was a source of great agony for them. My sister goes to see him sometimes, and then she sometimes writes to me. He never writes to me. We – we had – what shall I call it – differences. If you went to see him and told him that I had not gone to the devil, perhaps. . . ." He broke off abruptly, clearly agitated, and walked over to his window and stood staring out, then said. "Perhaps you'd better not. I – I don't want to impose on you."

I protested that he was not imposing at all, and promised that I would write to him as soon as I had paid my visit.

I met him several times after that, but he never mentioned the matter again.

I sailed from England about the middle of August and arrived in Montreal a week later. The long journey West was one of the most memorable experiences I have ever had. There were moments of weariness and dullness. But the very monotony was impressive. There was a grandeur about it. It was monotony of a really monumental kind. There were moments when, exhausted by the sheer impact of the landscape, I thought back with longing to the tidy, highly cultivated countryside of England and of France, to the sight of men and women working in the fields, to the steady succession of villages and towns, and everywhere the consciousness of nature humanized. But I also began to understand why Nick Solchuk was always longing for more space and more air, especially when we moved into the prairies, and the land became flatter until there seemed nothing, neither hill nor tree nor bush, to disturb the vast unbroken flow of land until in the far distance a thin, blue line marked the point where the prairie merged into the sky. Yet over all there was a strange tranquillity, all motion seemed suspended, and only the sun moved steadily, imperturbably West, dropping finally over the rim of the horizon, a blazing red ball, but leaving a superb evening light lying over the land still.

I was reminded of the promise I had made, but when I arrived in Edmonton, the task of settling down absorbed my time and energy so completely that I did nothing about it. Then, about the middle of October, I saw a brief report in the newspaper about the geophysical congress which had opened in Rome on the previous day, and I was mindful of my promise again. Before I could safely bury it in the back of my mind again, I sat down and wrote a brief letter to Nick's father, asking him when I could come out to visit him. Two weeks passed without an answer, and I decided to go and see him on the next Saturday without further formalities.

The day broke clear and fine. A few white clouds were in the metallic autumn sky and the sun shone coldly down upon the earth, as if from a great distance. I drove south as far as Wetaskiwin and then turned east. The paved highway gave way to gravel and got steadily worse. I was beginning to wonder whether I was going right, when I rounded a bend and a grain elevator hove like a signpost into view. It was now about three o'clock and I had arrived in Three Bear Hills, but, as Nick had told me, there were neither bears nor hills here, but only prairie, and suddenly the beginning of an embryonic street with a few buildings on either side like a small island in a vast sea, and then all was prairie again.

I stopped in front of the small general store and went in to ask for directions. Three farmers were talking to the storekeeper, a bald, bespectacled little man who wore a long, dirty apron and stood leaning against his counter. They stopped talking and turned to look at me. I asked where the Solchuk farm was.

Slowly scrutinizing me, the storekeeper asked, "You just new here?"

"Yes," I said.

"From the old country, eh?"

"Yes."

"You selling something?"

"No, no," I said. "I – I teach at the University."

"That so?" He turned to the other men and said, "Only boy ever went to University from around here was Solchuk's boy, Nick. Real brainy young kid, Nick. Two of 'em never got on together. Too different. You know."

They nodded slowly.

"But that boy of his – he's a real big-shot scientist now. You know them addem bombs and them hydrergen bombs. He helps make 'em."

"No, no," I broke in quickly. "That's not what he does. He's a geophysicist."

"What's that?" asked one of the men.

But before I could answer, the little storekeeper asked excitedly, "You know Nick?"

"Yes," I said, "we're friends. I've come to see his father."

"And where's he now? Nick, I mean."

"Right now he is in Rome," I said. "But he lives in London, and does research there."

"Big-shot, eh," said one of the men laconically, but with a trace of admiration in his voice, too.

"He's a big scientist, though, like I said. Isn't that so?" the storekeeper broke in.

"He's going to be a very important scientist indeed," I said, a trifle solemnly.

"Like I said," he called out triumphantly. "That's showing 'em. A kid from Three Bear Hills, Alberta. More power to him!" His pride was unmistakable. "Tell me, mister," he went on, his voice dropping, "does he remember this place sometimes? Or don't he want to know us no more?"

"Oh, no," I said quickly. "He often talks of this place, and of Alberta, and of Canada. Some day he plans to return."

"That's right," he said with satisfaction. He drew himself up to full height, banged his fist on the table and said, "I'm proud of that boy. Maybe old Solchuk don't think so much of him, but you tell him old Mister Marshall is proud of him." He came from behind the counter and almost ceremoniously escorted me out to my car and showed me the way to Solchuk's farm.

I had about another five miles to drive, and the road, hardly more now than two black furrows cut into the prairie, was uneven and bumpy. The land was fenced on both sides of the road, and at last I came to a rough wooden gate hanging loosely on one hinge, and beyond it there was a cluster of small wooden buildings. The largest of these, the house itself, seemed at one time to have been ochre-coloured, but the paint had worn off and it now looked curiously mottled. A few chickens were wandering about, pecking at the ground, and from the back I could hear the grunting and squealing of pigs.

I walked up to the house and, just as I was about to knock, the door was suddenly opened, and a tall, massively built old man stood before me.

"My name is . . ." I began.

But he interrupted me. "You the man wrote to me?" His voice, though unpolished, had the same deep timbre as Nick's.

"That's right," I said.

"You a friend of Nick?"

"Yes."

He beckoned me in with a nod of his head. The door was low and I had to stoop a bit to get into the room. It was a large, low-ceilinged room. A smallish window let in a patch of light which lit up the middle of the room but did not spread into the corners, so that it seemed as if it were perpetually dusk. A table occupied the centre, and on the far side there was a large wood stove on which stood a softly hissing black kettle. In the corner facing the entrance there was an iron bedstead, and the bed was roughly made, with a patchwork quilt thrown carelessly on top.

The old man gestured me to one of the chairs which stood around the table.

"Sit."

I did as he told me, and he sat down opposite me and placed his large calloused hands before him on the table. He seemed to study me intently for a while, and I scrutinized him. His face was covered by a three-days' stubble, but in spite of that, and in spite of the fact that it was a face beaten by sun and wind, it was clear that he was Nick's father. For Nick had the same determined mouth, and the same high cheek bones and the same dark, penetrating eyes.

At last he spoke. "You friend of Nick."

I nodded my head.

"What he do now?" he asked sharply. "He still tampering with the earth?"

His voice rose as if he were delivering a challenge, and I drew back involuntarily. "Why – he's doing scientific research, yes," I told him. "He's...."

"What God has made," he said sternly, "no man should touch."

Before I could regain my composure, he went on, "He sent you. What for? What he want?"

"Nothing," I said, "Nothing at all. He sent me to bring you greetings and to tell you he is well."

"And you come all the way from Edmonton to tell me?"

"Yes, of course."

A faint smile played about his mouth, and the features of his face softened. Then suddenly he rose from his chair and stood towering over me. "You are welcome in this house," he said.

The formality with which he spoke was quite extraordinary and seemed to call for an appropriate reply, but I could do little more than stammer a thank you, and he, assuming again a normal tone of voice, asked me if I cared to have coffee. When I assented he walked to the far end of the room and busied himself about the stove.

It was then that I noticed, just under the window, a rough little wooden table and on top of it a faded old globe made of cardboard, such as little children use in school. I was intrigued to see it there and went over to look at it more closely. The cheap metal mount was brown with rust, and when I lifted it and tried to turn the globe on its axis, I found that it would not rotate because part of it had been squashed and broken. I ran my hand over the deep dent, and suddenly the old man startled me.

"What you doing there?" Curiosity seemed mingled with suspicion in his voice and made me feel like a small child surprised by its mother in an unauthorized raid on the pantry. I set down the globe and turned. He was standing by the table with two big mugs of coffee in his hands.

"Coffee is hot," he said.

I went back to my chair and sat down, slightly embarrassed.

"Drink," he said, pushing one of the mugs over to me.

We both began to sip the coffee, and for some time neither of us said anything.

"That thing over there," he said at last, putting down his mug, "that thing you was looking at – he brought it home one day – he was a boy then – maybe thirteen-year-old Nick. The other day I found it up in the attic. I was going to throw it in the garbage. But I forgot. There it belongs. In the garbage. It is a false thing." His voice had now become venomous.

"False?" I said. "How is it false?"

He disregarded my question. "I remember," he went on, "he came home from school one day and we was all here in this room – all sitting around this table eating supper, his mother, his sister and me and Alex, too – the hired man like. And then sudden like Nick pipes up, and he says, we learned in school today, he says, how the earth is round like a ball, he says, and how it moves around and around the sun and never stops, he says. They learning you rubbish in school, I say. But he says, no, Miss McKenzie never told him no lies. Then I say she does, I say, and a son of mine shouldn't believe it. Stop your ears! Let not Satan come in!" He raised an outspread hand and his voice thundered as if he were a prophet armed. "But he was always a stubborn boy – Nick. Like a mule. He never listened to reason. I believe it, he says, because science has proved it and it is the truth. It is false, I cry, and you will not believe it. I believe it, he says. So then I hit him because he will not listen and will not obey. But he keeps shouting and shouting and shouting. 'She moves,' he shouts, 'she moves, she moves!'"

He stopped. His hands had balled themselves into fists, and the remembered fury sent the blood streaming into his face. He seemed now to have forgotten my presence and he went on speaking in a low murmuring voice, almost as if he were telling the story to himself.

"So the next day, or the day after, I go down to that school, and there is this little Miss McKenzie, so small and so thin that I could have crush her with my bare hands. What you teaching my boy Nick? I ask her. What false lies you stuffing in his head? What you telling him that the earth is round and that she moves for? Did Joshua tell the earth to stand still, or did he command the sun? So she says to me, I don't care what Joshua done, she says, I will tell him what science has discovered. With that woman I could get nowhere. So then I try to keep him away from school, and I lock him up in the house, but it was no good. He got out, and he run to the school like, and Miss McKenzie she sends me a letter to say she will sent up the inspectors if I try to keep him away from the school. And I could do nothing."

His sense of impotence was palpable. He sat sunk into himself as if he were still contemplating ways of halting the scientific education of his son.

"Two, three weeks after," he went on, "he comes walking in this door with a large paper parcel in his hand. Now, he calls out to me, now I will prove it to you, I will prove that she moves. And he tears off the paper from the box and takes out this – this thing, and he puts it on the table here. Here, he cries, here is the earth, and look, she moves. And he gives that thing a little push and it twirls around like. I have to laugh. A toy, I say to him, you bring me a toy here, not bigger than my hand, and it is supposed to be the world, this little toy here, with the printed words on coloured paper, this little cardboard ball. This Miss McKenzie, I say to him, she's turning you crazy in that school. But look, he says, she moves. Now I have to stop my laughing. I'll soon show you she moves, I say, for he is beginning to get me mad again. And I go up to the table and I take the toy thing in my hands and I smash it down like this."

He raised his fists and let them crash down on the table as if he meant to splinter it.

"That'll learn you, I cry. I don't think he could believe I had done it, because he picks up the thing and he tries to turn it, but it don't turn no more. He stands there and the tears roll down his cheeks, and then, sudden like, he takes the thing in both his hands and he throws it at me. And it would have hit me right in the face, for sure, if I did not put up my hand. Against your father, I cry, you will raise up your hand against your father. Asmodeus! I grab him by the arm, and I shake him and I beat him like he was the devil. And he makes me madder and madder because he don't cry or shout or anything. And I would have kill him there, for sure, if his mother didn't come in then and pull me away. His nose was bleeding, but he didn't notice. Only he looks at me and says, you can beat me and break my globe, but you can't stop her moving. That night my wife she make me swear by all that's holy that I wouldn't touch him no more. And from then on I never hit him again nor talk to him about this thing. He goes his way and I go mine."

He fell silent. Then after a moment he snapped suddenly, "You hold with that?"

"Hold with what?" I asked, taken aback.

"With that thing?" He pointed behind him at the little table and at the broken globe. His gnarled hands now tightly interlocked, he leaned forward in his chair and his dark, brooding eyes sought an answer from mine in the twilight of the room.

Alone with him there, I was almost afraid to answer firmly. Was it because I feared that I would hurt him too deeply if I did, or was I perhaps afraid that he would use violence on me as he had on Nick?

I cleared my throat. "Yes," I said then. "Yes, I believe that the earth is round and that she moves. That fact has been accepted now for a long time."

I expected him to round on me but he seemed suddenly to have grown very tired, and in a low resigned voice he said, "Satan has taken over all the world." Then suddenly he roused himself and hit the table hard with his fist, and cried passionately, "But not me! Not me!"

It was unbearable. I felt that I must break the tension, and I said the first thing that came into my mind. "You can be proud of your son in spite of all that happened between you. He is a fine man, and the world honours him for his work."

He gave me a long look. "He should have stayed here," he said quietly. "When I die, there will be nobody to look after the land. Instead he has gone off to tamper with God's earth."

His fury was now all spent. We sat for a while in silence, and then I rose. Together we walked out of the house. When I was about to get into my car, he touched me lightly on the arm. I turned. His eyes surveyed the vast expanse of sky and land, stretching far into the distance, reddish clouds in the sky and blue shadows on the land. With a gesture of great dignity and power he lifted his arm and stood pointing into the distance, at the flat land and the low-hanging sky.

"Look," he said, very slowly and very quietly, "she is flat, and she stands still."

It was impossible not to feel a kind of admiration for the old man. There was something heroic about him. I held out my hand and he took it. He looked at me steadily, then averted his eyes and said, "Send greetings to my son."

I drove off quickly, but had to stop again in order to open the wooden gate. I looked back at the house, and saw him still standing there, still looking at his beloved land, a lonely, towering figure framed against the darkening evening sky.

Further Reading

Huffman, G., *Canadiana.* Toronto: McClelland & Stewart Ltd., 1970

Klink, C., *Literary History of Canada: Canadian Literature in English.* University of Toronto Press, 1970

McInnis, E., *Canada: A Political and Social History.* Toronto: Rinehart & Co., 1959

Smith, A.J.M., *The Canadian Century.* Toronto: Gage Educational Publishing Ltd., 1973

Smith, A.J.M., *The Oxford Book of Canadian Verse.* Toronto: Oxford University Press, 1965

Stephens, D., *Contemporary Voices.* Toronto: Prentice Hall of Canada, Ltd., 1972

Thomas, C., *Our Nature - Our Voices: A Guidebook to English-Canadian Literature.* Toronto: New Press, 1972

Weaver, R. & Toye, W., *Oxford Anthology of Canadian Literature.* Toronto: Oxford University Press, 1973

Wilson, M., *Poetry of Mid-Century 1940/1960.* Toronto: McClelland & Stewart Ltd., 1967

Evolution of Canadian Literature in English (Volumes 1,2,3&4). Toronto: Holt, Rinehart & Winston, 1973

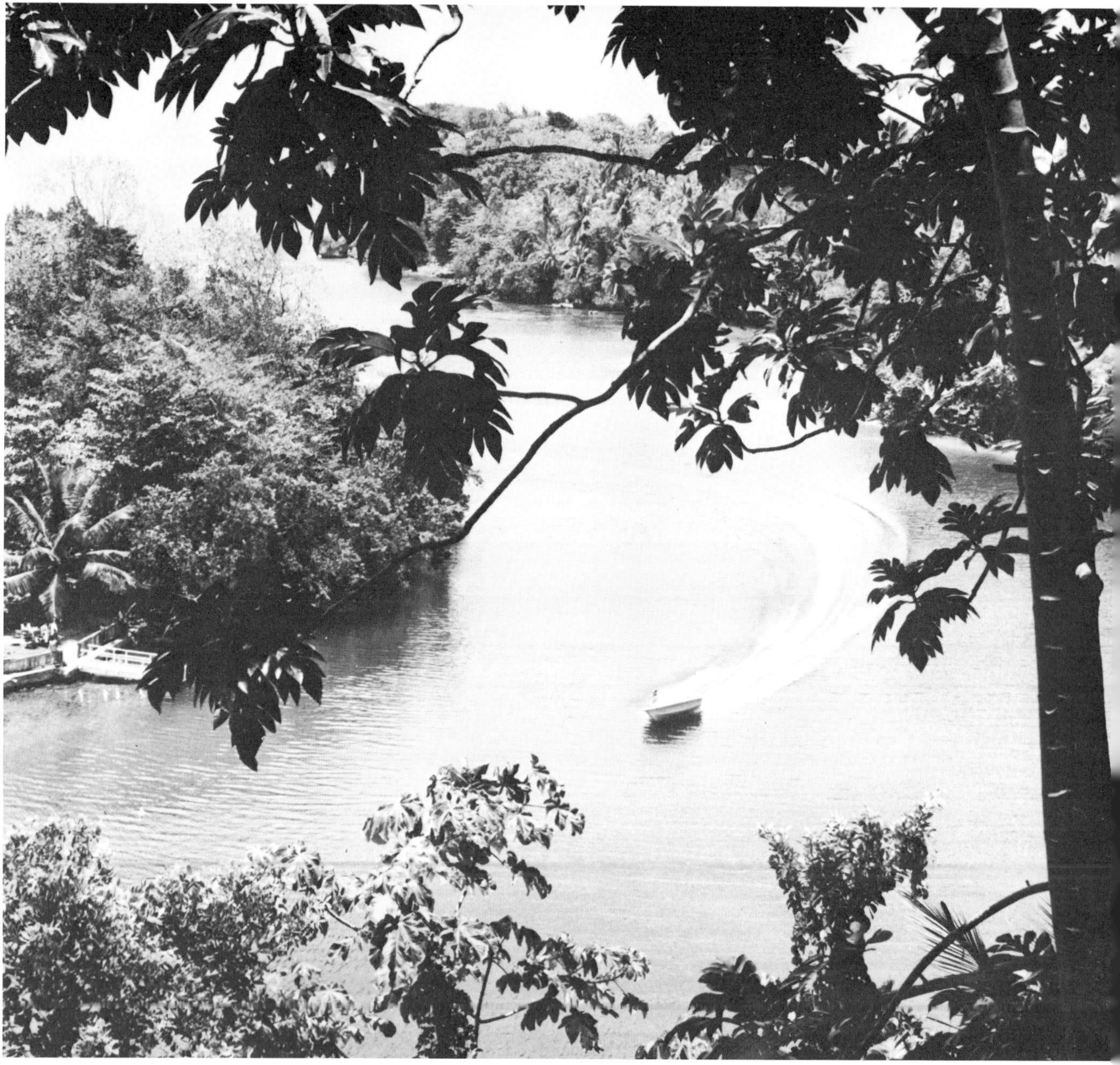

Patriciamay McBlane

...ty for Public Information, Jamaica

A Glimpse of the West Indies

Although claims have been made for an earlier starting date, the literature of the West Indies and of Guyana really began in the twentieth century. It is polyethnic in nature, coming from authors of various races and cultures. Claude McKay of Jamaica, publishing from 1912 to 1937, made the first significant contribution to modern literature of the West Indies. His high standards have been maintained by V.S. Naipaul and Samuel Selvon of Trinidad; Andrew Salkey of Panama; E. Mittelholzer, Jan Carew, and Wilson Harris of Guyana; George Lamming and Geoffrey Drayton of Barbados; A.L. Hendricks and Roger Mais of Jamaica; Derek Walcott of St. Lucia; and John Hearne of Canada. The writers of the West Indies are truly a multicultural lot.

Because writers of the West Indies present unusual characters with expressive dialects in colorful local situations, one may suspect that themes are limited. Fortunately, such is not the case. West Indian literature enjoys a broad international appeal. It has, in fact, played a very important part during the past thirty years in establishing African literature. The themes of West Indian literature deal with conflicts about class, race, religion, freedom, language, education, politics, and economics. These conflicts are often presented in literature as serious or bitter ironies which contain much zest and much optimism, and which often resolve themselves into a West Indian identity.

West Indian literature presents a pictorial mosaic of diverse groups of people who retain a West Indian identity. Their interesting dialects, resilient attitudes, and dynamic personalities are revealed in the selections "Titus Hoyt, I.A." and "Calypsonian." "Anancy" describes the importance of early beliefs, while "Jamaican Fragment" and "Blackout" deal with different aspects of the racial problem.

Anancy

Andrew Salkey

Andrew Salkey, born in Panama in 1928, moved to Jamaica at the age of two. Educated at Munro College, Salkey joined the Civil Service in 1951 and also began to write poetry and short stories for the BBC. In 1955, he was awarded a Guggenheim Fellowship and the Thomas Helmor Poetry prize. He has written two novels and now works free lance with the BBC World Service in England. "Anancy" depicts a legendary figure in West Indian and West African folklore who represents the cunning traits in man; a spider is also called "anancy" in the West Indies.

Anancy is a spider;
Anancy is a man;
Anancy's West Indian
And West African.

Sometimes, he wears a waistcoat;
Sometimes, he carries a cane;
Sometimes, he sports a top hat;
Sometimes, he's just a plain,
Ordinary, black, hairy spider.

WEST INDIES

Anancy is vastly cunning,
Tremendously greedy,
Excessively charming,
Hopelessly dishonest,
Warmly loving,
Firmly confident,
Fiercely wild,
A fabulous character,
Completely out of our mind
And out of his, too.

Anancy is a master planner,
A great user
Of other people's plans;
He pockets everybody's food,
Shelter, land, money, and more;
He achieves mountains of things,
Like stolen flour dumplings;
He deceives millions of people,
Even the man in the moon;
And he solves all the mysteries
On earth, in air, under sea.

And always,
Anancy changes
From a spider into a man
And from a man into a spider
And back again
At the drop of a sleepy eyelid.

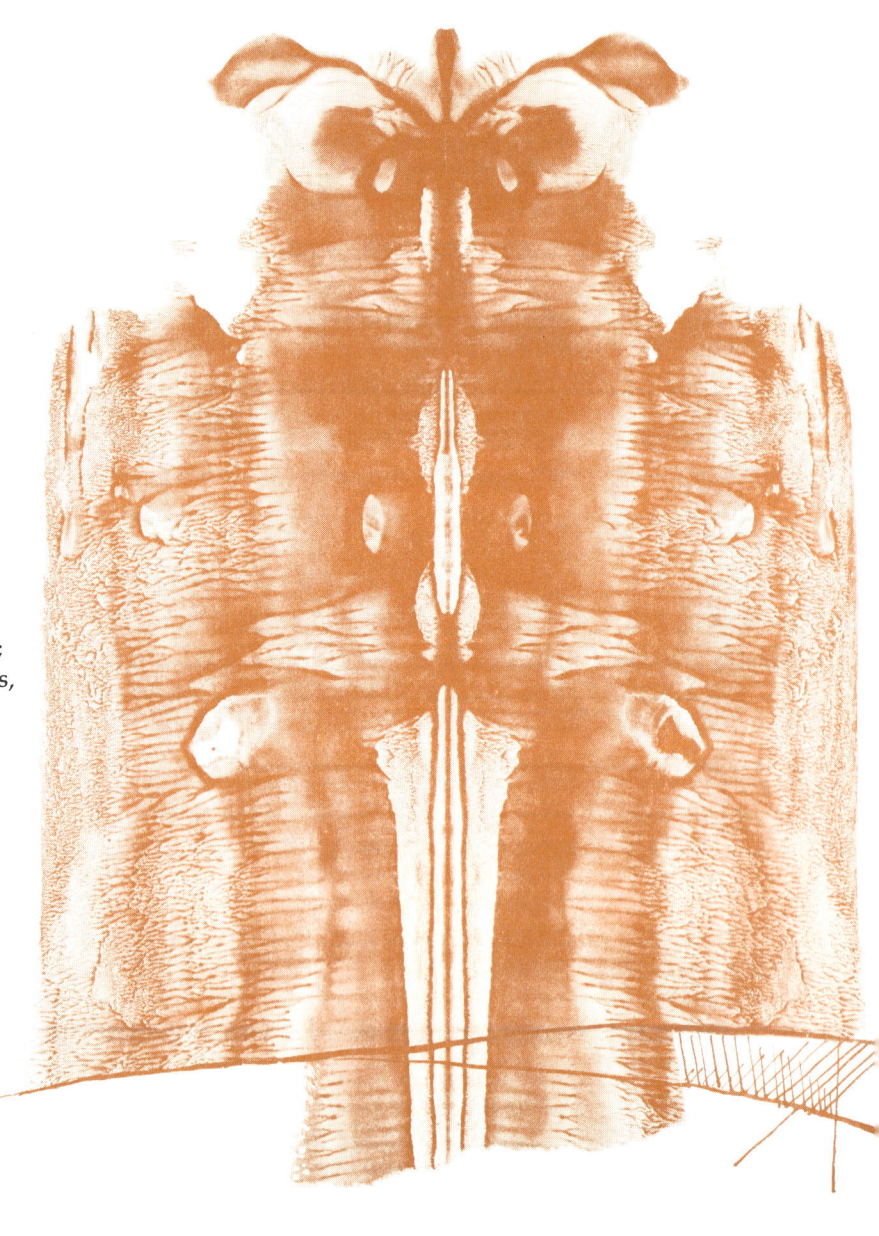

Flame-Heart

Claude McKay

Claude McKay (1890-1948), the first West Indian novelist and a leading poet, was born in Clarendon, Jamaica. He migrated to the United States and, later, to London, where he settled. McKay was a more significant writer of prose than of verse. His novels are *Banjo, Home to Harlem,* and *Banana Bottom.* In "Flame-Heart," McKay reflects with nostalgia on things typically Jamaican.

So much have I forgotten in ten years,
   So much in ten brief years! I have forgot
What time the purple apples come to juice,
   And what month brings the shy forget-me-not.
I have forgot the special, startling season
   Of the pimento's flowering and fruiting;

What time of year the ground doves brown the fields
   And fill the noonday with their curious fluting.
I have forgotten much, but still remember
The poinsettia's red, blood-red in warm December.

I still recall the honey-fever grass,
   But cannot recollect the high days when
We rooted them out of the ping-wing path
   To stop the mad bees in the rabbit pen.
I often try to think in what sweet month

WEST INDIES

    The languid painted ladies used to dapple
The yellow by-road mazing from the main,
    Sweet with the golden threads of the rose-apple.
I have forgotten-strange-but quite remember
The poinsettia's red, blood-red in warm December.

What weeks, what months, what time of the mild year
    We cheated school to have our fling at tops?
What days our wine-thrilled bodies pulsed with joy
    Feasting upon blackberries in the copse?
Oh some I know! I have embalmed the days,
    Even the sacred moments when we played,
All innocent of passion, uncorrupt,
    At noon and evening in the flame-heart's shade.
We were so happy, happy, I remember,
Beneath the poinsettia's red in warm December.

Pocomania

P.M. Sherlock

The son of a Methodist minister, Philip M. Sherlock was born in Jamaica in 1902 and educated locally, later receiving a London degree. After teaching at high school and university, he became vice-chancellor of the University of the West Indies. He has published history books and folk tales. "Pocomania" is a poem named after a religious sect in Jamaica which is characterized by its evocation of spirits in converts to enable them to have revelations and make prophesies. In part, the rhythm of the poem echoes the incantations of the religion.

Long Mountain, rise,
Lift you' shoulder, blot the moon.
Black the stars, hide the skies,
Long Mountain, rise, lift you' shoulder high.

Black of skin and white of gown
Black of night and candle light
White against the black of trees
And altar white against the gloom,
Black of mountain high up there
Long Mountain, rise,
Lift you' shoulder, blot the moon,
Black the stars, black the sky.

WEST INDIES

Africa among the trees
Asia with her mysteries
Weaving white in flowing gown
Black Long Mountain looking down
Sees the shepherd and his flock
Dance and sing and wisdom mock,

Dance and sing and falls away
All the civilized to-day
Dance and sing and fears let loose;
Here the ancient gods that choose
Man for victim, man for hate
Man for sacrifice to fate
Hate and fear and madness black
Dance before the altar white
Comes the circle closer still
Shepherd weave your pattern old
Africa among the trees
Asia with her mysteries.

Black of night and white of gown
White of altar, black of trees
'Swing de circle wide again
Fall and cry me sister now
Let de spirit come again
Fling away de flesh an' bone
Let de spirit have a home.'

Grunting low and in the dark
White of gown and circling dance
Gone to-day and all control
Now the dead are in control
Power of the past returns
Africa among the trees
Asia with her mysteries.

Black the stars, hide the sky
Lift you' shoulder, blot the moon.
Long Mountain rise.

Poem for My country

Basil Clare McFarlane

Basil McFarlane was born in Jamaica and, except for two years in the R.A.F. in England, has lived his life there. A journalist, civil servant, film and art critic, he was also a writer for Radio Jamaica.

I am Jamaica –
And I have seen my children grow
Out of their separate truths;
Out of the absolute truth of me:
Out of my soil
Into false shadows
And I have wept
So
that the strangers with sunglasses
and red faces
who survey my passive sorrow
call me beautiful
and Isle of Springs
And God!
I have no voice
to shout my disgust
When their vile trappings brush my skin
their filthy coppers reach my children's palms;
These palms: my flesh
my flesh beloved

But where, O where my spirit
where my self my fire?
Lost, I wander through a sunlit night
Beseeching beseeching my belly's result
to turn from other gods
to turn on me
the dawn
of their regard

Titus Hoyt, I.A.

V. S. Naipaul

Vidia S. Naipaul was born in Trinidad in 1932. He received his education in Trinidad and at Oxford University. *Miguel Street*, the book in which "Titus Hoyt, I. A." appears, is made up of many stories about the inhabitants of a fictional street.

This man was born to be an active and important member of a local road board in the country. An unkind fate had placed him in the city. He was a natural guide, philosopher and friend to anyone who stopped to listen.

Titus Hoyt was the first man I met when I came to Port of Spain, a year or two before the war.

My mother had fetched me from Chaguanas after my father died. We travelled up by train and took a bus to Miguel Street. It was the first time I had travelled in a city bus.

I said to my mother, 'Ma, look, they forget to ring the bell here.'

My mother said, 'If you ring the bell you damn well going to get off and walk home by yourself, you hear.'

And then a little later I said, 'Ma, look, the sea.'

People in the bus began to laugh.

My mother was really furious.

Early next morning my mother said, 'Look now, I giving you four cents. Go to the shop on the corner of this road, Miguel Street, and buy two hops bread for a cent apiece, and buy a penny butter. And come back quick.'

I found the shop and I bought the bread and the butter – the red, salty type of butter.

Then I couldn't find my way back.

I found about six Miguel Streets, but none seemed to have my house. After a long time walking up and down I began to cry. I sat down on the pavement, and got my shoes wet in the gutter.

Some little white girls were playing in a yard behind me. I looked at them, still crying. A girl wearing a pink frock came out and said, 'Why you crying?'

I said, 'I lost.'

She put her hands on my shoulder and said, 'Don't cry. You know where you live?'

I pulled out a piece of paper from my shirt pocket and showed her. Then a man came up. He was wearing white shorts and a white shirt, and he looked funny.

The man said, 'Why he crying?' In a gruff, but interested way.

The girl told him.

The man said, 'I will take him home.'

I asked the girl to come too.

The man said, 'Yes, you better come to explain to his mother.'

The girl said, 'All right, Mr Titus Hoyt.'

That was one of the first things about Titus Hoyt that I found interesting. The girl calling him 'Mr Titus Hoyt.' Not Titus, or Mr Hoyt, but Mr Titus Hoyt. I later realised that everyone who knew him called him that.

When we got home the girl explained to my mother what had happened, and my mother was ashamed of me.

Then the girl left.

Mr Titus Hoyt looked at me and said, 'He look like a intelligent little boy.'

My mother said in a sarcastic way, 'Like his father.'

Titus Hoyt said, 'Now, young man, if a herring and a half cost a penny and a half, what's the cost of three herrings?'

Even in the country, in Chaguanas, we had heard about that.

Without waiting, I said, 'Three pennies.'

Titus Hoyt regarded me with wonder.

He told my mother, 'This boy bright like anything, ma'am. You must take care of him and send him to a good school and feed him good food so he could study well.'

My mother didn't say anything.

When Titus Hoyt left, he said, 'Cheerio!'

That was the second interesting thing about him.

My mother beat me for getting my shoes wet in the gutter but she said she wouldn't beat me for getting lost.

For the rest of that day I ran about the yard saying, 'Cheerio! Cheerio!' to a tune of my own.

That evening Titus Hoyt came again.

My mother didn't seem to mind.

To me Titus Hoyt said, 'You can read?'

I said yes.

'And write?'

I said yes.

'Well, look,' he said, 'get some paper and a pencil and write what I tell you.'

I said, 'Paper and pencil?'

He nodded.

I ran into the kitchen and said, 'Ma, you got any paper and pencil?'

My mother said, 'What you think I is? A shopkeeper?'

Titus Hoyt shouted, 'Is for me, ma'am.'

My mother said, 'Oh.' In a disappointed way.

She said, 'In the bottom drawer of the bureau you go find my purse. It have a pencil in it.'

And she gave me a copy-book from the kitchen shelf.

Mr Titus Hoyt said, 'Now, young man, write. Write the address of this house in the top right-hand corner, and below that, the date.' Then he asked, 'You know who we writing this letter to, boy?'

I shook my head.

He said, 'Ha, boy! Ha! We writing to the *Guardian*, boy.'

I said, 'The *Trinidad Guardian*? The paper? What, *me* writing to the *Guardian*! But only big big man does write to the *Guardian*.'

Titus Hoyt smiled. 'That's *why* you writing. It go surprise them.'

I said, 'What I go write to them about?'

He said, 'You go write it now. Write. To the Editor, *Trinidad Guardian*. Dear Sir, I am but a child of eight (How old you is? Well, it don't matter anyway) and yesterday my mother sent me to make a purchase in the city. This, dear Mr Editor, was my first peregrination (p-e-r-e-g-r-i-n-a-t-i-o-n) in this metropolis, and I had the misfortune to wander from the path my mother had indicated –'

I said. 'Oh God, Mr Titus Hoyt, where you learn all these big words and them? You sure you spelling them right?'

Titus Hoyt smiled. 'I spend all afternoon making up this letter,' he said.

I wrote: '. . . and in this state of despair I was rescued by a Mr Titus Hoyt, of Miguel Street. This only goes to show, dear Mr Editor, that human kindness is a quality not yet extinct in this world.'

The *Guardian* never printed the letter.

When I next saw Titus Hoyt, he said, 'Well, never mind. One day, boy, one day, I go make them sit up and take notice of every word I say. Just wait and see.'

And before he left, he said, 'Drinking your milk?'

He had persuaded my mother to give me half a pint of milk every day. Milk was good for the brains.

It is one of the sadnesses of my life that I never fulfilled Titus Hoyt's hopes for my academic success.

I still remember with tenderness the interest he took in me. Sometimes his views clashed with my mother's. There was the business of the cobwebs, for instance.

Boyee, with whom I had become friendly very quickly, was teaching me to ride. I had fallen and cut myself nastily on the shin.

My mother was attempting to cure this with sooty cobwebs soaked in rum.

Titus Hoyt was horrified. 'You ain't know what you doing,' he shouted.

My mother said, 'Mr Titus Hoyt, I will kindly ask you to mind your own business. The day you make a baby yourself I go listen to what you have to say.'

Titus Hoyt refused to be ridiculed. He said, 'Take the boy to the doctor, man.'

I was watching them argue, not caring greatly either way.

In the end I went to the doctor.

Titus Hoyt reappeared in a new role.

He told my mother, 'For the last two three months I been taking the first-aid course with the Red Cross. I go dress the boy foot for you.'

That really terrified me.

For about a month or so afterwards, people in Miguel Street could tell when it was nine o'clock in the morning. By my shrieks. Titus Hoyt loved his work.

All this gives some clue to the real nature of the man.

The next step followed naturally.

Titus Hoyt began to teach.

It began in a small way, after the fashion of all great enterprises.

He had decided to sit for the external arts degree of London University. He began to learn Latin, teaching himself, and as fast as he learned, he taught us.

He rounded up three or four of us and taught us in the verandah of his house. He kept chickens in his yard and the place stank.

That Latin stage didn't last very long. We got as far as the fourth declension, and then Boyee and Errol and myself began asking questions. They were not the sort of questions Titus Hoyt liked.

'Boyee said, 'Mr Titus Hoyt, I think you making up all this, you know, making it up as you go on.'

Titus Hoyt said, 'But I telling you, I not making it up. Look, here it is in black and white.'

Errol said, 'I feel, Mr Titus Hoyt, that one man sit down one day and make all this up and have everybody else learning it.'

Titus Hoyt asked me, 'What is the accusative singular of *bellum?*'

Feeling wicked, because I was betraying him, I said to Titus Hoyt, 'Mr Titus Hoyt, when you was my age, how you woulda feel if somebody did ask you that question?'

And then Boyee asked, 'Mr Titus Hoyt, what is the meaning of the ablative case?'

So the Latin lessons ended.

But however much we laughed at him, we couldn't deny that Titus Hoyt was a deep man.

Hat used to say, 'He is a thinker, that man.'

Titus Hoyt thought about all sorts of things, and he thought dangerous things sometimes.

Hat said, 'I don't think Titus Hoyt like God, you know.'

Titus Hoyt would say, 'The thing that really matter is faith. Look, I believe that if I pull out this bicycle-lamp from my pocket here, and set it up somewhere, and really really believe in it and pray to it, what I pray for go come. That is what I believe.'

And so saying he would rise and leave, not forgetting to say, 'Cheerio!'

He had the habit of rushing up to us and saying, 'Silence, everybody. I just been thinking. Listen to what I just been thinking.'

One day he rushed up and said, 'I been thinking how this war could end. If Europe could just sink for five minutes all the Germans go drown –'

Eddoes said, 'But England go drown too.'

Titus Hoyt agreed and looked sad. 'I lose my head, man,' he said. 'I lose my head.'

And he wandered away, muttering to himself, and shaking his head.

One day he cycled right up to us when we talking about the Barbados-Trinidad cricket match. Things were not going well for Trinidad and we were worried.

Titus Hoyt rushed up and said, 'Silence. I just been thinking. Look, boys, it ever strike you that the world not real at all? It ever strike you that we have the only mind in the world and you just thinking up everything else? Like me here, having the only mind in the world, and thinking up you people here, thinking up the war and all the houses and the ships and them in the harbour. That ever cross your mind?'

His interest in teaching didn't die.

We often saw him going about with big books. These books were about teaching.

Titus Hoyt used to say, 'Is a science, man. The trouble with Trinidad is that the teachers don't have this science of teaching.'

And, 'Is the biggest thing in the world, man. Having the minds of the young to train. Think of that. Think.'

It soon became clear that whatever we thought about it Titus Hoyt was bent on training our minds.

He formed the Miguel Street Literary and Social Youth Club, and had it affiliated to the Trinidad and Tobago Youth Association.

We used to meet in his house which was well supplied with things to eat and drink. The walls of his house were now hung with improving quotations, some typed, some cut out of magazines and pasted on bits of cardboard.

I also noticed a big thing called 'Time-table.'

From this I gathered that Titus Hoyt was to rise at five-thirty, read Something from Greek philosophers until six, spend fifteen minutes bathing and exercising, another five reading the morning paper, and ten on breakfast. It was a formidable thing altogether.

Titus Hoyt said, 'If I follow the time-table I will be a educated man in about three four years.'

The Miguel Street Club didn't last very long.

It was Titus Hoyt's fault.

No man in his proper senses would have made Boyee secretary. Most of Boyee's minutes consisted of the names of people present.

And then we all had to read something.

The Miguel Street Literary and Social Club became nothing more than a gathering of film critics.

Titus Hoyt said, 'No, man. We just can't have all you boys talking about pictures all the time. I will have to get some propaganda for you boys.'

Boyee said, 'Mr Titus Hoyt, what we want with propaganda? Is a German thing.'

Titus Hoyt smiled. 'That is not the proper meaning of the word, boy. I am using the word in it proper meaning. Is education boy, that make me know things like that.'

Boyee was sent as our delegate to the Youth Association annual conference.

When he came back Boyee said, 'Is a helluva thing at that youth conference. Is only a pack of old, old people it have there.'

The attraction of the Coca-Cola and the cakes and the ice-cream began to fade. Some of us began staying away from meetings.

Titus Hoyt made one last effort to keep the club together.

One day he said, 'Next Sunday the club will go on a visit to Fort George.'

There were cries of disapproval.

Titus Hoyt said, 'You see, you people don't care about your country. How many of you know about Fort George? Not one of you here know about the place. But is history, man, your history, and you must learn about things like that. You must remember that the boys and girls of today are the men and women of tomorrow. The old Romans had a saying, you know. *Mens sana in corpore sano.* I think we will make the walk to Fort George.'

Still no one wanted to go.

Titus Hoyt said, 'At the top of Fort George it have a stream, and it cool cool and the water crystal clear. You could bathe there when we get to the top.'

We couldn't resist that.

The next Sunday a whole group of us took the trolley-bus to Mucurapo.

When the conductor came round to collect the fares, Titus Hoyt said, 'Come back a little later.' And he paid the conductor only when we got off the bus. The fare for everybody came up to about two shillings. But Titus Hoyt gave the conductor a shilling, saying, 'We don't want any ticket, man!' The conductor and Titus Hoyt laughed.

It was a long walk up the hill, red and dusty, and hot.

Titus Hoyt told us, 'This fort was built at a time when the French and them was planning to invade Trinidad.'

We gasped.

We had never realised that anyone considered us so important.

Titus Hoyt said, 'That was in 1803, when we was fighting Napoleon.'

We saw a few old rusty guns at the side of the path and heaps of rusty cannon-balls.

I asked, 'The French invade Trinidad, Mr Titus Hoyt?'

Titus Hoyt shook his head in a disappointed way. 'No, they didn't attack. But we was ready, man. Ready for them.'

Boyee said, 'You sure it have this stream up there you tell us about, Mr Titus Hoyt?'

Titus Hoyt said, 'What you think I is? A liar?'

Boyee said, 'I ain't saying nothing.'

We walked and sweated. Boyee took off his shoes.

Errol said, 'If it ain't have that stream up there, somebody going to catch hell.'

We got to the top, had a quick look at the graveyard where there were a few tombstones of British soldiers dead long ago; and we looked through the telescope at the city of Port of Spain large and sprawling beneath us. We could see the people walking in the streets as large as life.

Then we went looking for the stream.

We couldn't find it.

Titus Hoyt said, 'It must be here somewhere. When I was a boy I use to bathe in it.'

Boyee said, 'And what happen now? It dry up?'

Titus Hoyt said, 'It look so.'

Boyee got really mad, and you couldn't blame him. It was hard work coming up that hill, and we were all hot and thirsty.

He insulted Titus Hoyt in a very crude way.

Titus Hoyt said, 'Remember, Boyee, you are the secretary of the Miguel Street Literary and Social Club. Remember that you have just attended a meeting of the Youth Association as our delegate. Remember these things.'

Boyee said, 'Go to hell, Hoyt'.

We were aghast.

So the Literary Club broke up.

It wasn't long after that Titus Hoyt got his Inter Arts degree and set up a school of his own. He had a big sign placed in his garden:

TITUS HOYT. I.A. (London, External)
*Passes in the Cambridge
School Certificate Guaranteed*

One year the *Guardian* had a brilliant idea. They started the Needy Cases Fund to help needy cases at Christmas. It was popular and after a few years was called the Neediest Cases Fund. At the beginning of November the *Guardian* announced the target for the fund and it was a daily excitement until Christmas Eve to see how the fund rose. It was always front page news and everybody who gave got his name in the papers.

In the middle of December one year, when the excitement was high, Miguel Street was in the news.

Hat showed us the paper and we read:
FOLLOW THE EXAMPLE OF THIS TINYMITE!

The smallest and most touching response to our appeal to bring Yuletide cheer to the unfortunate has come in a letter from Mr Titus Hoyt, I.A., a headmaster of Miguel Street, Port of Spain. The letter was sent to Mr Hoyt by one of his pupils who wishes to remain anonymous. We have Mr Hoyt's permission to print the letter in full.

'Dear Mr Hoyt, I am only eight and, as you doubtless know, I am a member of the GUARDIAN Tinymites League. I read Aunt Juanita every Sunday. You, dear Mr Hoyt, have always extolled the virtue of charity and you have spoken repeatedly of the fine work the GUARDIAN Neediest Cases Fund is doing to bring Yuletide cheer to the unfortunate. I have decided to yield to your earnest entreaty. I have very little money to offer – a mere six cents, in fact, but take, it, Mr Hoyt, and send it to the GUARDIAN Neediest Cases Fund. May it bring Yuletide cheer to some poor unfortunate! I know it is not much. But, like the widow, I give my mite. I remain, dear Mr Hoyt, One of Your Pupils.'

And there was a large photograph of Titus Hoyt, smiling and pop-eyed in the flash of the camera.

Calypsonian

Samuel Selvon

Samuel Selvon was born in Trinidad of East Indian parents. From home and from England, he has written of Trinidadians in his novels. "Calypsonian" portrays a carefree calypso singer who turns to petty crime in duress. Nuances of the Trinidad dialect permit a very subtle and penetrating insight into character and into mixed emotions. Here, Selvon employs an idiom based on the rhythm and images of folk speech.

It had a time when things was really brown in Trinidad, and Razor Blade couldn't make a note nohow, no matter what he do, everywhere he turn, people telling him they ain't have work. It look like if work scarce like gold, and is six months now he ain't working.

Besides that, Razor Blade owe Chin parlour about five dollars, and the last time he went in for a sandwich and a sweet drink, Chin tell him no more trusting until he pay all he owe. Chin have his name in a copybook under the counter.

"Wait until the calypso season start," he tell Chin, "and I go be reaping a harvest. You remember last year how much money I had?"

But though Chin remember last year, that still ain't make him soften up, and it reach a position where he hungry, clothes dirty, and he see nothing at all to come, and this time so, the calypso season about three four months off.

On top of all that, rain falling nearly every day, and the shoes he have on have big hole in them, like if they laughing.

Was the rain what cause him to t'ief a pair of shoes from by a shoemaker shop in Park Street. Is the first time he ever t'ief, and it take him a long time to make up his mind. He stand up there on the pavement by this shoemaker shop, and he thinking things like Oh God when I tell you I hungry, and all the shoes around the table, on the ground, some capsize, some old and some new, some getting halfsole and some getting new heel.

It have a pair just like the one he have on.

The table cut up for so, as if the shoemaker blind and cutting the wood instead of the leather, and it have a broken calabash shell with some boil starch in it. The starch look like pap; he so hungry he feel he could eat it.

Well, the shoemaker in the back of the shop, and it only have few people sheltering rain on the pavement. It look so easy for him to put down the old pair and take up another pair – this time so, he done have his eye fix on a pair that look like Technic, and just his size, too, besides.

Razor Blade remember how last year he was sitting pretty – two-tone Technic, gaberdeen suit, hot tie. Now that he catching his royal, everytime he only making comparison with last year, thinking in his mind how them was the good old days, and wondering if they go ever come back again.

And it look to him as if t'iefing could be easy, because plenty time people does leave things alone and go away, like how now the shoemaker in the back of the shop, and all he have to do is take up a pair of shoes and walk off in cool blood.

Well, it don't take plenty to make a t'ief. All you have to do is have a fellar catching his royal, and can't get a work noway, and bam! By the time he make two three rounds he bounce something somewhere, an orange from a tray, or he snatch a bread in a parlour, or something.

Like how he bounce the shoes.

So though he frighten like hell and part of him going like a pliers, Razor Blade playing victor brave boy and whistling as he go down the road.

The only thing now is that he hungry.

Right there by Queen Street, in front of a chinee restaurant, he get an idea. Not an idea in truth; all he did think was: In for a shilling in for a pound. But when he think that, is as if he begin to realise that if he going to get stick for the shoes, he might as well start t'iefing black is white.

So he open now to anything: all you need is a start, all you need is a crank up, and it come easy after that.

What you think he planning to do? He planning to walk in the chinee restaurant and sit down and eat a major meal, and then out off without paying. It look so easy, he wonder why he never think of it before.

The waitress come up while he looking at the menu. She stand up there, with a pencil stick up on she ears like a real test, and when he take a pin-t at she he realise that this restaurant work only part-time as far as she concern, because she look as if she sleepy, she body bend up like a piece of copper wire.

What you go do? She must be only getting a few dollars from the chinee man, and she can't live on that.

He realise suddenly that he bothering about the woman when he himself catching his tail, so he shake his head and watch down at the menu.

He mad to order a portion of everything – fry rice, chicken chopsuey, roast pork, chicken chow-min, birdnest soup, chicken broth, and one of them big salad with big slice of tomato and onion.

He begin to think again about the last calypso season, when he was holding big, and uses to go up by the high-class chinee restaurant in St. Vincent Street. He think how is a funny thing how sometimes you does have so much food that you eat till you sick, and another time you can't even see you way to hustle a rock and mauby.

It should have some way that when you have the chance you could eat enough to last you for a week or a month, and he make a plan right there, that the next time he have money (oh God) he go make a big deposit in a restaurant, so that all he have to do is walk in and eat like stupidness.

But the woman getting impatient. She say: "You taking a long time to make up you mind, like you never eat in restaurant before."

And he think about the time when he had money, how no frowsy woman could have talk to him so. He remember how them waitresses used to hustle to serve him, and one night the talk get around that Razor Blade, the Calypsonian, was in the place, and they insist that he give them a number. Which one it was again? The one about Home and the Bachelor.

"Come, come make up you mind, mister, I have work to do."

So he order plain boil rice and chicken stew, because the way how he feeling, all them fancy chinee dish is only joke, he feel as if he want something like roast breadfruit and saltfish, something solid so when it go down in you belly you could feel it there.

And he tell the woman to bring a drink of Barbados rum first thing, because he know how long they does take to bring food in them restaurant, and he could coast with the rum in the meantime.

By the time the food come he feeling so hungry he could hardly wait, he fall down on the plate of rice and chicken as if is the first time he see food, and in three minute everything finish.

And is just as if he seeing the world for the first time, he feel like a million, he feel like a lord; he give a loud belch and bring up some of the chicken and rice to his throat; when he swallow it back down it taste sour.

He thinking how it had a time a American fellar hear a calypso in Trinidad and he went back to the States and he get it set up to music and thing, and he get the Andrews Sisters to sing it, and the song make money like hell, it was on Hit Parade and all; wherever you turn, you could hear people singing that calypso. This time so, the poor calypsonian who really write the song catching hell in Trinidad; it was only when some smart lawyer friend tell him about copyright and that sort of business that he wake up. He went to America; and how you don't know he get a lot of money after the case did fix up in New York?

Razor Blade know the story good; whenever he write a calypso, he always praying that some big-shot from America would hear it and like it, and want to set it up good. The Blade uses to go in Frederick Street and Marine Square by the one-two music shops, and look at all the popular songs, set up in notes and words, with the name of the fellar who write it big on the front, and sometimes his photograph too. And Razor Blade uses to think: But why I can't write song like that too, and have my name all over the place?

And when things was good with him, he went inside now and then, and tell the clerks and them that he does write calypsos. But they only laugh at him, because they does think that calypso is no song at all, that what is song is numbers like "I've Got You Under My Skin" and "Sentimental Journey", what real American composers write.

And the Blade uses to argue that every dog has his day, and that a time would come when people singing calypso all over the world like stupidness.

He thinking about all that as he lean back there in the chinee man restaurant.

Is to peel off now without paying!

The best way is to play brassface, do as if you own the damn restaurant, and walk out cool.

So he get up and he notice the waitress not around (she must be serving somebody else) and he take time and walk out, passing by the cashier who writing something in a book.

But all this time, no matter how boldface you try to be, you can't stop part of you from going like a pliers, clip clip, and he feel as if he want to draw his legs together and walk with two foot as one.

When the waitress find out Razor Blade gone without paying, she start to make one set of noise, and a chinee man from the kitchen dash outside to see if he could see him, but this time so Razor Blade making races down Frederick Street.

The owner of the restaurant tell the woman she have to pay for the food that Razor Blade eat, that was she fault, and she begin to cry big water, because is a lot of food that Razor Blade put away, and she know that that mean two three dollars from she salary.

This time so, Razor Blade laughing like hell; he quite down by the Railway

Station, and he know nobody could catch him now.

One set of rain start to fall suddenly; Razor Blade walking like a king in his new shoes, and no water getting up his foot this time, so he ain't even bothering to shelter.

And he don't know why, but same time he get a sharp idea for a calypso. About how a man does catch his royal when he can't get a work noway. The calypso would say about how he see some real hard days; he start to think up words right away as he walking in the rain:

It had a time in this colony
When everybody have money excepting me
I can't get a work no matter how I try
It look as if good times pass me by.

He start to hum it to the tune of an old calypso (Man Centipede Bad Too Bad) just to see how it shaping up.

And he think about One Foot Harper, the one man who could help him out with a tune.

It had a big joke with One Foot one time. Somebody t'ief One Foot crutch one day when he was catching a sleep under a weeping willow tree in Woodford Square, and One Foot had to stay in the square for a whole day and night. You could imagine how he curse stink; everybody only standing up and laughing like hell; nobody won't lend a hand, and if wasn't for Razor Blade, now so One Foot might still be waiting under the weeping willow tree for somebody to get a crutch for him.

But the old Blade help out the situation, and since that time, the both of them good friends.

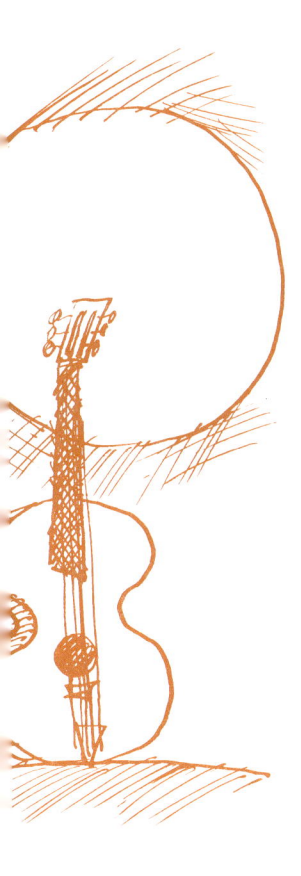

So Razor Blade start making a tack for the tailor shop which part One Foot does always be hanging out, because One Foot ain't working noway, and every day he there by the tailor shop, sitting down on a soapbox and talking whole day.

But don't fret you head One Foot ain't no fool; it had a time in the old days when they uses to call him King of Calypso, and he was really good. If he did have money, or education business, is a sure thing he would have been up the ladder, because he was the first man who ever had the idea that calypsonians should go away and sing in America and England. But people only laugh at One Foot when he say that.

Razor Blade meet One Foot in a big old talk about the time when the Town Hall burn down (One Foot saying he know the fellar who start the fire). When One Foot see him, he stop arguing right away and he say:

"What happening paleets, long time no see."

Razor Blade say: "Look man, I have a sharp idea for a calypso. Let we go in the back of the shop and work it out."

But One Foot feeling comfortable on the soapbox. He say:

"Take ease, don't rush me. What about the shilling you have for me, that you borrow last week?"

The Blade turn his pockets inside out, and a pair of dice roll out, and a penknife fall on the ground.

"Boy, I ain't have a cent. I broken. I bawling. If you stick me with a pin you won't draw blood."

"Don't worry with that kind of talk, is so with all-you fellars, you does borrow a man money and then forget his address."

"I telling you man," Razor Blade talk as if he in hurry, but is only to get away from the topic, "you don't believe me?"

But the Foot cagey. He say, "All right, all right, but I telling you in front that if you want money borrow again, you come to the wrong man. I ain't lending you a nail till you pay me back that shilling that you have for me." The Foot move off the soapbox, and stand up balancing on the crutch.

"Come man, do quick," Razor Blade make as if to go behind the shop in the backroom. Same time he see Rahamut, the Indian tailor.

"What happening Indian, things looking good with you."

Rahamut stop stitching a khaki pants and look at the Blade.

"You and One Foot always writing calypso in this shop, all-you will have to give me a commission."

"Well, you know how it is, sometimes you up, sometimes you down. Right now I so down that bottom and I same thing."

"Well, old man is a funny thing but I never see you when you up."

"Ah, but wait till the calypso season start."

"Then you won't come round here at all. Then you is bigshot, you forget small fry like Rahamut."

Well, Razor Blade don't know what again to tell Rahamut, because is really true all what the Indian saying about he and One Foot hanging out behind the shop. And he think about these days when anybody tell him anything, all he could say is: "Wait till the calypso season start up," as if when the calypso season start up God go come to earth, and make everybody happy.

So what he do is he laugh kiff-kiff and give Rahamut a pat on the back, like they is good friends.

Same time One Foot come up, so they went and sit down by a break-up table.

Razor Blade say: "Listen to these words old man, you never hear calypso like this in you born days," and he start to give the Foot the words.

But from the time he start, One Food chock his fingers in his ears and bawl out: "Oh God, old man, you can't think up something new, is the same old words every year."

"But how you mean, man," the Blade say, "this is calypso father. Wait until you hear the whole thing."

They begin to work on the song, and One Foot so good that in two twos he fix up a tune. So Razor Blade pick up a empty bottle and a piece of stick, and One Foot start beating the table, and is so they getting on, singing this new calypso that they invent.

Well, Rahamut and other Indian fellar who does help him out with the sewing come up and listen.

"What you think of this new number, papa?" the Blade ask Rahamut.

Rahamut scratch his head and say: "let me get that tune again."

So they begin again, beating on the table and the bottle, and Razor Blade imagine that he singing to a big audience in the Calypso Tent, so he putting all he have in it.

When they finished the fellar who does help Rahamut say: "That is hearts."

But Rahamut say: "Why you don't shut you mouth? What all-you Indian know about calypso?"

And that cause a big laugh, everybody begin to laugh kya-kya, because Rahamut himself is a Indian.

One Foot turn to Razor Blade and say: "Listen to them two Indian how they arguing about we creole calypso. I never see that in my born days!"

Rahamut say: "Man I is a creolise Trinidadian, *oui*."

Razor Blade say: "All right, joke is joke, but all-you think it good? It really good?"

Rahamut want to say yes, it good, but he beating about the bush, he hemming and hawing, he saying: "Well, it so-so" and "it not so bad," and "I hear a lot of worse ones."

But the fellar who does help Rahamut, he getting on as if he mad, he only hitting Razor Blade and One Foot on the shoulder and saying how he never hear a calypso like that, how it sure to be the Road March for next year Carnival. He swinging his hands all about in the air while he talking, and his hand hit Rahamut hand and Rahamut get a chook in his finger with a needle he was holding.

Well, Rahamut put the finger in his mouth and start to suck it, and he turn round and start to abuse the other tailor fellar, saying why you don't keep you tail quiet, look you make me chook my hand with the blasted needle?

"Well, what happen for that? You go dead because a needle chook you?" the fellar say.

Big argument start up; they forget all about Razor Blade calypso and start to talk about how people does get blood poison from pin and needle chook.

Well, it don't have anything to write down as far as the calypso concern. Razor Blade memorise the words and tune, and that is the case. Is so a calypso born, cool cool, without any fuss. It so all them big numbers like "Yes, I Catch Him Last Night", and "That Is a Thing I Can Do Anytime Anywhere", and "Old Lady Your Bloomers Falling Down ", born right there behind Rahamut tailor shop.

After the big talk about pin and needle Rahamut and the fellar who does assist him went back to finish off a zootsuit that a fellar was going to call for in the evening.

Now Razor Blade want to ask One Foot to borrow him a shilling, but he don't know how to start, especially as he owe him already. So he begin to talk sweet, praising up the tune that One Foot invent for the calypso, saying he never hear a tune so sweet, that the melody smooth like sweetoil.

But as soon as he start to come like that, the old Foot begin to get cagey, and say, "Oh God, old man, don't mamaguile me."

The Blade not so very fussy, because a solid meal in his belly. But same time he trying to guile One Foot into lending him a little thing, he get an idea.

He begin to tell One Foot how he spend the morning, how he ups the shoes from the shoemaker shop in Park Street, and how he eat big for nothing.

One Foot say: "I bet you get in trouble, all-you fellars does take some brave risk, *oui.*"

Razor say: "Man, it easy as kissing hand, is only because you have one foot and can't run fast, that's why you talking so."

Foot say: "No jokes about my one foot."

Razor say: "But listen, man, you too stupid again! You and me could work up a good scheme to get some money. If you t'iefing, you might as well t'ief big."

"Is you is the t'ief, not me."

"But listen, man, Foot," the Blade gone down low in voice, "I go do everything, all I want you to do is to keep watchman for me, to see if anybody coming."

"What is the scheme you have?"

To tell truth, the old Blade ain't have nothing cut and dry in the old brain; all he thinking is that he go make a big t'ief somewhere where have money. He scratch his head and pull his ears like he did see Spencer Tracy do in a picture, and he say: "What about the Roxy Theatre down St. James?"

Same time he talking, he feeling excitement in his body, like if waves going up and coming down and he hold on to One Foot hand.

The Foot say: "Well yes, the day reach when you really catching you royal. I never thought I would see the time when my good friend Razor Blade turn t'ief. Man, you sure to get catch. Why you don't try for a work somewhere until the calypso season start up?"

"I tired try to get work. It ain't have work noway."

"Well, you ain't no t'ief. You sure to get catch, I tell you."

"But, man, look how I get away with the shoes and the meal! I tell you all you have to do is play boldface and you could commit murder and get away free."

The Foot start to hum a old calypso:

> *"If a man have money today . . .*
> *He could commit murder and get away free*
> *And live in the Governor's company. . . .*

The Blade begin to get vex. "So you don't like the idea? You think I can't get away with it?"

"You ain't have no practice. You is a novice. Crime does not pay."

"You is a damn coward!"

"Us calypsonians have to keep we dignity."

"You go to hell! If you won't help me I go do it by myself, you go see! And I not t'iefing small, I t'iefing big! If I going down the river, I making sure is for plenty money, and not for no small time job."

"Well, papa, don't say I ain't tell you you looking for trouble."

"Man Foot, the trouble with you is you only have one foot so you can't think like me."

The Foot get hot. He say: "Listen, I tell you already no jokes about my one foot, you hear? I ain't taking no jokes about that. Curse my mother, curse my father, but don't tell me nothing about my foot."

The Blade relent. "I sorry, Foot, I know you don't like nobody to give you jokes.

Same time Rahamut call out and ask why they keeping so much noise, if they think they in the fishmarket.

So they finish the talk. Razor Blade tell One Foot he would see him later, and One Foot say: "Righto, boy, don't forget the words for the song. And I warning you for the last time to keep out of trouble."

But the minute he leave the tailor shop Razor Blade only thinking how easy it go be to pull off this big deal. He alone would do it, without any gun, too, besides.

Imagine the Foot saying he is a novice! All you need is brassface; play brazen; do as if you is a saint, as if you still have you mother innocent features, and if anybody ask you anything, lift up you eyebrows and throw you hands up in the air and say: "Oh Lord, who, *me?*"

He find himself quite round by the Queen's Park Savannah, walking and thinking. And he see a old woman selling orange. The woman as if she sleeping in the heat, she propping up she chin with one hand, and she head bend down. Few people passing; Razor Blade size up the situation in one glance.

He mad to bounce a orange from the tray, just to show that he could do it and get away. Just pass up near – don't even look down at the tray – and just lift one up easy as you walking, and put it in you pocket.

He wish One Foot was there to see how easy it was to do.

But he hardly put the orange in his pocket when the old woman jump up and start to make one set of noise, bawling out: "T'ief, t'ief! Look a man t'ief a orange from me! Help! Hold him! Don't let 'im get away!"

And as if that bawling start the pliers working on him right away; he forget every thing he was thinking, and he start to make races across the Savannah.

WEST INDIES

He look back and he see three fellars chasing him. And is just as if he can't feel nothing at all, as if he not running, as if he standing up in one spot. The only thing is the pliers going clip clip, and he gasping: Oh God! Oh God!

Jamaican Fragment

A. L. Hendricks

Born in Jamaica in 1922, A. L. Hendricks was educated at Jamaica College and then in London. He has been a broadcaster in England since 1950, and has published a volume of poems, *On This Mountain,* in 1965.

Every day I walk a half-mile from my home to the tramcar lines in the morning, and from the lines to my home in the evening. The walk is pleasant. The road on either side is flanked by red- and green-roofed bungalows, green lawns and gardens. The exercise is good for me and now and then I learn something from a little incident.

One morning, about half-way between my front gate and the tram track, I noticed two little boys playing in the garden of one of the more modest cottages. They were both very little boys, one was four years old perhaps, the other five. The bigger of the two was a sturdy youngster, very dark, with a mat of coarse hair on his head and coal-black eyes. He was definitely a little Jamaican – a strong little Jamaican. The other little fellow was smaller, but also sturdy – he was white, with hazel eyes and light-brown hair. Both were dressed in blue shirts and khaki pants: they wore no shoes and their feet were muddy. They were not conscious of my standing there watching them; they played on. The game, if it could be called a game, was not elaborate. The little white boy strode imperiously up and down and every now and then shouted imperiously at his bigger playmate. The little brown boy shuffled along quietly behind him and did what he was told.

"Pick up that stick!" The dark boy picked it up.

"Jump into the flowers!" The dark boy jumped.

"Get me some water!" The dark boy ran inside. The white boy sat down on the lawn.

I was amazed. Here before my eyes, a white baby, for they were little more than babies, was imposing his will upon a little black boy. And the little black boy submitted. I puzzled within myself as I went down the road. Could it be that the little dark boy was the son of a servant in the home and therefore had to do the white boy's bidding? No. They were obviously dressed alike, the little dark boy was of equal class with his playmate. No. They were playmates, the little dark boy was a neighbour's child. I was sure of that. Then how was it that he obeyed so faithfully the white boy's orders? Was it that even at his early age he sensed that in his own country he would be at the white man's beck and call? Could he in such youth divine a difference between himself and the white boy? And did the little white youngster so young, such a baby, realize that he would grow to dominate the black man? Was there an indefinable quality in the white man that enabled his baby, smaller and younger than his playmate, to make him his slave? Was there really some difference between a white man and a black man? Something that made the white superior? I could find no answer. I could not bring myself to believe such a thing, and yet, with my own eyes I had seen a little dark boy take orders from a little white boy – a little white boy obviously his social equal, and younger and smaller. Were we as a race really inferior? So inferior that even in our infancy we realized our deficiencies, and accepted a position as the white man's servant?

For a whole day I puzzled over this problem. For a whole day my faith in my people was shaken. When I passed that afternoon the little boys were not there. That evening I thought deeply on the subject.

The next morning the boys were there again, and a man was standing at the gate watching them. I stopped and looked, just to see what the white boy was making his little servant do. To my utter astonishment the little dark boy was striding imperiously up and down the lawn, while the white youngster walked abjectly behind him.

"Get me a banana!" The little white boy ran into the house and reappeared shortly with a banana. "Peel it for me!" The little white boy skinned the banana and handed it to his dark master.

I saw it now. This was indeed a game, a game I had played as a child. Each boy took it in turn every alternate day to be the boss, the other the slave. It had been great fun to me as a youngster. I smiled as I remembered. I looked at the man standing by the gate. He was a white man. I remembered what I had thought yesterday. He, no doubt, I thought to myself, was wondering if the black race is superior to the white. I laughed gently to myself. How silly grown-ups are, how clever we are, how wonderfully able we are to impute deep motives to childish actions! How suspicious we are when we have been warped by prejudice! This man, I said to myself, will puzzle all day on whether the blacks will eventually arise and rule the world because he thinks he sees a little black boy realizing at a tender age his superiority over the white. I will save him his puzzle. I will explain it to him. I went across to him.

"I know what you're thinking," I said. "You're thinking that maybe the black race is superior to the white, because you just saw the little dark youngster on the lawn ordering the little white boy around. Don't think that, it's a game they play. Alternate days one is boss, the other the servant. It's a grand game. I used to play it and maybe so did you. Yesterday I saw the little white boy bossing the dark one and I worried all day over the dark boy's realization of his inferiority so young in life! We are silly, we grown-ups, aren't we?"

The man was surprised at my outburst. He looked at me smiling.

"I know all about the game," he said. "The boys are brothers – my sons." He pointed to a handsome brown woman on the veranda who had just come out to call in the children. "That's my wife," he said.

I smiled. My spirit laughed within me. This is Jamaica, I said in my heart, this is my country – my people. I looked at the white man. He smiled at me. "We'll miss the tram if we don't hurry," he said.

Blackout

Roger Mais

Roger Mais (1905-1955) was a painter and dramatist as well as a writer. Many of his stories deal with characters attempting to cope with social situations and impulses that they find difficult to understand.

The city was in partial blackout; the street lights had not been turned on, because of the wartime policy of conserving electricity; and the houses behind their discreet *aurelia* hedges were wrapped in an atmosphere of exclusive respectability.

The young woman waiting at the bus stop was not in the least nervous, in spite of the wave of panic that had been sweeping the city about bands of hooligans roaming the streets after dark and assaulting unprotected women. She was a sensible young woman to begin with, who realised that one good scream would be sufficient to bring a score of respectable suburban householders running to her assistance. On the other hand she was an American, and fully conscious of the tradition of American young women that they don't scare easily.

Even that slinking black shadow that seemed to be materialising out of the darkness at the other side of the street did not disconcert her. She was only slightly curious now that she observed that the shadow was approaching her, slowly.

It was a young man dressed in conventional shirt and pants, and wearing a pair of canvas shoes. That was what lent the suggestion of slinking to his movements, because he went along noiselessly – that, and the mere suggestion of a stoop. He was very tall. There was a curious look of hunger and unrest about his eyes. But the thing that struck her immediately was the fact that he was black; the other particulars scarcely made any impression at all in comparison. In her country not every night a white woman could be nonchalantly approached by a black man. There was enough novelty in all this to intrigue her. She seemed to remember that any sort of adventure might be experienced in one of these tropical islands of the West Indies.

"Could you give me a light, lady?" the man said.

It is true she was smoking, but she had only just lit this one from the stub of the cigarette she had thrown away. The fact was she had no matches. Would he believe her, she wondered? "I am sorry. I haven't got a match."

The young man looked into her face, seemed to hesitate an instant and said, his brow slightly wrinkled in perplexity: "But you are smoking."

There was no argument against that. Still, she was not particular about giving him a light from the cigarette she was smoking. It may be stupid, but there was a suggestion of intimacy about such an act, simple as it was, that, call it what you may, she could not accept just like that.

There was a moment's hesitation on her part now, during which time the man's steady gaze never left her face. There was pride and challenge in his look, curiously mingled with quiet amusement.

She held out her cigarette toward him between two fingers.

"Here," she said, "you can light from that."

In the act of bending his head to accept the proffered light, he came quite close to her. He did not seem to understand that she meant him to take the lighted cigarette from her hand. He just bent over her hand to light his.

Presently he straightened up, inhaled a deep lungful of soothing smoke and exhaled again with satisfaction. She saw then that he was smoking the half of a cigarette, which had been clinched and saved for future consumption.

"Thank you," said the man, politely; and was in the act of moving off when he noticed that instead of returning her cigarette to her lips she had casually, unthinkingly flicked it away. He observed this in the split part of a second that it took him to say those two words. It was almost a whole cigarette she had thrown away. She had been smoking it with evident enjoyment a moment before.

He stood there looking at her, with cold speculation.

In a way it unnerved her. Not that she was frightened. He seemed quite decent in his own way, and harmless; but he made her feel uncomfortable. If he had said something rude she would have preferred it. It would have been no more than she would have expected of him. But instead, this quiet contemptuous look. Yes, that was it. The thing began to take on definition in her mind. How dare he; the insolence!

"Well, what are you waiting for?" she said, because she felt she had to break the tension somehow.

"I am sorry I made you waste a whole cigarette," he said.

She laughed a little nervously. "It's nothing," she said, feeling a fool.

"There's plenty more where that came from, eh?" he asked.

"I suppose so."

This won't do, she thought, quickly. She had no intention of standing at a street corner jawing with – well, with a black man. There was something indecent about it. Why doesn't he move on? As though he had read her thoughts he said:

"This is the street, lady. It's public."

Well, anyway, she didn't have to answer him. She could snub him quietly, the way she should have properly done from the start.

"It's a good thing you're a woman," he said.

"And if I were a man?"

"As man to man maybe I'd give you something to think about," he said, still in that quiet, even voice.

In America they lynch them for less than this, she thought.

"This isn't America," he said. "I can see you are an American. In this country there are only men and women. You'll learn about it." She could only humour him. Find out what his ideas were about this question, anyway. It would be something to talk about back home. Suddenly she was intrigued.

"So in this country there are only men and women, eh?"

"That's right. So to speak there is only you an' me, only there are hundreds and thousands of us. We seem to get along somehow without lynchings and burnings and all that."

"Do you really think that all men are created equal?"

"It don't seem to me there is any sense in that. The facts show it ain't so. Look at you an' me, for instance. But that isn't to say you're not a woman, the same way as I am a man. You see what I mean?"

"I can't say I do."

"You will, though, if you stop here long enough."

She threw a quick glance in his direction.

The man laughed.

"I don't mean what you're thinking," he said. "You're not my type of woman. You don't have anything to fear under that heading."

"Oh!"

"You're waiting for the bus, I take it. Well, that's it coming now. Thanks for the light."

"Don't mention it," she said, with a nervous sort of giggle.

He made an attempt to move along as the bus came up. He stood there quietly aloof, as though in the consciousness of a male strength and pride that was justly his. There was something about him that was at once challenging and disturbing. He had shaken her supreme confidence in some important sense.

As the bus moved off she was conscious of his eyes' quiet scrutiny, without the interruption of artificial barriers, in the sense of dispassionate appraisement, as between man and woman, any man, any woman.

She fought resolutely against the very natural desire to turn her head and take a last look at him. Perhaps she was thinking about what the people on the bus might think. And perhaps it was just as well that she did not see him bend forward with that swift hungry movement, retrieving from the gutter the half-smoked cigarette she had thrown away.

Jamaica Market

Agnes Maxwell-Hall

Born in 1894 in Montego Bay, Jamaica, Agnes Maxwell-Hall was educated in London, Boston, and New York. Besides writing, she operated a dairy in the Jamaican mountains at Kempshot.

Honey, pepper, leaf-green limes,
Pagan fruit whose names are rhymes,
Mangoes, breadfruit, ginger-roots
Granadillas, bamboo shoots,
Cho-cho, ackees, tangerines,
Lemons, purple Congo-Beans,
Sugar, okras, folanuts,
Citrons, hairy coconuts,
Fish, tobacco, native hats,
Golden bananas, woven mats,
Plantain, wild-thyme, pallid leeks,
Pigeons with their scarlet beaks,
Oranges and saffren yams,
Baskets, ruby guava jams,
Turtles, goat-skins, cinnamon,
Allspice, conch-shells, golden rum.
Black skins, babel – The sun
That burns all colours into one.

Further Reading

Lamming, G., *In the Castle of My Skin.* Toronto: Collier–Macmillan Canada Ltd., 1970

Harris, W., *Palace of the Peacock.* London: Faber and Faber, 1960

Naipaul, V.S., *A House for Mr. Biswas.* Middlesex, England: Penguin Books Ltd., 1961

Ramchand, K., *West Indian Narrative.* Don Mills, Ontario: Thomas Nelson and Sons Ltd., 1966

Breman, P., *You Better Believe It.* Baltimore: Penguin Books Ltd., 1973

Moore, G., *The Chosen Tongue.* London: Longman's, 1969

James, L., *The Islands in Between.* London: Oxford University Press, 1968

Salkey, A., *West Indian Stories.* London: Faber and Faber, 1960

Mais, R., *The Three Novels of Roger Mais.* Norwich, England: Fletcher & Son Ltd., 1966

Ramchand, K., *The West Indian Novel and Its Background.* London: Faber and Faber, 1970

Information Services, Ghana

tion Services, Ghana

Information Services, Ghana

ation Services, Ghana

Information Services, Ghana

Zambia Information Services

Information Services

A Glimpse of Africa

A written literature was first established in Africa by European settlers and by those Africans who reacted to the ways of the politically dominant whites. The realistic fiction of Alan Paton and Peter Abrahams demonstrates this reaction, as do earlier works published in *Imvo Zabantsunde,* a South African literary newspaper established independently of the missionaries in the 1880's.

Modern African literature is directed toward revealing African life as it is seen by Africans. African literature has virtually exploded in little more than two decades - with new writers developing themes that are both universal and particular to African situations. The themes centre on materialism, racial conflict, self-identity, conflict between the old and the new, alienation, symbol in folklore, female emancipation, superstitions, and provincialism - in short, the current themes of British and American writers.

In this section of *Literary Glimpses of the Commonwealth* certain African cultural characteristics are reflected, and an opportunity for comparison with the West Indies is provided. A strong allegiance to the ruling spirit is shown in "The Rain Came" and "Abiku." The African struggle against external forces is presented in "The Gentlemen of the Jungle" and "Dead Men's Path." Reactions to reality and to a fading heritage are revealed in "Telephone Conversation" and "Once upon a Time."

African and West Indian selections lend themselves to comparisons. For example, "Telephone Conversation" (African) and "Blackout" (West Indian) explore the interaction between races.

Abiku

Wole Soyinka

Born in 1934 in Western Nigeria, Wole Soyinka has become the most topical playwright of Nigeria. After local schooling, he attended Leeds University to receive a B.A. (Honours) in English Literature. In 1960 he returned to Nigeria to become actor, director, and playwright, and to help found the Nigerian Theatre.

In vain your bangles cast
Charmed circles at my feet
I am Abiku, calling for the first
And the repeated time.

Must I weep for goats and cowries
For palm oil and the sprinkled ash?
Yams do not sprout in amulets
To earth Abiku's limbs.

So when the snail is burnt in his shell,
Whet the heated fragment, brand me
Deeply on the breast. You must know him
When Abiku calls again.

I am the squirrel teeth, cracked
The riddle of the palm. Remember
This, and dig me deeper still into
The god's swollen foot.

AFRICA

Once and the repeated time, ageless
Though I puke; and when you pour
Libations, each finger points me near
The way I came, where

The ground is wet with mourning
White dew suckles flesh-birds
Evening befriends the spider, trapping
Flies in wind-froth;

Night, and Abiku sucks the oil
From lamps. Mothers! I'll be the
Suppliant snake coiled on the doorstep
Yours the killing cry.

The ripest fruit was saddest;
Where I crept, the warmth was cloying.
In the silence of webs, Abiku moans, shaping
Mounds from the yolk.

The Rain Came

Grace A. Ogot

Grace Ogot was born in 1930 at Bustere, Kenya, and trained as a nurse and midwife in Uganda and in England. She became a scriptwriter and an announcer for the BBC in the 1950's and married Dr. Allan Ogot, chairman of history at Nairobi University, in 1959. Her writings include a novel, *The Promised Land*, a short story collection, *Land without Thunder*, and tales for children.

The chief was still far from the gate when his daughter Oganda saw him. She ran to meet him. Breathlessly she asked her father, "What is the news, great Chief? Everyone in the village is anxiously waiting to hear when it will rain." Labong'o held out his hands for his daughter but he did not say a word. Puzzled by her father's cold attitude Oganda ran back to the village to warn the others that the chief was back.

The atmosphere in the village was tense and confused. Everyone moved aimlessly and fussed in the yard without actually doing any work. A young woman whispered to her co-wife, "If they have not solved this rain business today, the chief will crack." They had watched him getting thinner and thinner as the people kept on pestering him. "Our cattle lie dying in the fields," they reported. "Soon it will be our children and then ourselves. Tell us what to do to save our lives, oh great Chief." So the chief had daily pleaded with the Almighty through the ancestors to deliver them from their great distress.

Instead of calling the family together and giving them the news immediately,

Labong'o went to his own hut, a sign that he was not to be disturbed. Having replaced the shutter, he sat in the dimly lit hut to contemplate.

It was no longer a question of being the chief of hunger-stricken people that weighed Labong'o's heart. It was the life of his only daughter that was at stake. At the time when Oganda came to meet him, he saw the glittering chain shining around her waist. The prophecy was complete. "It is Oganda, Oganda, my only daughter, who must die so young." Labong'o burst into tears before finishing the sentence. The chief must not weep. Society had declared him the bravest of men. But Labong'o did not care any more. He assumed the position of a simple father and wept bitterly. He loved his people, the Luo, but what were the Luo for him without Oganda? Her life had brought a new life in Labong'o's world and he ruled better than he could remember. How would the spirit of the village survive his beautiful daughter? "There are so many homes and so many parents who have daughters. Why choose this one? She is all I have." Labong'o spoke as if the ancestors were there in the hut and he could see them face to face. Perhaps they were there, warning him to remember his promise on the day he was enthroned when he said aloud, before the elders, "I will lay down my life, if necessary, and the life of my household, to save this tribe from the hands of the enemy." "Deny! Deny!" he could hear the voice of his forefathers mocking him.

When Labong'o was made chief he was only a young man. Unlike his father he ruled for many years with only one wife. But people mocked him secretly because his only wife did not bear him a daughter. He married a second, a third and a fourth wife. But they all gave birth to male children. When Labong'o married a fifth wife, she bore him a daughter. They called her Oganda, meaning "beans", because her skin was very smooth. Out of Labong'o's twenty children, Oganda was the only girl. Though she was the chief's favourite, her mother's co-wives swallowed their jealous feelings and showered her with love. After all, they said, Oganda was a girl whose days in the royal family were numbered. She would soon marry at a tender age and leave the enviable position to someone else.

Never in his life had he been faced with such an impossible decision. Refusing to yield to the rain-maker's request would mean sacrificing the whole tribe, putting the interests of the individual above those of the society. More than that. It would mean disobeying the ancestors, and most probably wiping the Luo people from the surface of the earth. On the other hand, to let Oganda die as a ransom for the people would permanently cripple Labong'o spiritually. He knew he would never be the same chief again.

The words of Nditi, the medicine-man, still echoed in his ears. "Podho, the ancestor of the Luo, appeared to me in a dream last night and he asked me to speak to the chief and the people," Nditi had said to the gathering of tribesmen. "A young woman who has not known a man must die so that the country may have rain. While Podho was still talking to me, I saw a young woman standing at the lakeside, her hands raised above her head. Her skin was as a tender young deer's. Her tall slender figure stood like a lonely reed at the river bank. Her sleepy eyes wore a sad look like that of a bereaved mother. She wore a gold ring on her left ear and a glittering brass chain around her waist. As I still marvelled at the beauty of this young woman, Podho told me, 'Out of all the women in this land, we have chosen this one. Let her offer herself a sacrifice to the lake monster! And on that day, the rain will come down in torrents. Let everyone stay at home on that day, lest he be carried away by the floods.'"

Outside there was a strange stillness, except for the thirsty birds that sang lazily on the dying trees. The blinding midday heat had forced the people into their huts. Not far away from the chief's hut two guards were snoring away quietly. Labong'o removed his crown and the large eagle-head that hung loosely on his shoulders. He left the hut and, instead of asking Nyabogo the messenger to beat the drum, he went straight and beat it himself. In no time the whole household had assembled under the *siala* tree where he usually addressed them. He told Oganda to wait a while in her grandmother's hut.

When Labong'o stood to address his household his voice was hoarse and tears choked him. He started to speak but words refused to leave his lips. His wives and sons knew there was danger, perhaps their enemies had declared war on them. Labong'o's eyes were red and they could see he had been weeping. At last he told them, "One whom we love and treasure will be taken away from us. Oganda is to die." Labong'o's voice was so faint that he could not hear it himself. But he continued, "The ancestors have chosen her to be offered as a sacrifice to the lake monster in order that we may have rain."

For a moment there was dead silence among the people. They were completely stunned; and as some confused murmur broke out Oganda's mother fainted and was carried off to her own hut. But the other people rejoiced. They danced around singing and chanting, "Oganda is the lucky one to die for the people; if it is to save the people, let Oganda go."

In her grandmother's hut Oganda wondered what the whole family was discussing about her that she could not hear. Her grandmother's hut was well away from the chief's court and much as she strained her ears, she could not hear what they were saying. "It must be marriage," she concluded. It was an accepted custom for the family to discuss their daughter's future marriage behind her back. A faint smile played on Oganda's lips as she thought of the several young men who swallowed saliva at the mere mention of her name.

There was Kech, the son of an elder in a neighbouring clan. Kech was very handsome. He had sweet, meek eyes and roaring laughter. He could make a wonderful father, Oganda thought. But they would not be a good match. Kech was a bit too short to be her husband. It would humiliate her to have to look down at Kech each time she spoke to him. Then she thought of Dimo, the tall young man who had already distinguished himself as a brave warrior and an outstanding wrestler. Dimo loved Oganda, but Oganda thought he would make a cruel husband, always quarrelling and ready to fight. No, she did not like him. Oganda fingered the glittering chain on her waist as she thought of Osinda. A long time ago when she was quite young Osinda had given her that chain and, instead of wearing it around her neck several times, she wore it round her waist where it could permanently stay. She heard her heart pounding so loudly as she thought of him. She whispered, "Let it be you they are discussing, Osinda the lovely one. Come now and take me away...."

The lean figure in the doorway startled Oganda who was rapt in thought about the man she loved. "You have frightened me, Grandma," said Oganda laughing. "Tell me, is it my marriage you were discussing? You can take it from me that I won't marry any of them." A smile played on her lips again. She was coaxing her grandma to tell her quickly, to tell her they were pleased with Osinda.

In the open space outside the excited relatives were dancing and singing. They were coming to the hut now, each carrying a gift to put at Oganda's feet. As their singing got nearer Oganda was able to hear what they were saying: "If it is to save the people, if it is to give us rain, let Oganda go. Let Oganda die for her people and for her ancestors." Was she mad to think that they were singing about her? How could she die? She found the lean figure of her grandmother barring the door. She could not get out. The look on her grandmother's face warned her that there was danger around the corner. "Mother, it is not marriage then?" Oganda asked urgently. She suddenly felt panicky, like a mouse cornered by a hungry cat. Forgetting that there was only one door in the hut, Oganda fought desperately to find another exit. She must fight for her life. But there was none.

She closed her eyes, leapt like a wild tiger through the door, knocking her grandmother flat to the ground. There outside in mourning garments Labong'o stood motionless, his hands folded at the back. He held his daughter's hand and led her away from the excited crowd to the little red-painted hut where her mother was resting. Here he broke the news officially to his daughter.

For a long time the three souls who loved one another dearly sat in darkness. It was no good speaking. And even if they tried, the words could not have come out.

In the past they had been like three cooking-stones, sharing their burdens. Taking Oganda away from them would leave two useless stones which would not hold a cooking-pot.

News that the beautiful daughter of the chief was to be sacrificed to give the people rain spread across the country like wind. And at sunset the chief's village was full of relatives and friends who had come to congratulate Oganda. Many more were on their way, coming, carrying their gifts. They would dance till morning to keep her company. And in the morning they would prepare her a big farewell feast. All these relatives thought it a great honour to be selected by the spirits to die in order that the society might live. "Oganda's name will always remain a living name among us," they boasted.

Of course it was an honour, a great honour, for a woman's daughter to be chosen to die for the country. But what could the mother gain once her only daughter was blown away by the wind? There were so many other women in the land, why choose her daughter, her only child? Had human life any meaning at all? – other women had houses full of children while Oganda's mother had to lose her only child!

In the cloudless sky the moon shone brightly and the numerous stars glittered. The dancers of all age groups assembled to dance before Oganda, who sat close to her mother sobbing quietly. All these years she had been with her people she thought she understood them. But now she discovered that she was a stranger among them. If they really loved her as they had always professed, why were they not sympathetic? Why were they not making any attempt to save her? Did her people really understand what it felt like to die young? Unable to restrain her emotions any longer, she sobbed loudly as her age-group got up to dance. They were young and beautiful and very soon they would marry and have their own children. They would have husbands to love and little huts for themselves. They would have reached maturity. Oganda touched the chain around her waist as she thought of Osinda. She wished Osinda were there too, among her friends.

"Perhaps he is ill," she thought gravely. The chain comforted Oganda – she would die with it around her waist and wear it in the underground world.

In the morning a big feast of many different dishes was prepared for Oganda so that she could pick and choose. "People don't eat after death," they said. The food looked delicious but Oganda touched none of it. Let the happy people eat. She contented herself with sips of water from a little calabash.

The time for her departure was drawing near and each minute was precious. It was a day's journey to the lake. She was to walk all night, passing through the great forest. But nothing could touch her, not even the denizens of the forest. She was already anointed with sacred oil. From the time Oganda received the sad news she had expected Osinda to appear any moment. But he was not there. A relative told her that Osinda was away on a private visit. Oganda realized that she would never see her dear one again.

In the afternoon the whole village stood at the gate to say good-bye and to see her for the last time. Her mother wept on her neck for a long time. The great chief in a mourning skin came to the gate barefooted and mingled with the people – a simple father in grief. He took off his wrist bracelet and put it on his daughter's wrist, saying, "You will always live among us. The spirit of our forefathers is with you."

Tongue-tied and unbelieving Oganda stood there before the people. She had nothing to say. She looked at her home once more. She could hear her heart beating so painfully within her. All her childhood plans were coming to an end. She felt like a flower nipped in the bud never to enjoy the morning dew again. She looked at her weeping mother and whispered, "Whenever you want to see me, always look at the sunset. I will be there."

Oganda turned southwards to start her trek to the lake. Her parents, relatives, friends and admirers stood at the gate and watched her go. Her beautiful, slender figure grew smaller and smaller till she mingled with the thin dry trees in the forest.

As Oganda walked the lonely path that wound its way in the wilderness, she sang a song and her own voice kept her company.

> "The ancestors have said Oganda must die;
> The daughter of the chief must be sacrificed.
> When the lake monster feeds on my flesh,
> The people will have rain;
> Yes, the rain will come down in torrents.
> The wind will blow, the thunder will roar.
> And the floods will wash away the sandy beaches
> When the daughter of the chief dies in the lake.
> My age-group has consented,
> My parents have consented,
> So have my friends and relatives;
> Let Oganda die to give us rain.
> My age-group are young and ripe,
> Ripe for womanhood and motherhood;
> But Oganda must die young,
> Oganda must sleep with the ancestors.
> Yes, rain will come down in torrents."

The red rays of the setting sun embraced Oganda and she looked like a burning candle in the wilderness.

The people who came to hear her sad song were touched by her beauty. But they all said the same thing: "If it is to save the people, if it is to give us rain, then be not afraid. Your name will for ever live among us."

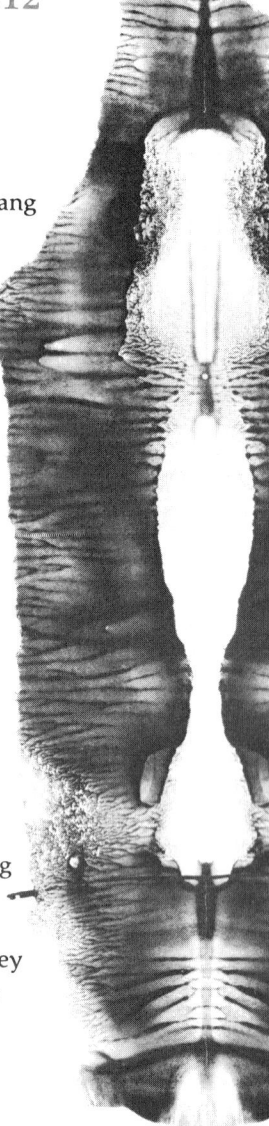

At midnight Oganda was tired and weary. She could walk no more. She sat under a big tree and, having sipped water from her calabash, she rested her head on the tree trunk and slept.

When she woke up in the morning the sun was high in the sky. After walking for many hours she reached the *tong*, a strip of land that separated the inhabited part of the country from the sacred place – *kar lamo*. No lay man could enter this place and come out alive – only those who had direct contact with the spirits and the Almighty were allowed to enter his holy of holies. But Oganda had to pass through this sacred land on her way to the lake, which she had to reach at sunset.

A large crowd gathered to see her for the last time. Her voice was now hoarse and painful but there was no need to worry any more. Soon she would not have to sing. The crowd looked at Oganda sympathetically, mumbling words she could not hear. But none of them pleaded for her life. As Oganda opened the gate a child, a young child, broke loose from the crowd and ran towards her. The child took a small ear-ring from her sweaty hands and gave it to Oganda, saying, "When you reach the world of the dead, give this ear-ring to my sister. She died last week. She forgot this ring." Oganda, taken aback by this strange request, took the little ring and handed her precious water and food to the child. She did not need them now. Oganda did not know whether to laugh or cry. She had heard mourners sending their love to their sweethearts, long dead, but this idea of sending gifts was new to her.

Oganda held her breath as she crossed the barrier to enter the sacred land. She looked appealingly at the crowd but there was no response. Their minds were too preoccupied with their own survival. Rain was the precious medicine they were longing for and the sooner Oganda could get to her destination the better.

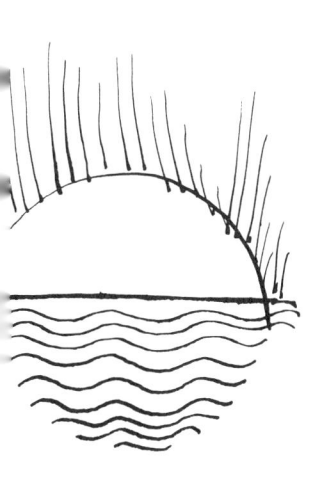

A strange feeling possessed the princess as she picked her way in the sacred land. There were strange noises that often startled her and her first reaction was to take to her heels. But she remembered that she had to fulfil the wish of her people. She was exhausted, but the path was still winding. Then suddenly the path ended on sandy land. The water had retreated miles away from the shore, leaving a wide stretch of sand. Beyond this was the vast expanse of water.

Oganda felt afraid. She wanted to picture the size and shape of the monster, but fear would not let her. The people did not talk about it, nor did the crying children who were silenced at the mention of its name. The sun was still up but it was no longer hot. For a long time Oganda walked ankle-deep in the sand. She was exhausted and longed desperately for her calabash of water. As she moved on she had a strange feeling that something was following her. Was it the monster? Her hair stood erect and a cold paralysing feeling ran along her spine. She looked behind, sideways and in front, but there was nothing except a cloud of dust.

Oganda began to hurry but the feeling did not leave her and her whole body seemed to be bathing in its perspiration.

The sun was going down fast and the lake shore seemed to move along with it.

Oganda started to run. She must be at the lake before sunset. As she ran she heard a noise coming from behind. She looked back sharply and something resembling a moving bush was frantically running after her. It was about to catch up with her.

Oganda ran with all her strength. She was now determined to throw herself into the water even before sunset. She did not look back but the creature was upon her. She made an effort to cry out, as in a nightmare, but she could not hear her own voice. The creature caught up with Oganda. A strong hand grabbed her. But she fell flat on the sand and fainted.

When the lake breeze brought her back to consciousness a man was bending over her. "O...!" Oganda opened her mouth to speak, but she had lost her voice. She swallowed a mouthful of water poured into her mouth by the stranger.

"Osinda, Osinda! Please let me die. Let me run, the sun is going down. Let me die. Let them have rain."

Osinda fondled the glittering chain around Oganda's waist and wiped tears from her face. "We must escape quickly to an unknown land," Osinda said urgently. "We must run away from the wrath of the ancestors and the retaliation of the monster."

"But the curse is upon me, Osinda, I am no good for you any more. And moreover the eyes of the ancestors will follow us everywhere and bad luck will befall us. Nor can we escape from the monster."

Oganda broke loose, afraid to escape, but Osinda grabbed her hands again. "Listen to me, Oganda! Listen! Here are two coats!" He then covered the whole of Oganda's body, except her eyes, with a leafy attire made from the twigs of *bwombwe*. "These will protect us from the eyes of the ancestors and the wrath of the monster. Now let us run out of here." He held Oganda's hand and they ran from the sacred land, avoiding the path that Oganda had followed.

The bush was thick and the long grass entangled their feet as they ran. Half-way through the sacred land they stopped and looked back. The sun was almost touching the surface of the water. They were frightened. They continued to run, now faster, to avoid the sinking sun.

"Have faith, Oganda – that thing will not reach us."

When they reached the barrier and looked behind them, trembling, only a tip of the sun could be seen above the water's surface.

"It is gone! It is gone!" Oganda wept, hiding her face in her hands.

AFRICA

"Weep not, the daughter of the chief. Let us run, let us escape."

There was a lightning flash in the distance. They looked up, frightened.

That night it rained in torrents as it had not done for a long, long time.

New Life in Kyerefaso

Efua Theodora Sutherland

Efua Theodora Sutherland was born in Ghana in 1924 and educated there and in London. She taught school, founded both the Ghana Drama Studio and Writers' Workshop, and helped establish the magazine *Okyeame* for new writers.

Shall we say
Shall we put it this way
Shall we say that the maid of Kyerefaso, Foruwa, daughter of the Queen Mother, was as a young deer, graceful in limb? Such was she, with head held high, eyes soft and wide with wonder. And she was light of foot, light in all her moving.

Stepping springily along the water path like a deer that has strayed from the thicket, springily stepping along the water path, she was a picture to give the eye a feast. And nobody passed her by but turned to look at her again.

Those of her village said that her voice in speech was like the murmur of a river quietly flowing beneath shadows of bamboo leaves. They said her smile would sometimes blossom like a lily on her lips and sometimes rise like sunrise.

The butterflies do not fly away from the flowers, they draw near. Foruwa was the flower of her village.

So shall we say,

Shall we put it this way, that all the village butterflies, the men, tried to draw near her at every turn, crossed and crossed her path? Men said of her, 'She shall be my wife, and mine, and mine and mine.'

But suns rose and set, moons silvered and died and as the days passed Foruwa grew more lovesome, yet she became no one's wife. She smiled at the butterflies and waved her hand lightly to greet them as she went swiftly about her daily work:

'Morning, Kweku

Morning, Kwesi

Morning, Kodwo'

but that was all.

And so they said, even while their hearts thumped for her:

'Proud!

Foruwa is proud . . . and very strange'

And so the men when they gathered would say:

'There goes a strange girl. She is not just stiff-in-the-neck proud, not just breasts-stuck-out I-am-the-only-girl-in-the-village proud. What kind of pride is hers?'

The end of the year came round again, bringing the season of festivals. For the gathering in of corn, yams and cocoa there were harvest celebrations. There were bride-meetings too. And it came to the time when the Asafo companies should hold their festival. The village was full of manly sounds, loud musketry and swelling choruses.

The path-finding, path-clearing ceremony came to an end. The Asafo marched on toward the Queen Mother's house, the women fussing round them, prancing round them, spreading their cloths in their way.

'O*see*!' rang the cry. 'O*see*!' to the manly men of old. They crouched like leopards upon the branches.

> Before the drums beat
> Before the danger drums beat, beware!
> Before the horns moaned
> Before the wailing horns moaned, beware!

They were upright, they sprang. They sprang. They sprang upon the enemy. But now, blood no more! No more thundershot on thundershot.

But still we are the leopards on the branches. We are those who roar and cannot be answered back. Beware, we are they who cannot be answered back.

There was excitement outside the Queen Mother's courtyard gate.

'Gently, gently,' warned the Asafo leader. 'Here comes the Queen Mother.

> Spread skins of the gentle sheep in her way.
> Lightly, lightly walks our Mother Queen.
> Shower her with silver,
> Shower her with silver for she is peace.'

And the Queen Mother stood there, tall, beautiful, before the men, and there was silence.

'What news, what news do you bring?' she quietly asked.

'We come with dusty brows from our pathfinding, Mother. We come with tired, thorn-pricked feet. We come to bathe in the coolness of your peaceful stream. We come to offer our manliness to new life.'

The Queen Mother stood there, tall and beautiful and quiet. Her fanbearers stood by her and all the women clustered near. One by one the men laid their guns at her feet and then she said:

'It is well. The gun is laid aside. The gun's rage is silenced in the stream. Let your weapons from now on be your minds and your hands' toil.

'Come maidens, women all, join the men in dance for they offer themselves to new life.'

There was one girl who did not dance.

'What, Foruwa!' urged the Queen Mother. 'Will you not dance? The men are tired of parading in the ashes of their grandfathers' glorious deeds. That should make you smile. They are tired of the empty croak: "We are men, we are men."

'They are tired of sitting like vultures upon the rubbish heaps they have piled upon the half-built walls of their grandfathers. Smile, then, Foruwa, smile.

'Their brows shall now indeed be dusty, their feet thorn-pricked, and "I love my land" shall cease to be the empty croaking of a vulture upon the rubbish heap. Dance, Foruwa, dance!'

Foruwa opened her lips and this was all she said: 'Mother, I do not find him here.'

'Who? Who do you not find here?'

'He with whom this new life shall be built. He is not here, Mother. These men's faces are empty; there is nothing in them, nothing at all.'

'Alas, Foruwa, alas, alas! What will become of you, my daughter?'

'The day I find him, Mother, the day I find the man, I shall come running to you, and your worries will come to an end.'

'But, Foruwa, Foruwa,' argued the Queen Mother, although in her heart she understood her daughter, 'five years ago your rites were fulfilled. Where is the child of your womb? Your friend Maanan married. Your friend Esi married. Both had their rites with you.'

'Yes, Mother, they married and see how their steps once lively now drag in the dust. The sparkle has died out of their eyes. Their husbands drink palm wine the day long under the mango trees, drink palm wine and push counters across the draughtboards all the day, and are they not already looking for other wives? Mother, the man I say is not here.'

This conversation had been overheard by one of the men and soon others heard what Foruwa had said. That evening there was heard a new song in the village.

'*There was a woman long ago,*
Tell that maid, tell that maid,
There was a woman long ago,
She would not marry Kwesi,
She would not marry Kwaw,
She would not, would not, would not.
One day she came home with hurrying feet,
I've found the man, the man, the man,
Tell that maid, tell that maid,
Her man looked like a chief.
Tell that maid, tell that maid,
Her man looked like a chief,
Most splendid to see,
But he turned into a python,
He turned into a python
AND HE SWALLOWED HER UP.'

From that time onward there were some in the village who turned their backs on Foruwa when she passed.

Shall we say

Shall we put it this way

Shall we say that a day came when Foruwa with hurrying feet came running to her mother? She burst through the courtyard gate; and there she stood in the courtyard, joy all over. And a stranger walked in after her and stood in the courtyard beside her, stood tall and strong as a pillar. Foruwa said to the astonished Queen Mother:

'Here he is, Mother, here is the man.'

The Queen Mother took a slow look at the stranger standing there strong as a forest tree, and she said:

'You carry the light of wisdom on your face, my son. Greetings, you are welcome. But who are you, my son?'

'Greetings, Mother,' replied the stranger quietly. 'I am a worker. My hands are all I have to offer your daughter, for they are all my riches. I have travelled to see how men work in other lands. I have that knowledge and my strength. That is all my story.'

Shall we say,

Shall we put it this way,
strange as the story is, that Foruwa was given in marriage to the stranger.

There was a rage in the village and many openly mocked saying, 'Now the proud one eats the dust.'

Yet shall we say,
Shall we put it this way
that soon, quite soon, the people of Kyerefaso began to take notice of the stranger in quite a different way.

'Who,' some said, 'is this who has come among us? He who mingles sweat and song, he for whom toil is joy and life is full and abundant?'

'See,' said others, 'what a harvest the land yields under his ceaseless care.'

'He has taken the earth and moulded it into bricks. See what a home he has built, how it graces the village where it stands.'

'Look at the craft of his fingers, baskets or *kente*, stool or mat, that man makes them all.'

'And our children swarm about him, gazing at him with wonder and delight.'

Then it did not satisfy them any more to sit all day at their draughtboards under the mango trees.

'See what Foruwa's husband has done,' they declared; 'shall the sons of the land not do the same?'

And soon they began to seek out the stranger to talk with him. Soon they too were toiling, their fields began to yield as never before, and the women laboured joyfully to bring in the harvest. A new spirit stirred the village. As the carelessly built houses disappeared one by one, and new homes built after the fashion of the stranger's grew up, it seemed as if the village of Kyerefaso had been born afresh.

The people themselves became more alive and a new pride possessed them. They were no longer just grabbing from the land what they desired for their stomachs' present hunger and for their present comfort. They were looking at the land with new eyes, feeling it in their blood, and thoughtfully building a permanent and beautiful place for themselves and their children.

'Osee!' It was festival time again. 'Osee!' Blood no more. Our fathers found for us the paths. We are the roadmakers. They bought for us the land with their blood, We shall build it with our strength. We shall create it with our minds.

Following the men were the women and children. On their heads they carried every kind of produce that the land had yielded and crafts that their fingers had created. Green plantains and yellow bananas were carried by the bunch in large white wooden trays. Garden eggs, tomatoes, red oil-palm nuts warmed by the sun were piled high in black earthen vessels. Oranges, yams, maize filled shining brass trays and golden calabashes. Here and there were children proudly carrying colourful mats, baskets and toys which they themselves had made.

'The Queen Mother watched the procession gathering on the new village playground now richly green from recent rains. She watched the people palpitating in a massive dance toward her where she stood with her fanbearers outside the royal house. She caught sight of Foruwa. Her load of charcoal in a large brass tray which she had adorned with red hibiscus danced with her body. Happiness filled the Queen Mother when she saw her daughter thus.

Then she caught sight of Foruwa's husband. He was carrying a white lamb in his arms, and he was singing happily with the men. She looked on him with pride. The procession had approached the royal house.

'See!' rang the cry of the Asafo leader. 'See how the best in all the land stands. See how she stands waiting, our Queen Mother. Waiting to wash the dust from our brow in the coolness of her peaceful stream. Spread skins of the gentle sheep in her way, gently, gently. Spread the yield of the land before her. Spread the craft of your hands before her, gently, gently.

'Lightly, lightly walks our Queen Mother, for she is peace.'

The Gentlemen of the Jungle

Jomo Kenyatta

Jomo Kenyatta was born on a farm in 1891 at Ichaweri, in Kikuyu country, southwest of mount Kenya. During the 1930's he travelled to Russia and Eastern Europe more than once, and he also studied anthropology at the London School of Economics. Politically, he became active in a number of nationalistic movements: the East African Association in 1921, the Pan-African Congress in 1945, and the Kenya African Union in 1946. He was sentenced to seven years in prison, in 1952, for "managing the Mau Mau terrorist organization" – a charge he always denied. But Britain then moved toward African majority rule, and by 1963 Kenyatta became first president of the Republic of Kenya. His books – *Facing Mount Kenya* (1938) and *Kenya: Land of Conflict* (1944) – deal with social issues affecting his country.

Once upon a time an elephant made a friendship with a man. One day a heavy thunderstorm broke out, the elephant went to his friend, who had a little hut at the edge of the forest, and said to him: "My dear good man, will you please let me put my trunk inside your hut to keep it out of this torrential rain?" The man, seeing what situation his friend was in, replied: "My dear good elephant, my hut is very small, but there is room for your trunk and myself. Please put your trunk in gently." The elephant thanked his friend, saying: "You have done me a good deed and one day I shall return your kindness." But what followed? As soon as the elephant put his trunk inside the hut, slowly he pushed his head inside, and finally flung the man out in the rain, and then lay down comfortably inside his friend's hut, saying: "My dear good friend, your skin is harder than mine, and as there is not enough room for both of us, you can afford to remain in the rain while I am protecting my delicate skin from the hailstorm."

The man, seeing what his friend had done to him, started to grumble; the animals in the nearby forest heard the noise and came to see what was the matter. All stood around listening to the heated argument between the man and his friend the elephant. In this turmoil the lion came along roaring, and said in a loud voice: "Don't you all know that I am the King of the Jungle! How dare anyone disturb the peace of my kingdom?" On hearing this the elephant, who was one of the high ministers in the jungle kingdom, replied in a soothing voice, and said: "My lord, there is no disturbance of the peace in your kingdom. I have only been having a little discussion with my friend here as to the possession of this little hut which your lordship sees me occupying." The lion, who wanted to have "peace and tranquillity" in his kingdom, replied in a noble voice, saying: "I command my ministers to appoint a Commission of Enquiry to go thoroughly into this matter and report accordingly." He then turned to the man and said: "You have done well by establishing friendship with my people, especially with the elephant, who is one of my honourable ministers of state. Do not grumble any more, your hut is not lost to you. Wait until the sitting of my Imperial Commission, and there you will be given plenty of opportunity to state your case. I am sure that you will be pleased with the findings of the Commission." The man was very pleased by these sweet words from the King of the Jungle, and innocently waited for his opportunity, in the belief that naturally the hut would be returned to him.

The elephant, obeying the command of his master, got busy with other ministers to appoint the Commision of Enquiry. The following elders of the jungle were appointed to sit in the Commission: (1) Mr. Rhinoceros; (2) Mr. Buffalo; (3) Mr. Alligator; (4) The Rt. Hon. Mr. Fox to act as chairman; and (5) Mr. Leopard to act as Secretary to the Commission. On seeing the personnel, the man protested and asked if it was not necessary to include in this Commission a member from his side. But he was told that it was impossible, since no one from his side was well enough educated to understand the intricacy of jungle law. Further, that there was nothing to fear, for the members of the Commission were all men of repute for their impartiality in justice, and as they were gentlemen chosen by God to look after the interests of races less adequately endowed with teeth and claws, he might rest assured that they would investigate the matter with the greatest care and report impartially.

The Commission sat to take the evidence. The Rt. Hon. Mr. Elephant was first called. He came along with a superior air, brushing his tusks with a sapling which Mrs. Elephant had provided, and in an authoritative voice said: "Gentlemen of the Jungle, there is no need for me to waste your valuable time in relating a story which I am sure you all know. I have always regarded it as my duty to protect the interests of my friends, and this appears to have caused the misunderstanding between myself and my friend here. He invited me to save his hut from being blown away by a hurricane. As the hurricane had gained access owing to the unoccupied space in the hut, I considered it necessary, in my friend's own interests, to turn the undeveloped space to a more economic use by sitting in it myself; a duty which any of you would undoubtedly have performed with equal readiness in similar circumstances."

After hearing the Rt. Hon. Mr. Elephant's conclusive evidence, the Commission called Mr. Hyena and other elders of the jungle, who all supported what Mr. Elephant had said. They then called the man, who began to give his own account of the dispute. But the Commission cut him short, saying: "My good man, please confine yourself to relevant issues. We have already heard, the circumstances from various unbiased sources; all we wish you to tell us is whether the undeveloped space in your hut was occupied by anyone else before Mr. Elephant assumed his position?" The man began to say: "No, but " But at this point the Commission declared that they had heard sufficient evidence from both sides and retired to consider their decision. After enjoying a delicious meal at the expense of the Rt. Hon. Mr. Elephant, they reached their verdict, called the man, and declared as follows: "In our opinion this dispute has arisen through a regrettable misunderstanding due to the backwardness of your ideas. We consider that Mr. Elephant has fulfilled his sacred duty of protecting your interests. As it is clearly for your good that the space should be put to its most economic use, and as you yourself have not yet reached the stage of expansion which would enable you to fill it, we consider it necessary to arrange a compromise to suit both parties. Mr. Elephant shall continue his occupation of your hut, but we give you permission to look for a site where you can build another hut more suited to your needs, and we will see that you are well protected."

The man, having no alternative, and fearing that his refusal might expose him to the teeth and claws of members of the Commission, did as they suggested. But no sooner had he built another hut than Mr. Rhinoceros charged in with his horn lowered and ordered the man to quit. A Royal Commission was again appointed to look into the matter, and the same finding was given. This procedure was repeated until Mr. Buffalo, Mr. Leopard, Mr. Hyena and the rest were all accommodated with new huts. Then the man decided that he must adopt an effective method of protection, since Commissions of Enquiry did not seem to be of any use to him. He sat down and said: *"Ng'enda thi ndagaga motegi,"* which literally means "there is nothing that treads on the earth that cannot be trapped," or in other words, you can fool people for a time, but not for ever.

Early one morning, when the huts already occupied by the jungle lords were all beginning to decay and fall to pieces, he went out and built a bigger and better hut a little distance away. No sooner had Mr. Rhinoceros seen it than he came rushing in, only to find that Mr. Elephant was already inside, sound asleep. Mr. Leopard next came in at the window, Mr. Lion, Mr. Fox and Mr. Buffalo entered the doors, while Mr. Hyena howled for a place in the shade and Mr. Alligator basked on the roof. Presently they all began disputing about their rights of penetration, and from disputing they came to fighting, and while they were all embroiled together the man set the hut on fire and burnt it to the ground, jungle lords and all. Then he went home, saying: "Peace is costly, but it's worth the expense," and lived happily ever after.

Dead Men's Path

Chinua Achebe

Chinua Achebe, born in 1930 in eastern Nigeria, is one of Africa's foremost writers. He became the Director of External Broadcasting for the Nigerian Broadcasting Corporation in 1954 but left that position in 1966 to write full time.

Michael Obi's hopes were fulfilled much earlier than he had expected. He was appointed headmaster of Ndume Central School in January 1949. It had always been an unprogressive school, so the Mission authorities decided to send a young and energetic man to run it. Obi accepted this responsibility with enthusiasm. He had many wonderful ideas and this was an opportunity to put them into practice. He had had sound secondary school education which designated him a 'pivotal teacher' in the official records and set him apart from the other headmasters in the mission field. He was outspoken in his condemnation of the narrow views of these older and often less educated ones.

'We shall make a good job of it, shan't we?' he asked his young wife when they first heard the joyful news of his promotion.

'We shall do our best,' she replied. 'We shall have such beautiful gardens and everything will be just *modern* and delightful . . .' In their two years of married life she had become completely infected by his passion for 'modern methods' and his denigration of 'these old and superannuated people in the teaching field who would be better employed as traders in the Onitsha market'. She began to see herself already as the admired wife of the young headmaster, the queen of the school.

The wives of the other teachers would envy her position. She would set the fashion in everything . . . Then, suddenly, it occurred to her that there might not be other wives. Wavering between hope and fear, she asked her husband, looking anxiously at him.

'All our colleagues are young and unmarried,' he said with enthusiasm which for once she did not share. 'Which is a good thing,' he continued.

'Why?'

'Why? They will give all their time and energy to the school.'

Nancy was downcast. For a few minutes she became sceptical about the new school; but it was only for a few minutes. Her little personal misfortune could not blind her to her husband's happy prospects. She looked at him as he sat folded up in a chair. He was stoop-shouldered and looked frail. But he sometimes surprised people with sudden bursts of physical energy. In his present posture, however, all his bodily strength seemed to have retired behind his deep-set eyes, giving them an extraordinary power of penetration. He was only twenty-six, but looked thirty or more. On the whole, he was not unhandsome.

'A penny for your thoughts, Mike,' said Nancy after a while, imitating the woman's magazine she read.

'I was thinking what a grand opportunity we've got at last to show these people how a school should be run.' Ndume School was backward in every sense of the word. Mr. Obi put his whole life into the work, and his wife hers too. He had two aims. A high standard of teaching was insisted upon, and the school compound was to be turned into a place of beauty. Nancy's dream-gardens came to life with the coming of the rains, and blossomed. Beautiful hibiscus and allamanda hedges in brilliant red and yellow marked out the carefully tended school compound from the rank neighbourhood bushes.

One evening as Obi was admiring his work he was scandalized to see an old woman from the village hobble right across the compound, through a marigold flower-bed and the hedges. On going up there he found faint signs of an almost disused path from the village across the school compound to the bush on the other side.

'It amazes me,' said Obi to one of his teachers who had been three years in the school, 'that you people allowed the villagers to make use of this footpath. It is simply incredible.' He shook his head.

'The path,' said the teacher apologetically, 'appears to be very important to them. Although it is hardly used, it connects the village shrine with their place of burial.'

'And what has that got to do with the school?' asked the headmaster.

'Well, I don't know,' replied the other with a shrug of the shoulders. 'But I remember there was a big row some time ago when we attempted to close it.'

'That was some time ago. But it will not be used now,' said Obi as he walked away. 'What will the Government Education Officer think of this when he comes to inspect the school next week? The villagers might, for all I know, decide to use the schoolroom for a pagan ritual during the inspection.'

Heavy sticks were planted closely across the path at the two places where it entered and left the school premises. These were further strengthened with barbed wire.

Three days later the village priest of *Ani* called on the headmaster. He was an old man and walked with a slight stoop. He carried a stout walking-stick which he usually tapped on the floor, by way of emphasis, each time he made a new point in his argument.

'I have heard,' he said after the usual exchange of cordialities, 'that our ancestral footpath has recently been closed . . . '

'Yes,' replied Mr. Obi. 'We cannot allow people to make a highway of our school compound.'

'Look here, my son,' said the priest bringing down his walking-stick, 'this path was here before you were born and before your father was born. The whole life of this village depends on it. Our dead relatives depart by it and our ancestors visit us by it. But most important, it is the path of children coming in to be born . . . '

Mr. Obi listened with a satisfied smile on his face.

'The whole purpose of our school,' he said finally, 'is to eradicate just such beliefs as that. Dead men do not require footpaths. The whole idea is just fantastic. Our duty is to teach your children to laugh at such ideas.'

'What you say may be true,' replied the priest, 'but we follow the practices of our fathers. If you re-open the path we shall have nothing to quarrel about. What I always say is: let the hawk perch and let the eagle perch.' He rose to go.

'I am sorry,' said the young headmaster. 'But the school compound cannot be a thoroughfare. It is against our regulations. I would suggest your constructing another path, skirting our premises. We can even get our boys to help in building it. I don't suppose the ancestors will find the little detour too burdensome.'

'I have no more words to say,' said the old priest, already outside.

Two days later a young woman in the village died in childbed. A diviner was immediately consulted and he prescribed heavy sacrifices to propitiate ancestors insulted by the fence.

Obi woke up next morning among the ruins of his work. The beautiful hedges were torn up not just near the path but right round the school, the flowers trampled to death and one of the school buildings pulled down . . . That day, the white Supervisor came to inspect the school and wrote a nasty report on the state of the premises but more seriously about the 'tribal-war situation developing between the school and the village, arising in part from the misguided zeal of the new headmaster'.

And This, At Last

John Nagenda

John Nagenda was born in 1938 in Gahini, Uganda. He played for Uganda's national cricket team and, as a college student, edited the Makerere Journal, *Penpoint*. Since graduation, many of Nagenda's stories and poems have appeared in *Transitions* and other journals.

The young reporter was really very young, and this would be his first job of note. Indeed the editor had chosen him precisely because of this. He wanted a picture of innocence to confront the gouty, irate old boy with. Through the years the old man had refused to give interviews altogether, or gave them only to laugh at the newspapermen. Perhaps, somehow, the young man might appear so innocent that the other would take pity on him, decide that he was not worth laughing at. There was no harm in trying, anyway.

'Get him to talk about those barbaric wars they had. I want this article smelling of blood.' The editor was seated in a large and very comfortable swivel-chair, with a copy of *Playboy* conveniently to hand. 'And try to get something on sex out of him. Apart from that he won't have anything interesting to offer, except possibly talk about food, if I know anything about these duffers. I'm not interested in his food.

I'm thinking of starting a feature which we can probably call "Before . . ." and we might launch it with this man. Two or three paragraphs and a bloodthirsty sketch of a man waving a spear, his teeth and chest bared and possibly the sun a small half-ball somewhere behind him on a single-line horizon – you know the sort of thing.'

The editor's office gave you the impression that it was full of yesterday's cigarette smoke. You felt that here the whole world shrank until nothing had any meaning except newspaper copy – little letters and figures became almost alive and could be imagined giving silently transmitted orders concerning all that went on in this room. Three paragraphs was a man's life and a lurid illustration all his desires and beliefs.

Already, in preparation for the meeting with the old warrior, the reporter could not help comparing all this with a totally different life where physical strength and endurance were the major assets a man could have. But at the same time he was slightly revolted at the idea of half-naked men rushing about the lovely countryside hurling spears at each other, leaving puddles of blood in the grass. Together with all this was the more immediate and practical feeling that his career might depend on this interview. At last, after months of writing, he was being sent out on his first assignment.

And so here he was, bright and eager-looking, but very scared inside, willing himself to knock. In his hand he held a blue notebook and tucked away in his shirt pocket was a blue Biro. But even before he knocked, just as he had convinced himself that he was going to knock, the door opened and he found himself face to face with his quarry. At this irreverent thought, he smiled in spite of himself, but then broke off abruptly as he found the other's eyes looking down at him, dispassionately and most penetratingly. Immediately he was disconcerted and confused. He had not quite known what the old man would be like. But on the whole he had expected a sulky, bad-tempered, dried-up old fossil to whom he would have to speak slowly and simply, in a voice louder than normal. On his way up he had thought: Pathetic old duffer – no more women, no more explosions of movement achieved in a sudden overflow of emotion, probably no one really to miss him when he goes, the blood almost still in his veins, the old body smelling lingeringly of age. And he had felt a tolerant contempt for the old savage and a corresponding self-satisfaction with his own lot. But now in one moment nothing was so clear any more and he could not decide who was the quarry.

'Ah, youth, youth,' said the other. 'The time when we can still blush and cry into our coffee! Come in.'

The house had obviously been built for comfort. Cosy old straw chairs, a mellow-looking walking-stick in the corner, two sleepy spears on which the years had settled so that now they looked disused, a gourd, hanging up, which had gone black with time. It was a house full of old memories, of voices now forever silent and faces gone still and empty. The young newspaperman felt almost as if he knew the people who had passed through this house. And the silence was absolute, so that to look through the window and watch the sunlight racing over the ground until it touched the far hills, and to see, far away, the noiseless movement of a car whose only sign that it was moving was the dust following, and to remember that only two hours ago he had been standing before his editor – all this seemed impossible.

'Sit down, sit down,' the old man said, almost as if he grudged the younger the privilege of seeing all this for the first time. 'Let me see – you want an interview. Do you understand, young man, that you are the first newshound I've allowed in here since, since . . . oh, my God, since when? It must have been after the wedding of my eldest grandchild, fifteen years ago. But you fellows keep on hounding a man, hounding a man . . . '

He was silent and the young newspaperman could not decide whether he was remembering the wedding, or what, and himself kept quiet, so that the silence settled again and the very house seemed to doze.

'And so he is dead,' the old man said, and the boy knew that somehow the man had left the other memories behind and was talking about the interview. 'That's what you want to see me about, isn't it? Well, listen, boy, you are lucky, because somehow you remind me of another young man of your age, only he was your age sixty years ago and more – and was myself. I like you, boy, otherwise I might never have opened my mouth to the papers again. And now he is dead. It becomes increasingly lonely and cold the longer you stay. All your friends gone. On your own. Your wife gone and your children gone. Your grandchildren too full of life to be bothered.'

The old man had a disconcerting habit of hopping from one subject to another without notice and then hopping back again. But somehow it was powerful, so that he carried the boy with him and together they moved into the past, the one realistically, the other in imagination. A small bird came and alighted on the window and inquisitively nodded its head up and down, eavesdropping, and then perhaps felt something in the air and with a reproving twitter flew off for merrier pastimes.

'He and I grew up together in the same village. I was a bit older, perhaps three months. Their house was the nearest to ours and was about three hundred yards away. Between us lay a green sea of *matoke* leaves, standing oily in the haze of the sun, nudging their way heavenwards. And then a wind would sweep through them and their murmur would seem to fill the sky. When the rain fell, the chorus from those *matoke* plants was like nothing I can describe. You would feel as if life itself were spattering against and into a womb. So must the first people have thought. I am bothering you?'

Before even the boy could answer, while he was still searching for the words to tell the man that all this meant something to him, like a man who has been away a long time from home and suddenly returns in the moonlight, the old man went on.

'You town boys, what do you know? Have you uncovered the *empumumpu*, that heart-like object growing at the end of a stalk which itself is at the end of the bunch of *matoke*? And this *empumumpu* was made up of layer after layer of itself which you went on pulling off until the core lay gleaming and naked and infant-brown in your hands. And you smelled it. And it smelled like fecundity. The *matoke* garden was more than a garden of food – it was our mother.'

And he paused as the light began to fade out of the sky. And then he barked out some laughter as if deriding himself. But the past refused to relinquish him, so that even then he was only half aware of the boy. He was a long way off. A sudden urge to laugh seized the young reporter at remembering what his idea of the old man had been.

'Suddenly we were men. We became men earlier in those days. All at once the resilient soft, the unyielding firm soft of the young women began to excite us. And we began to watch for their golden skin where their dresses hid them from the direct sun. And their breasts where they pressed against the sky. We were then, perhaps, about thirteen to fifteen. One day I was walking through the bush when I saw her – Nambi or Mother-of-Earth or anybody – by the river, without any clothes on, washing herself. That is one of the climaxes of my life. I plucked her away bit by bit, for all the world as if she was *empumumpu*, until, like it, she lay gleaming and new to the sun. She must be dead these many years, but then she was only starting to live. And the same sun shines on. Life does not wither, does not grow old. It is we who do.'

The boy fought to control his smile as he recalled his editor telling him to probe the man about sex. For what the old man was talking about and the sex the editor had demanded were so dissimilar as to be comic. But there was nowhere in this atmosphere where his laughter could go when once it left his mouth, and mercifully he controlled himself.

A pause descended, as if the ghost of that long-ago day was here in the room. Furtively the dark was creeping in, subtly, like a very ghost. Almost brusquely the old man pulled himself away from the image of the maiden.

'Then came the war, our final big war. There still is in my ears the lapping, sucking sound of that water against the shore. The dark trees prick the angry, heaped-up sky, and the water itself is of oil, and green-black. Whichever way you looked, the canoes full of our men stole silently, with a grim, terrible humour, upon the island. What was in our hearts then? Individually I mean, not collectively. Collectively it was courage, courage, courage. But individually, well, I was thinking of my home among the *matoke*, and so was my friend, as he told me later, the one who is now dead. And if a spear struck you as you ran towards the enemy, you did not pull it out, for then you pulled your blood out and your life. You just ran on until afterwards, when you were looked after. My God, but it was a brave sight and an awesome sight, watching the great multitude of men, moving forever on, some of them with spears laughing out of their bodies. And you never, if you could help it, suffered a spear to come into you from the back.'

To the boy the man had become the opening through which immense vistas of the past could be discerned. It was as if by his words a curtain was raised and you looked through to a new world which you had not even suspected existed, and you held your breath. And wherever you looked there was a new light and everything appeared bigger than you remembered seeing before. The boy thought, And in my job I sit pecking away at a typewriter. What manner of man am I? What manner of men are we all nowadays? We are doomed to sterility and civilisation.

If he had not been so sunk in thoughts of his own, he would have seen on the man's face a look of wonder dawning as he grew silent, looking into himself. Even after all these years, he marvelled, the smell of blood was still in his head, and moved him still as once it did! Despite the years and the new order which he had thought had made him sterile, there was again a sound of thunder in him, and he could almost believe that he was still living as he had lived. It was as if all life had suddenly returned to him.

But gradually the present returned, the thunder sank and the smell of blood slowly thinned and vanished.

'I brought away two women,' he went on, 'and a number of goats, and . . . here, reach me that spear . . . thank you . . . and this spear as well. They pulled it out of my ribs. He who is now dead – I can't, funny isn't it, I can't bring myself to speak his name – we were together throughout.'

Slowly the ghosts rose and subsided and inside the room it was quite dark.

'We became blood brothers after that. We cut ourselves at the naval and bathed some nuts in the blood and ate the nuts and swore eternal blood-brothership. If one of us were ever in need, the other would share with him, even to a split nut. What does he mean, dying now, and leaving me alone? Tell me that! Do you know that he and I were yesterday the only surviving members of that victorious campaign? What else do you want to know? That we prospered and grew fat around the stomachs and sat down by the fire of an evening and re-lived that battle? That still the wind would sweep through the *matoke* and the rain spatter against and enter the womb of that garden? The *Bazungu*[1] came and stayed and now they are on their way out. But all that you know. You know also that my brother has died, and now there is myself alone and I stand with the heavens against my head, like a gnarled old tree which nobody wants anymore. And yet for my own sake I want to tell you something which might nail the ghost of this one who has just died.'

Little dots of yellow light had begun to wink all over the countryside and the gathering bloom was now complete. And still the old man pondered, and memories crowded in around him. The boy thought, Funny that I do not even know what he looks like. I forgot to see. And to him it was a moment of urgency, as when one has lost something very near which then attains importance and unapproachability for ever.

[1] Bazungu – Europeans

'Ah that's it! You know one day his wife was almost dying with fever and I had gone to see what I could do. He sat on one side of her, and I on the other. Then he lifted his eyes, which were heavy with sleep, across the shivering body of the woman, and whispered, "The thud of one's spear against an enemy's body, as it goes into him – that is a lovely sound and we've heard it you and I!" He said that, over the body of a woman he loved and whom he tended constantly for two months before she lived again. And now he is dead!'

For the first time the old man's voice cracked and the boy saw a distant light caught for a moment in the tears which coursed their way unheeded down the old cheeks. Even the shock about the thud of the spear became understandable to the boy and he knew that he too would have thrilled to that bizarre sound. It was then he knew that he could not report this interview. In the hands of his editor he knew how it would look. And to him this would be the final betrayal, as if all the man's life and what it stood for had been wiped away and replaced. Almost it would be as if the old man had lived in vain. And seeing the tears, a quick dart of pain went through him and he was overwhelmed with sadness. At the same time he began to panic to get away to his own world. The old man saw this and said nothing. Almost abruptly the boy rose up to go.

'Thank you, sir, thank you so much'. He knew his words were inadequate. Quickly he let himself out of the house and began to walk away.

'Here,' the old man shouted behind him, and as the boy turned he saw faintly the dark length of the old man, standing in the doorway, and over beyond, far away, the twinkling lights of the city. 'Here, you have forgotten your notebook!'

Piano and Drums

G. Okara

When at break of day at a riverside
I hear jungle drums telegraphing
the mystic rhythm, urgent, raw
like bleeding flesh, speaking of
primal youth and the beginning,
I see the panther ready to pounce,
the leopard snarling about to leap
and the hunters crouch with spears poised;

And my blood ripples, turns torrent,
topples the years and at once I'm
in my mother's lap a suckling;
at once I'm walking simple
paths with no innovations,
rugged, fashioned with the naked
warmth of hurrying feet and groping hearts
in green leaves and wild flowers pulsing.

Then I hear a wailing piano
solo speaking of complex ways
in tear-furrowed concerto;
of far-away lands

and new horizons with
coaxing diminuendo, counterpoint,
crescendo. But lost in the labyrinth
of its complexities, it ends in the middle
of a phrase at a daggerpoint.

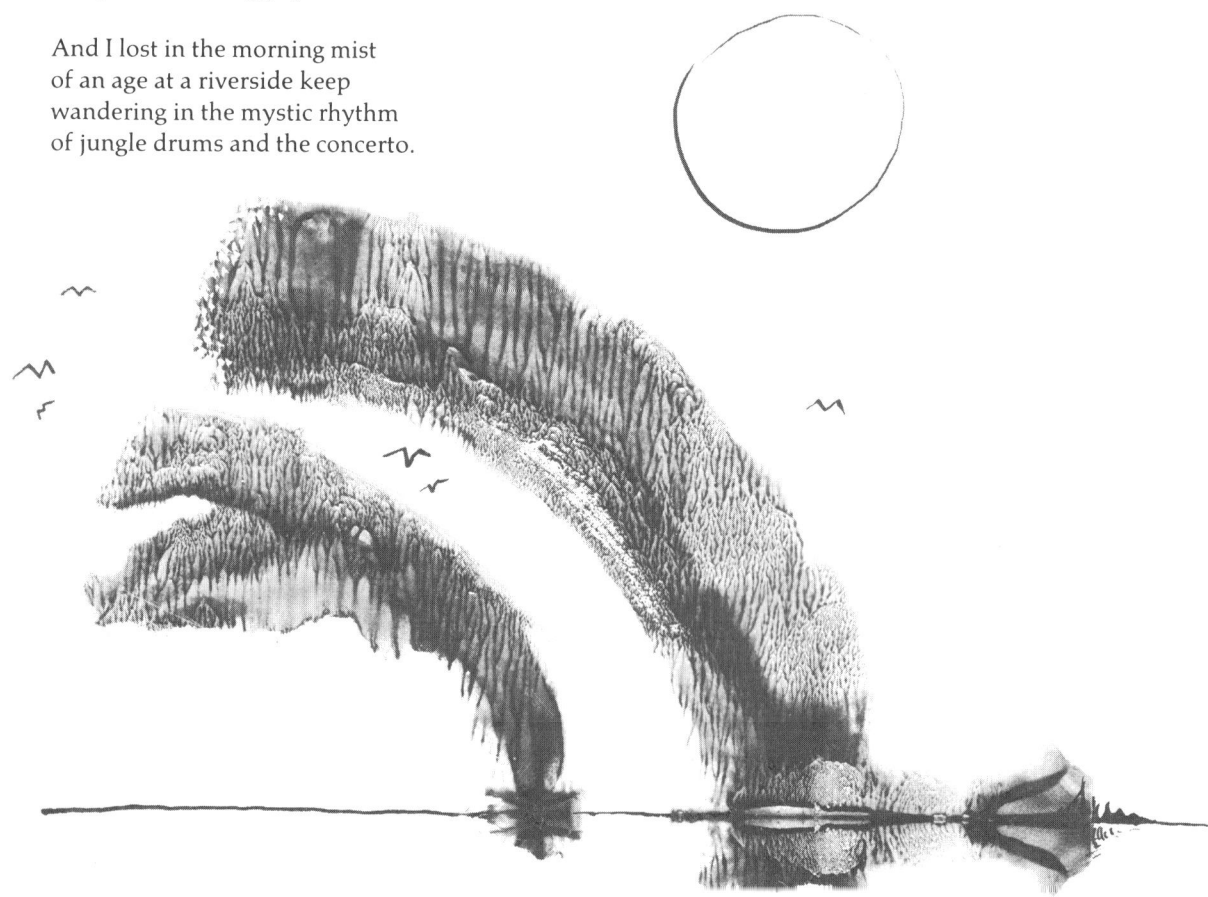

And I lost in the morning mist
of an age at a riverside keep
wandering in the mystic rhythm
of jungle drums and the concerto.

Telephone Conversation

Wole Soyinka

The price seemed reasonable, location
Indifferent. The landlady swore she lived
Off premises. Nothing remained
But self-confession. 'Madam,' I warned
'I hate a wasted journey – I am African.'
Silence. Silenced transmission of
Pressurised good-breeding. Voice, when it came,
Lipstick-coated, long gold-rolled
Cigarette-holder pipped. Caught I was, foully.

'HOW DARK?' . . . I had not misheard . . . 'ARE YOU LIGHT
OR VERY DARK?' Button B. Button A. Stench
Of rancid breath of public hide-and-speak.
Red booth. Red pillar-box. Red double-tiered
Omnibus squelching tar. It *was* real! Shamed
By ill-mannered silence, surrender
Pushed dumbfoundment to beg simplification.
Considerate she was, varying the emphasis –

'ARE YOU DARK? OR VERY LIGHT?' Revelation came.
'You mean – like plain or milk chocolate?'
Her assent was clinical, crushing in its light
Impersonality. Rapidly, wave-length adjusted,

I chose, 'West African sepia' – and as an afterthought,
'Down in my passport.' Silence for spectroscopic
Flight of fancy, till truthfulness clanged her accent
Hard on the mouthpiece 'WHAT'S THAT?', conceding,
'DON'T KNOW WHAT THAT IS.' 'Like brunette.'
'THAT'S DARK, ISN'T IT?' 'Not altogether.
'Facially, I am brunette, but madam, you should see
'The rest of me. Palm of my hand, soles of my feet
'Are a peroxide blonde. Friction, caused –
'Foolishly, madam – by sitting down, has turned
'My bottom raven black – One moment madam!'
 – sensing
Her receiver rearing on the thunder clap
About my ears – 'Madam,' I pleaded, 'wouldn't
you rather
'See for yourself?'

Once upon a Time

Gabriel Okara

Gabriel Okara was born in Western Nigeria in 1921 to the house of Prince Sampson Okara. He attended school in Nigeria and later obtained a degree in journalism from Northern University, Illinois, U.S.A.. He has written novels, short stories, poetry, and film scripts and now works for the Rivers State Ministry of Information, Port Harcourt, Nigeria.

Once upon a time, son,
they used to laugh with their hearts
and laugh with their eyes;
but now they only laugh with their teeth,
while their ice-block-cold eyes
search behind my shadow.

There was a time indeed
they used to shake hands with their hearts;
but that's gone, son.
Now they shake hands without hearts
while their left hands search
my empty pockets.

"Feel at home," "Come again,"
they say, and when I come
again and feel
at home, once, twice,
there will be no thrice –
for then I find doors shut on me.

So I have learned many things, son.
I have learned to wear many faces
like dresses – homeface,
officeface, streetface, hostface, cock-
tailface, with all their conforming smiles
like a fixed portrait smile.

And I have learned too
to laugh with only my teeth
and shake hands without my heart.

AFRICA

I have also learned to say, "Goodbye,"
when I mean "Goodriddance";
to say "Glad to meet you,"
without being glad; and to say "It's been
nice talking to you," after being bored.

But believe me, son.
I want to be what I used to be
when I was like you. I want
to unlearn all these muting things,
Most of all, I want to relearn
how to laugh, for my laugh in the mirror
shows only my teeth like a snake's bare fangs!

So show me, son,
how to laugh; show me how
I used to laugh and smile
once upon a time when I was like you.

A Meditation on Man

Kenneth Kaunda

Born in 1924, Dr. Kenneth Kaunda became president of Zambia after the country became independent in 1964. He is the author of several publications which include: *Zambia Shall be Free, Black Government, Humanism in Zambia and its Implementation,* and *A Humanist in Africa.*

If I were a poet I would write a very long poem in praise of Man and make all my children learn it by heart. Our discussions have confirmed my conviction that only the recovery of a sense of the centrality of Man will get politics back on the right track. How can we teach our people to appreciate the preciousness and dignity of Man in a world where we have been conditioned to think in terms of millions and thousands; where we can shrug off the news that ten thousand people have died in an earthquake or even one hundred in an air crash with a momentary wince of regret and a feeling of relief that the earthquake occurred somewhere else and we were not travelling on the aeroplane? How can we humanise our politics in Zambia so that the humblest and least well endowed of our citizens occupies a central place in Government's concern? The point of departure must surely be to look afresh at Man – not Man *for* anything or Man *as* anything but Man in himself – and sing his praises unashamedly. For until every person learns self-valuation, it is pointless trying to humanise Government and other great institutions within which Man tends to be submerged. If a person has no self-appreciation how can he expect others to treat him as he deserves? By self-appreciation I do not, of course, mean pride or conceit but rather a realistic recognition both of one's possibilities and limitations. Such an exercise is an essential prelude to any new thinking on political policy in which we may engage.

Let me try to put my thoughts about the nature of Man into some kind of order.

Man is an animal. The fact that he shares the same ancestry as lower forms of life is not something of which we need be ashamed. It makes his achievements all the more impressive that they emanate from a being who is as susceptible as other forms of life to natural hazards – heat and cold, hunger and thirst, disease and so on. Indeed, Man is less well equipped than most other animals for the battle of survival. Is it not amazing what this frail creature has achieved by using his mind and imagination in place of lost instincts? Yet it is tragic that having created or invented all kinds of protections against natural hazards, his greatest hazard is his neighbour. The most dangerous threats both to his survival and his progress come from the failure of his social instincts, his inability to live in community and to make his highest faculty, love, the law of his being.

But every time Man is confronted with a decision he finds himself at a crossroads. The choice is between rejoining his animal ancestors and struggling against his lower self in order to achieve spiritual freedom. There is a price to be paid either way. To align oneself with the animal world is to sacrifice dignity for comfort. To choose human freedom is to purify one's spirit through suffering and sacrifice. And by every decision he makes, Man shows whether he belongs to the past or the future; whether he is a biological dead-end or a new departure in evolution, thrusting upwards into the realm of the Spirit.

Reading the works of Teilhard de Chardin I am exhilarated by the majestic vision he unfolds of a Universe, all of whose component parts are moving toward some great goal. Such a picture is both comforting and challenging: comforting, because it means that there is after all a point and purpose in life, there are great forces at work with which we can co-operate; and challenging because we are encouraged to be better than our best to speed along this process whereby Man is thrusting like an underground seed upwards toward the light.

I suppose that Man is evolving now in his mind rather than through his physical make-up. It would be foolish to claim that we are wiser or better in a moral sense than were our ancestors of hundreds of years ago, yet I do believe that we understand more about ourselves and our place in the Universe. And we can trace the evolution of our conscience even through the legal structure of our society. We no longer regard slavery, the subordination of women, child labour and racial discrimination as either inevitable or desirable. I hope that in the not-too-distant future the evolution of our conscience will take us to the point where we recognise War as the wasteful and degrading thing that it is and a totally irrelevant solution to our problem.

Within the mind of Man, the evolutionary process has been speeded up immeasurably. I suppose it took the creatures we call birds hundreds of thousands of years to evolve to the point where they could fly. Man has solved this problem in half a century! Granted, every new area of discovery produces a new set of problems; the greater the circle of light, the larger the surrounding area of darkness. And the most difficult of these problems are those concerned with social living. Yet just as we evolved Plato, Beethoven, Shakespeare and Einstein, pacemakers in the sciences and arts, who have given us a greater appreciation of truth and beauty, so we shall evolve social pacemakers – men who will teach us fundamental truths about life in community. I believe that Gandhi and Bertrand Russell are two such men. We have moved on from the Survival of the Fittest to the Survival of the Highest – and what an exciting era this is both to observe and participate in!

So I glory in the fact that Man shares a common heritage with the animal world. It is through the struggle against his animal instincts that his conscience develops and he slowly humanises himself.

What about those qualities which are unique in Man? I would give priority to his capacity for suffering. As an exponent of the philosophy of non-violence, I have given much thought to the role and function of suffering in human life and I am convinced that Man alone of all life has the capacity to suffer as opposed to merely feeling pain. Suffering is the ability to understand and use pain in a constructive way. Did not Jesus Christ, the very pattern of Man, use suffering, and only suffering to accomplish his work? Pain brings out the very highest or the very lowest in Man – it will either degrade him and reduce him to the animal, or it can be used creatively to accomplish some purpose. Strike a dog and it will feel pain, and that is all; strike a child and he will suffer, not because he feels an unpleasant sensation but because he senses a change in relationship. The key to the philosophy of non-violence is that it transforms pain into suffering. It welcomes the pain inflicted by others and uses it to alter relationships.

The very attempts of modern societies to insulate themselves from suffering have resulted in a refusal of love, for the willingness to love and be loved makes suffering inevitable. And in the refusal of love, modern man feels pain without the possibility of transforming it into suffering. In trying to shut out suffering, Man only turns it into something useless and degrading. To be a Man implies a willingness to accept the responsibility and dignity of suffering; where this capacity is lost, Man once again takes his place in the animal world.

Man too has a name. I am not thinking of the label given to the whole species but to the means by which we are identified and distinguished from each other. The people of Africa are rich in names. It is the product of their humanism. To be known by name is to be dependent, linked with the one who utters it, and to know all a man's names is to have a special claim upon him. In Africa, our names are of many sorts. There is our tribal or clan name. Then there is often a special name which describes some experience or desirable attributes or records some significant event. My own middle name is Buchizya – the Unexpected One – because I was born long after natural expectancy had died in my parents. Often, there is added to this string of names the so-called Christian name, which was originally given to baptised Christians by missionaries to show that they had broken with their old life and now belonged to Christ. Very often the use of this Christian name degenerated into a matter of mere convenience. It was less trouble to the White Man to dub a servant John or David than to go to the trouble of learning his true name, which would be to demean himself and come down to the African's level.

I could go on for a long time on the significance of names in our culture. The importance of Man having a name is that it speaks both of his uniqueness and of his dependence upon others. Because he is called by name there is no one else on earth quite like him. This is, of course, literally true because no other individual can share the same point in space and time. Every man is unrepeatable once and for all. Yet he is a dependent being – a member of a family, a work situation and a community. And because he has a name it is possible to enter into relationship with him. Is it not the tension between that element in his nature in which he differs from all others and the element which he shares with them that produces most of the great things of which he is capable?

Man was intended to be an end in himself; this is surely implied by the Bible's claim that he is 'made in the image of God' and has been given 'dominion over all living things'. But he has been reduced to a means. The industrialist uses him as a means to wealth. To the demagogue he is the means to power, to the selfish lover the means of gratification. The war-monger uses him as cannon-fodder; to the economist he is a statistic; to the mass entertainer, he is an instrument to be manipulated. Everywhere Man is being used. And once he becomes a means to an end then all his abilities and activities can be exploited and organised to serve the interests of the nation, the State or the society. He ceases to be the absolute standard by which all systems should be measured. Instead he has to twist his personality and reduce his stature in order to fit into the system. I feel that there is a paradox here. The social and political units of the modern world are at one and the same time so large that Man is lost within them, yet so small that he cannot realise his potentiality. In the modern mass institution, he is physically too small to count, yet morally and intellectually he dwarfs it.

A politician like myself must always be alive to this danger of using man as a means rather than an end. We can so easily subordinate him to the interests of national pride, international prestige or what is called efficient government. And we can only avoid doing this by having faith in him and creating the conditions of life which will enable him to justify this faith.

No doubt the critics will claim that I expect too much of Man and the theologians will take issue with me for not giving due weight to Original Sin or the evil inherent in personal and social life which seems so often to have frustrated all Man's hopes and dreams. Their comments are, no doubt, justified. I can only retort that there are enough critics *against* Man. I am *for* him! Theologians, political scientists, sociologists and psychologists have had a good innings denigrating Man. It is time his defenders entered the lists. Possibly I do not take this volume of criticism as seriously as I ought because as far as I am concerned Man is not an abstraction, the subject of a theological sermon or a philosophical thesis. Man means my mother, my wife, my children, my friends, the citizens of my country. They deserve my faith. They shall have it.

Further Reading

Achebe, C., *Things Fall Apart.* Toronto: Heinemann Educational Books Ltd., 1958

Achebe, C., *No Longer at Ease.* Toronto: Heinemann Educational Books Ltd., 1960

Nquqi, J., *Weep Not, Child.* Toronto: Heinemann Educational Books Ltd., 1964

Abrahams, P., *Tell Freedom.* New York: The Macmillan Co., 1954

Komey, E.A., and Mphahlele, E., *Modern African Stories.* London: Faber and Faber Ltd., 1964

Moore, G., and Beier, U., *Modern Poetry from Africa.* Baltimore: Penguin Books Ltd., 1963

Roscoe, A.A., *Mother Is Gold.* London: Cambridge University Press, 1971

Beier, U., *Introduction to African Literature.* London: Longmans, Green and Co. Ltd., 1967

Killam, G.D., *African Writers on African Writing.* Evanston: Northwestern University Press, 1973

Harry S. Black

Black

Government of India

Harry S. Black

Government of India

ment of India

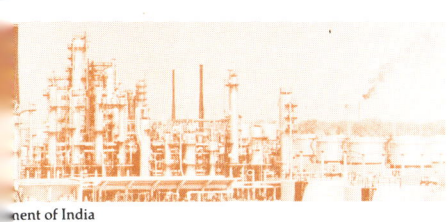

A Glimpse of Asia

The real birth of English literature in India came when James Augustus Hicky founded *Hicky's Bengal Gazette* in 1780 and Sir William Jones (1746-1794), a supreme court judge, founded the Bengal Asiatic Society and became the first English Sanskrit scholar.

Writings by the British stationed in India were varied and abundant. These were to culminate in the writings of Rudyard Kipling (1865-1936). Kipling's successors – E.M. Forster, Sir Malcolm Darling, Leonard Woolf, Edward Thompson, and George Orwell – supported independent rule for India and saw a more intricate people in a more complex society.

The stream of writing which was to maintain vitality in Asia was that set out by Ram Mohan Roy (1774-1833). He offered his successors a model of clarity which was supported by Vivekananda (1862-1902), who insisted upon precision and concreteness. Throughout the literature of the past and the present runs the pervading influence of the Vedas, which set out much of the Asian culture.

Those Indian novelists for whom fiction became an end in itself, and not a vehicle for other truths, began to write in the 1930's. From these, three outstanding writers emerge: Mulk Raj Anand, who writes with indignation and passion about the cruelties of caste and living conditions of the poor; R.K. Narayan, who writes with dry, ironic humour about the middle class family; and Raja Rao, who established the main theme and logic of the Indian novel.

Asian literature is steeped in the religious concepts of the people. "Gitanjali" and "On Learning to Be an Indian" reveal the influence of tradition. "The Cabuliwallah" shows the relationships between people and the resulting patterns of personal and social development in India.

Literature continues to be enriched by talented Asian writers who contribute the oldest and richest culture available to the English-speaking world.

Gitanjali (Song Offerings)

Rabindranath Tagore

Rabindranath Tagore (1861-1941), born in Calcutta, studied law in England but returned to India to establish the famous Santiniketan, an unconventional school at Bolpur. He was awarded the Nobel prize for literature in 1913 and was knighted in 1915. A poet, philosopher, and educator, Tagore urged social reforms prior to political freedom.

I ask for a moment's indulgence to sit by thy side. The works that I have in hand I will finish afterwards.

Away from the sight of thy face my heart knows no rest nor respite, and my work becomes an endless toil in a shoreless sea of toil.

To-day the summer has come at my window with its sighs and murmurs; and the bees are plying their minstrelsy at the court of the flowering grove.

Now it is time to sit quiet, face to face with thee, and to sing dedication of life in this silent and overflowing leisure.

19

If thou speakest not I will fill my heart with thy silence and endure it. I will keep still and wait like the night with starry vigil and its head bent low with patience.

The morning will surely come, the darkness will vanish, and thy voice pour down in golden streams breaking through the sky.

Then thy words will take wing in songs from every one of my birds' nests, and thy melodies will break forth in flowers in all my forest groves.

29

He whom I enclose with my name is weeping in this dungeon. I am ever busy building this wall all around; and as this wall goes up into the sky day by day I lose sight of my true being in its dark shadow.

I take pride in this great wall, and I plaster it with dust and sand lest a least hole should be left in this name; and for all the care I take I lose sight of my true being.

30

I came out alone on my way to my tryst. But who is this that follows me in the silent dark?

I move aside to avoid his presence but I escape him not.

He makes the dust rise from the earth with his swagger; he adds his loud voice to every word that I utter.

He is my own little self, my lord, he knows no shame; but I am ashamed to come to thy door in his company.

69

The same stream of life that runs through my veins night and day runs through the world and dances in rhythmic measures.

It is the same life that shoots in joy through the dust of the earth in numberless blades of grass and breaks into tumultuous waves of leaves and flowers.

It is the same life that is rocked in the ocean-cradle of birth and of death, in ebb and in flow.

I feel my limbs are made glorious by the touch of this world of life. And my pride is from the life-throb of ages dancing in my blood this moment.

73

Deliverance is not for me in renunciation, I feel the embrace of freedom in a thousand bonds of delight.

Thou ever pourest for me the fresh draught of thy wine of various colours and fragrance, filling this earthen vessel to the brim.

My world will light its hundred different lamps with thy flame and place them before the altar of thy temple.

No, I will never shut the doors of my senses. The delights of sight and hearing and touch will bear thy delight.

Yes, all my illusions will burn into illumination of joy, and all my desires ripen into fruits of love.

84

It is the pang of separation that spreads throughout the world and gives birth to shapes innumerable in the infinite sky.

It is this sorrow of separation that gazes in silence all night from star to star and becomes lyric among rustling leaves in rainy darkness of July.

It is this overspreading pain that deepens into loves and desires, into sufferings and joys in human homes; and this it is that ever melts and flows in songs through my poet's heart.

Miracle

Kartar Singh Duggal

Kartar Singh Duggal, born in 1917, is a distinguished short story writer in Punjabi.

"And then the Guru went into the wilderness. It was very hot. The scorching sun beat relentlessly on rock and sand; the scrub and trees were withered and burnt. And it was absolutely still. Not a man for miles around. Not a trace of life."

"And what happened then, mother?" I asked anxiously.

"The Guru walked on. He was lost in his thoughts. His disciple got very thirsty and begged for water. Water in that place! The Guru said: 'Man, have patience. Thou canst drink to thy heart's content when we get to the next village'. But the disciple was extremely thirsty and would not listen, so that the Guru became very anxious. There was no water in that waste land and he knew that when the disciple became difficult, he made things difficult for everyone else. The Guru explained once more: 'There is no water anywhere. Resign thyself to thy fate and be patient.' But the disciple sat down and refused to move another step. The Guru was amused at the disciple's stubbornness and closed his eyes to meditate. When he opened his eyes he saw the disciple writhing like a fish out of water. So the Guru smiled and said: 'Brother, on the top of this hill there is a hut in which dwelleth a Dervish. Go thou to him, and ask for water. In these parts only his well hath any water.'"

"And then, Mummy?" I asked very excited now to know whether or not the disciple got the water.

"The disciple was so thirsty that as soon as he heard of water he ran up the hill. The hot afternoon, the thirst and then the uphill journey! He found the hut with great difficulty, and when he got there he was out of breath and drenched in sweat. He salaamed the Dervish and begged for water. The Dervish pointed to the well. As the disciple moved to the well, a thought came into the Dervish's mind and he asked: 'Good man? Whence hast thou come?' The disciple replied: 'I am a companion of the Great Guru. We have walked into this wilderness and I grew very thirsty but there was no water down below.' When the Dervish heard of the Guru he was full of wrath and turned the disciple out of his hut. So he came down again to the Guru quite tired out and told him of what had passed. The Guru listened and smiled. 'Go back,' he advised, 'this time with humility in thine heart. Tell him that thou art the companion of another Dervish.' The disciple retraced his steps cursing and muttering to himself, but the Dervish refused to budge. 'I will not give a drop of water to the companion of an unbeliever,' he said and turned the disciple away. Now the disciple was in a very bad state. His lips were parched and cracked. He felt that he was going to die. The Guru heard the whole story. 'Praised be the Almighty, the Formless One,' exclaimed the Guru and asked the disciple to go to the Dervish yet another time. The disciple did as he was commanded and for the third time climbed the rocky hill. He fell at the feet of the Dervish and asked for just a few drops to slake his thirst, but the holy man was consumed with the fire of hate and harshly refused the disciple's request. "If thy Guru styles himself a holy man,' he taunted, 'cannot he give his disciple a palmful of water?' The disciple came back and collapsed at the Guru's feet. The Guru patted him on the back and asked him to be of good cheer. When the disciple recovered, the Guru asked him to pick up a big stone which lay in front of them.

The disciple did as he was told. And all at once water spouted out of the ground, so that within a few minutes there was water all around them. Meanwhile the Dervish who had need of water went to his well and found it absolutely dry. He looked down and saw a flowing stream. He also saw the Guru and his disciple sitting beneath an acacia tree. In great anger the Dervish put his weight against a huge boulder and rolled it down the hill. The disciple saw the enormous boulder coming down and shrieked with terror, but the Guru remained calm and merely exhorted him to praise the Almighty, the Formless one. When the boulder came upon him, he calmly put out his hand and stopped it with his palm. And to this day the rock bears the imprint of the hand of the Guru. Now at the site stands a temple known as the Temple of the Guru's Palm and a whole town has grown up about it. There is also a railway station called the 'Holy Palm.'"

I was thoroughly enjoying the tale. But when it came to the Guru holding back the boulder with his hand, it gave me a peculiar feeling. It was not possible; how could a man hold back a boulder the size of a hill? And how could the rock have received the imprint of his palm? I did not believe a word of it. "Someone must have carved it later on," said I, and I argued with my mother for a long time. I was willing to believe that there was a spring beneath a stone; there were many scientific ways of locating underground seams of water. But for a human being to stop a mountain landslide, that I refused to believe.

My mother looked at me and fell silent.

"Can anyone stop an avalanche?" I would say with a snigger whenever I recalled the legend. Many times was the tale told in our village temple, but the business of holding back the boulder was too much for me to stomach; when they told us the same story at school, I protested and began to argue with the teacher.

"Nothing is impossible for men of faith," replied my teacher and silenced me. I remained quiet but did not believe a word of what he had said. I wanted to yell at the top of my voice: "How can anyone stop a big boulder rolling down a hill with the palm of his hand?"

Not long afterwards I heard that an 'incident' had taken place at the Temple of the Guru's Palm. Those days there were many 'incidents' taking place. And whenever there was an 'incident' no fires were lit in our home and we slept on the floor as during days of mourning. What the 'incident' was, I did not know.

Our village was not far from the Temple of the Guru's Palm. As soon as the news came, my mother left the house. I went with her, and with me, my little sister. All the way my mother's eyes were moist with tears. I wondered what the word 'incident' meant.

When we reached the Temple we heard a strange tale.

Far away in a distant city the white man had opened fire on an unarmed crowd of Indians and killed many of them. Amongst the dead were young men, old men, women and children. Those that remained had been bundled into a train and were being sent to a prison in another city. The prisoners were hungry and thirsty, but the order was that the train was to run through without stopping anywhere. When the news came to the Temple, every one who had heard this was aflame with anger. How could a trainload of thirsty people pass by the Temple where the Guru had performed a miracle to quench the thirst of one disciple! The train carried not only thirsty, but also hungry and wounded men and women. The inhabitants of the Holy Palm asked for the train to be stopped at their railway station. A written request was addressed to the Station Master. Long distance telephone calls were made and many telegrams sent. But the white man had ordained that the train was not to stop and he refused to change his orders. The people of Holy Palm decided otherwise. They piled the platform high with loaves of bread, curried lentils, sweet rice pudding and canisters of water.

The trains were known to come like the sudden storms of summer and vanish with the speed of hurricanes. How could anyone stop a train!

My mother's friend told us the rest.

"The first one on the rail-track was the father of my children. Then his friends lay alongside him and alongside them we their wives. The engine started whistling frantically from a long distance. It began to slow down. But all said and done it was made of steel and had to take its time to come to a standstill. The wheels of the locomotive ran over many men. But no one moved from his place. All along the track we chanted: "Praise be to the Almighty, the Formless One – praise be . . . the Formless One." And the train stopped. "Praise be to the Almighty, the Formless One," the chant went on in unison. And then the train went backwards. This time the men under it were cut up again. Streams of blood flowed on either side of the railtrack right up to the brick-built culvert near the bridge."

I heard the story and was amazed. The whole day I did not utter a word.

When we were returning to our village that evening my mother began to tell my sister the story of the Temple of the Palm. She told her how the Guru came that way with his disciple; how the disciple thirsted for water; how the Guru sent him to the Dervish on top of the hill; how the Dervish turned him back three times; how the Guru asked his disciple to pick up a rock; how the spring burst forth from under it and the well of the Dervish dried up; how the Dervish had hurled the boulder; and how the Guru had said: "Praise be to the Almighty, the Formless One," and stopped it with the palm of his hand.

"But how can any one hold back a big boulder?" interrupted my little sister.

"And why not," I burst in. "If the train which comes like a storm can be held, why not a boulder down a mountain?"

And then tears came rolling down my mother's cheeks.

Translated by Khushwant Singh

The Cabuliwallah

(The Fruitseller from Cabul)

Rabindranath Tagore

Mini, my five year old daughter, cannot live without chattering. I really believe that in all her life she has not wasted one minute in silence. Her mother is often vexed at this, and would stop her prattle, but I do not. To see Mini quiet is unnatural and I cannot bear it for long. Because of this, our conversations are always lively.

One morning, for instance, when I was in the midst of the seventeenth chapter of my new novel, Mini stole into the room, and putting her hand into mine, said: "Father! Ramdayal the door-keeper calls a crow a krow! He doesn't know anything, does he?"

Before I could explain the language differences in this country, she was on the trace of another subject. "What do you think, Father? Shola says there is an elephant in the clouds, blowing water out of his trunk, and that is why it rains!"

The child had seated herself at my feet near the table, and was playing softly, drumming on her knees. I was hard at work on my seventeenth chapter, where Pratap Singh, the hero, had just caught Kanchanlata, the heroine, in his arms, and was about to escape with her by the third-story window of the castle, when all of a sudden Mini left her play, and ran to the window, crying: "A Cabuliwallah! a Cabuliwallah!" Sure enough, in the street below was a Cabuliwallah passing slowly along. He wore the loose, soiled clothing of his people, and a tall turban; there was a bag on his back, and he carried boxes of grapes in his hand.

I cannot tell what my daughter's feelings were at the sight of this man, but she began to call him loudly. Ah, I thought, he will come in and my seventeenth chapter will never be finished! At this exact moment the Cabuliwallah turned and looked up at the child. When she saw this she was overcome by terror, fled to her mother's protection, and disappeared. She had a blind belief that inside the bag which the big man carried were two or three children like herself. Meanwhile, the pedlar entered my doorway and greeted me with a smiling face.

So precarious was the position of my hero and my heroine that my first impulse was to stop and buy something, especially since Mini had called to the man. I made some small purchases, and a conversation began about Abdurrahman, the Russians, the English, and the Frontier Policy.

As he was about to leave, he asked: "And where is the little girl, sir?"

I, thinking that Mini must get rid of her false fear, had her brought out. She stood by my chair, watching the Cabuliwallah and his bag. He offered her nuts and raisins but she would not be tempted, and only clung closer to me, with all her doubts increased. This was their first meeting.

One morning, however, not many days later, as I was leaving the house I was startled to find Mini seated on a bench near the door, laughing and talking with the great Cabuliwallah at her feet. In all her life, it appeared, my small daughter had never found so patient a listener, except for her father. Already the corner of her little sari was stuffed with almonds and raisins, gifts from her visitor. "Why did you give her those?" I said, and taking out an eight-anna piece, handed it to him. The man accepted the money without delay, and slipped it into his pocket.

Alas, on my return an hour later, I found the unfortunate coin had made twice its own worth of trouble! The Cabuliwallah had given it to Mini, and her mother seeing the bright round object, had pounced on the child with: "Where did you get that eight-anna piece?"

"The Cabuliwallah gave it to me." said Mini cheerfully.

"The Cabuliwallah gave it to you!" cried her mother much shocked. "O Mini! how could you take it from him?"

Entering at this moment, I saved her from impending disaster, and proceeded to make my own inquiries. I found that it was not the first or the second time the two had met. The Cabuliwallah had overcome the child's first terror by a judicious bribery of nuts and almonds, and the two were now great friends.

They had many quaint jokes which afforded them a great deal of amusement. Seated in front of him, and looking with all her tiny dignity on his gigantic frame, Mini would ripple her face with laughter, and begin "O Cabuliwallah! Cabuliwallah! what have you got in your bag?"

He would reply in the nasal accents of a mountaineer: "An elephant!" Not much cause for merriment, perhaps, but how they both enjoyed their joke! And for me, this child's talk with a grown-up man always had in it something strangely fascinating.

Then the Cabuliwallah, not to be caught behind, would take his turn with: "Well, little one, and when are you going to the father-in-law's house?"

Now most small Bengali maidens have heard long ago about the father-in-law's house, but we, being a little modern, had kept these things from our child, and at this question Mini must have been a trifle bewildered. But she would not show it, and with instant composure replied: "Are you going there?"

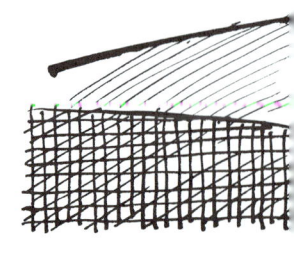

Among men of the Cabuliwallah's class, however, it is well known that the words "father-in-law's house" have a double meaning. It is a euphemism for jail, the place where we are well cared for at no expense. The sturdy pedlar would take my daughter's question in this sense. "Ah," he would say, shaking his fist at an invisible policeman, "I will thrash my father-in-law!" Hearing this, and picturing the poor, uncomfortable relative, Mini would go into peals of laughter, joined by her formidable friend.

These were autumn mornings, the time of year when kings of old went forth to conquest; and I, never stirring from my little corner in Calcutta, would let my mind wander over the whole world. At the very name of another country, my heart would go out to it, and at the sight of a foreigner in the streets, I would fall to weaving a network of dreams: the mountains, the glens, the forests of his distant homeland with a cottage in its setting, and the free and independent life of far-away wilds. Perhaps these scenes of travel pass in my imagination all the more vividly because I lead a vegetable existence such that a call to travel would fall upon me like a thunderbolt. In the presence of this Cabuliwallah I was immediately transported to the foot of mountains, with narrow defiles twisting in and out amongst their towering, arid peaks. I could see the string of camels bearing merchandise, and the company of turbaned merchants carrying queer old firearms, and some of their spears down toward the plains. I could see – but at this point Mini's mother would intervene, imploring me to "beware of that man."

Unfortunately Mini's mother is a very timid lady. Whenever she hears a noise in the street or sees people coming toward the house, she always jumps to the conclusion that they are either thieves, drunkards, snakes, tigers, malaria, cockroaches, caterpillars, or an English sailor. Even after all these years of experience, she is not able to overcome her terror. Thus she was full of doubts about the Cabuliwallah, and used to beg me to keep a watchful eye on him.

I tried to gently laugh her fear away, but then she would turn on me seriously and ask solemn questions.

Were children never kidnapped?

Was it, then, not true that there was slavery in Cabul?

Was it so very absurd that this big man should be able to carry off a tiny child?

I told her that, though not impossible, it was highly improbable. But this was not enough, and her dread persisted. As her suspicion was unfounded, however, it did not seem right to forbid the man to come to the house, and his familiarity went unchecked.

Once a year, in the middle of January, Rahmun the Cabuliwallah was in the habit of returning to his country and as the time approached he would be very busy going from house to house collecting his debts. This year, however, he always found time to come and see Mini. It would have seemed to an outsider that there was some conspiracy between them, for when he would not come in the morning, he would appear in the evening.

Even to me it was a little startling now and then, to *suddenly* surprise this tall, loose-garmented man of bags in the corner of a dark room; but when Mini would run in, smiling, with her "O Cabuliwallah! Cabuliwallah!" and the two friends so far apart in age would subside into their old laughter and their old jokes, I felt reassured.

One morning, a few days before he had made up his mind to go, I was correcting my proof sheets in my study. It was chilly weather. Through the window the rays of the sun touched my feet, and the slight warmth was very welcome. It was almost eight o'clock, and the early pedestrians were returning home with their heads covered. All at once I heard an uproar in the street, and, looking out, saw Rahmun bound and being led away between two policemen, followed by a crowd of curious boys. There were blood-stains on the clothes of the Cabuliwallah, and one of the policemen carried a knife. Hurrying out, I stopped them and inquired what it all meant. Partly from one, partly from another, I gathered that a certain neighbor had owed the pedlar something for a Rampuri shawl, but had falsely denied having bought it, and that in the course of the quarrel Rahmun had struck him. Now, in the heat of his excitement, the prisoner began calling his enemy all sorts of names. Suddenly, from a verandah of my house my little Mini appeared, with her usual exclamation: "O Cabuliwallah! Cabuliwallah!" Rahmun's face lighted up as he turned to her. He had no bag under his arm today, so she could not discuss the elephant with him. She at once therefore proceeded to the next question: "Are you going to the father-in-law's house?" Rahmun laughed and said: "Just where I am going, little one!" Then seeing that the reply did not amuse the child, he held up his fettered hands. "Ah," he said. "I would have thrashed that old father-in-law, but my hands are bound!"

On a charge of murderous assault, Rahmun was sentenced to many years of imprisonment.

Time passed and he was forgotten. The accustomed work in the accustomed place was ours, and the thought of the once free mountaineer spending his years in prison seldom occurred to us. Even my light-hearted Mini, I am ashamed to say, forgot her old friend. New companions filled her life. As she grew older she spent more of her time with girls, so much in fact that she came no more to her father's room. I was scarcely on speaking terms with her.

Many years passed. It was autumn once again and we had made arrangements for Mini's marriage; it was to take place during the Puja holidays. With the goddess Durga returning to her seasonal home in Mount Kailas, the light of our home was also to depart, leaving our house in shadows.

The morning was bright. After the rains, there was a sense of cleanness in the air, and the rays of the sun looked like pure gold; so bright that they radiated even to the sordid brick walls of our Calcutta lanes. Since early dawn, the wedding-pipes had been sounding, and at each beat my own heart throbbed. The wailing tune,

Bhairavi, seemed to intensify my pain at the approaching separation. My Mini was to be married tonight.

From early morning, noise and bustle pervaded the house. In the courtyard the canopy had to be slung on its bamboo poles; the tinkling chandeliers should be hung in each room and verandah; there was great hurry and excitement. I was sitting in my study, looking through the accounts, when some one entered; saluting respectfully, and stood before me. It was Rahmun the Cabuliwallah, and at first I did not recognize him. He had no bag, nor the long hair, nor the same vigor that he used to have. But he smiled, and I knew him again.

"When did you come, Rahmun? I asked him.

"Last evening," he said, "I was released from jail."

The words struck harsh upon my ears. I had never talked with anyone who had wounded his fellowman, and my heart shrank when I realized this, for I felt that the day would have been better-omened if had he not turned up.

"There are ceremonies going on," I said, "and I am busy. Could you perhaps come another day?"

At once he turned to go; but as he reached the door he hesitated, and said: "May I not see the little one, sir, for a moment?" It was his belief that Mini was still the same. He had pictured her running to him as she used to do, calling "O Cabuliwallah! Cabuliwallah!" He had imagined that they would laugh and talk together, just as in the past. In fact, in memory of those former days he had brought, carefully wrapped up in paper, a few almonds and raisins and grapes, somehow obtained from a countryman – his own little fund was gone.

I said again: "There is a ceremony in the house, and you will not be able to see any one today."

The man's face fell. He looked wistfully at me for a moment, said "Good morning," and went out.

I felt a little sorry, and would have called him back, but saw that he was returning of his own accord. He came close up to me holding out his offerings, and said: "I brought these few things, sir, for the little one. Will you give them to her?"

I took them and was going to pay him, but he caught my hand and said: "You are very kind sir! Keep me in your recollection; do not offer me money! You have a little girl; I too have one like her in my own home. I thought of my own, and brought fruits to your child, not to make a profit for myself."

Saying this, he put his hand inside his big loose robe and brought out a small dirty piece of paper. With great care he unfolded this, and smoothed it out with both hands on my table. It bore the impression of a little hand, not a photograph, not a drawing. The impression of an ink-smeared hand laid flat on the paper. This touch of his own little daughter had been always on his heart, as he had come year after year to Calcutta to sell his wares in the streets.

Tears came to my eyes. I forgot that he was a poor Cabuli fruitseller, while I was – but no, was I more than he? He was also a father.

That impression of the hand of his little Parbati in her distant mountain home reminded me of my own little Mini, and I immediately sent for her from the inner apartment. Many excuses were raised, but I would not listen. Clad in the red silk of her wedding-day, with the sandal paste on her forehead, and adorned as a young bride, Mini came and stood bashfully before me.

The Cabuliwallah was staggered at the sight of her. There was no hope of reviving their old friendship. At last he smiled and said: "Little one, are you going to your father-in-law's house?"

But Mini now understood the meaning of the word "father-in-law", and she could not reply to him as in the past. She flushed at the question and stood before him with her bride's face looking down.

I remembered the day when the Cabuliwallah and my Mini first met, and I felt sad. When she had gone, Rahmun heaved a deep sigh and sat down on the floor. The idea had suddenly come to him that his daughter also must have grown up during this long time, and that he would have to make friends with her all over again. Surely he would not find her as he used to know her; besides, what might have happened to her in these eight years?

The marriage-pipes sounded, and the mild autumn sun streamed around us. But Rahmun sat in the little Calcutta lane, and saw before him the barren mountains of Afghanistan.

I took out a bank-note and gave it to him, saying: "Go back to your own daughter, Rahmun, in your own country, and may the happiness of your meeting bring good fortune to my child!"

After giving this gift, I had to eliminate some of the festivities. I could not have the electric lights, nor the military band, and the ladies of the house were saddened. But to me the wedding-feast was brighter because of the thought that in a distant land a long-lost father met again with his only child.

Street Cries

Sarojini Naidu

When dawn's first cymbals beat upon the sky,
Rousing the world to labor's various cry,
To tend the flock, to bind the mellowing grain,
From ardent toil to forge a little gain,
And fasting men go forth on hurrying feet,
Buy bread, buy bread, rings down the eager street.

When the earth falters and the waters swoon
With the implacable radiance of noon,
And in dim shelters koels[1] hush their notes,
And the faint, thirsting blood in languid throats
Craves liquid succor from the cruel heat,
Buy fruit, buy fruit, steals down the panting street.

When twilight twinkling o'er the gay bazaars,
Unfurls a sudden canopy of stars,
When lutes are strung and fragrant torches lit
On white roof terraces where lovers sit
Drinking together of life's poignant sweet,
Buy flowers, buy flowers, floats down the singing street.

---

[1] koel – the cuckoo of India

The Letter

Dhumektu

Dhumektu is the pseudonym of Gaurishanker Goverdhanram Joshi. He has published plays, novels, short stories, and biographies, as well as an autobiography. A leading writer in Gujarati, a Bombay dialect, he turned to short story writing in his later years and became known as a master in this area.

In the gray sky of early dawn stars still glowed, as happy memories light up a life that is nearing its close. An old man was walking through the town, now and again drawing his tattered cloak tighter to shield his body from the cold and biting wind. From some houses standing apart came the sound of grinding mills and the sweet voices of women singing at their work, and these sounds helped him along his lonely way. Except for the occasional bark of a dog, the distant steps of a workman going early to work or the screech of a bird disturbed before its time, the whole town was wrapped in deathly silence. Most of its inhabitants were still in the arms of sleep, a sleep which grew more and more profound on account of the intense winter cold; for the cold used sleep to extend its sway over all things even as a false friend lulls his chosen victim with caressing smiles. The old man, shivering at times but fixed of purpose, plodded on till he came out of the town gate on to a straight road. Along this he now went at a somewhat slower pace, supporting himself on his old staff.

On one side of the road was a row of trees, on the other the town's public garden. The night was darker now and the cold more intense, for the wind was blowing straight along the road and on it there only fell, like frozen snow, the faint light of the morning star. At the end of the garden stood a handsome building of the newest style and light gleamed through the crevices of its closed doors and windows.

Beholding the wooden arch of this building, the old man was filled with the joy that the pilgrim feels when he first sees the goal of his journey. On the arch hung an old board with the newly painted letters POST OFFICE. The old man went in quietly and squatted on the veranda. The voices of the two or three people busy at their routine work could be heard faintly through the wall.

"Police Superintendent," a voice inside called sharply. The old man started at the sound, but composed himself again to wait. But for the faith and love that warmed him he could not have borne the bitter cold.

Name after name rang out from within as the clerk read out the English addresses on the letters and flung them to the waiting postmen. From long practice he had acquired great speed in reading out the titles – Commissioner, Superintendent, Diwan Sahib, Librarian – and in flinging out the letters.

In the midst of this procedure a jesting voice from inside called, "Coachman Ali!"

The old man got up, raised his eyes to Heaven in gratitude and, stepping forward, put his hand on the door.

"Godul Bhai!"

"Yes. Who's there?"

"You called out Coachman Ali's name, didn't you? Here I am. I have come for my letter."

"It is a madman, sir, who worries us by calling every day for letters that never come," said the clerk to the postmaster.

The old man went back slowly to the bench on which he had been accustomed to sit for five long years.

Ali had once been a clever shikari. As his skill increased so did his love for the hunt, till at last it was as impossible for him to pass a day without it as it is for the opium eater to forgo his daily portion. When Ali sighted the earth-brown partridge, almost invisible to other eyes, the poor bird, they said, was as good as in his bag. His sharp eyes would see the hare crouching in its form. When even the dogs failed to see the creature cunningly hidden in the yellow-brown scrub, Ali's eagle eyes would catch sight of its ears; and in another moment it was dead. Besides this, he would often go with his friends, the fishermen.

But when the evening of his life was drawing in, he left his old ways and suddenly took a new turn. His only child, Miriam, married and left him. She went off with a soldier to his regiment in the Punjab, and for the last five years he had had no news of this daughter for whose sake alone he dragged on a cheerless existence. Now he understood the meaning of love and separation. He could no longer enjoy the sportsman's pleasure and laugh at the bewildered terror of the young partridges bereft of their parents.

Although the hunter's instinct was in his very blood and bones, such a loneliness had come into his life since the day Miriam had gone away that now, forgetting his sport, he would become lost in admiration of the green cornfields. He reflected deeply and came to the conclusion that the whole universe is built up through love and that the grief of separation is inescapable. And seeing this, he sat down under a tree and wept bitterly. From that day he had risen each morning at four o'clock to walk to the post office. In his whole life he had never received a letter, but with a devout serenity born of hope and faith he continued and was always the first to arrive.

The post office, one of the most uninteresting buildings in the world, became his place of pilgrimage. He always occupied a particular seat in a particular corner of the building, and when people got to know his habit they laughed at him. The postmen began to make a game of him. Even though there was no letter for him, they would call out his name for the fun of seeing him jump and come to the door. But with boundless faith and infinite patience he came every day – and went away empty-handed.

While Ali waited, peons would come for their firms' letters and he would hear them discussing their masters' scandals. These smart young peons in their spotless turbans and creaking shoes were always eager to express themselves. Meanwhile the door would be thrown open and the postmaster, a man with a head as sad and inexpressive as a pumpkin, would be seen sitting on his chair inside. There was no glimmer of animation in his features; and such men usually prove to be village schoolmasters, office clerks, or postmasters.

One day he was there as usual and did not move from his seat when the door was opened.

"Police Commissioner!" the clerk called out, and a young fellow stepped forward briskly for the letters.

"Superintendent!" Another peon came; and so the clerk, like a worshiper of Vishnu, repeated his customary thousand names.

At last they had all gone. Ali too got up and, saluting the post office as though it housed some precious relic, went off, a pitiable figure, a century behind his time.

"That fellow," asked the postmaster, "is he mad?"

"Who, sir? Oh, yes," answered the clerk. "No matter what sort of weather, he has been here every day for the last five years. But he doesn't get many letters."

"I can understand that! Who does he think will have time to write to him every day?"

"But he's a bit touched, sir. In the old days he committed many sins; and maybe he shed blood within some sacred precincts and is paying for it now," the clerk added in support to his statement.

"Madmen are strange people," the postmaster said.

"Yes. Once I saw a madman in Ahmedabad who did absolutely nothing but make little heaps of dust. Another had a habit of going every day to the river in order to pour water on a certain stone!"

"Oh, that's nothing," chimed in another. "I knew one madman who paced up and down all day long, another who never ceased declaiming poetry, and a third who would slap himself on the cheek and then begin to cry out because he was being beaten."

And everyone in the post office began talking of lunacy. All working-class people have a habit of taking periodic rests by joining in general discussion for a few minutes. After listening a little, the postmaster got up and said:

"It seems as though the mad live in a world of their own making. To them, perhaps, we too, appear mad. The madman's world is rather like the poet's, I should think!"

He laughed as he spoke the last words, looking at one of the clerks who wrote indifferent verse. Then he went out and the office became still again.

For several days Ali had not come to the post office. There was no one with enough sympathy or understanding to guess the reason, but all were curious to know what had stopped the old man. At last he came again; but it was a struggle for him to breathe, and on his face were clear signs of his approaching end. That day he could not contain his impatience.

"Master Sahib," he begged the postmaster, "have you a letter from my Miriam?"

The postmaster was in a hurry to get out to the country.

"What a pest you are, brother!" he exclaimed.

"My name is Ali," answered Ali absentmindedly.

"I know! I know! But do you think we've got your Miriam's name registered?"

"Then please note it down, brother. It will be useful if a letter should come when I am not here." For how should the villager who had spent three quarters of his life hunting know that Miriam's name was not worth a pice to anyone but her father?

The postmaster was beginning to lose his temper. "Have you no sense?" he cried. "Get away! Do you think we are going to eat your letter when it comes?" And he walked off hastily. Ali came out very slowly, turning after every few steps to gaze at the post office. His eyes were filling with tears of helplessness, for his patience was exhausted, even though he still had faith. Yet how could he still hope to hear from Miriam?

Ali heard one of the clerks coming up behind him and turned to him.

"Brother!" he said.

The clerk was surprised, but being a decent fellow he said, "Well?"

"Here, look at this!" and Ali produced an old tin box and emptied five golden guineas into the surprised clerk's hands. "Do not look so startled," he continued.

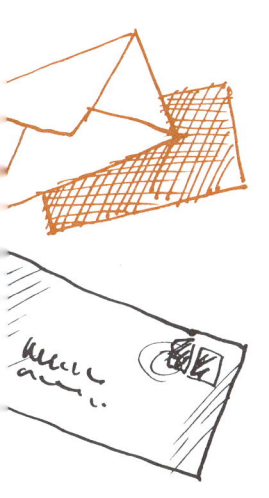

"They will be useful to you, and they can never be so to me. But will you do one thing?"

"What?"

"What do you see up there?" said Ali, pointing to the sky.

"Heaven."

"Allah is there, and in His presence I am giving you this money. When it comes, you must forward my Miriam's letter to me."

"But where – where am I to send it?" asked the utterly bewildered clerk.

"To my grave."

"What?"

"Yes. It is true. Today is my last day: my very last, alas! And I have not seen Miriam, I have had no letter from her." Tears were in Ali's eyes as the clerk slowly left him and went on his way with the five golden guineas in his pocket.

Ali was never seen again and no one troubled to inquire after him.

One day, however, trouble came to the postmaster. His daughter lay ill in another town and he was anxiously waiting for news from her. The post was brought in and the letters piled on the table. Seeing an envelope of the color and shape he expected, the postmaster eagerly snatched it up. It was addressed to coachman Ali, and he dropped it as though it had given him an electric shock. The haughty temper of the official had quite left him in his sorrow and anxiety and had laid bare his human heart. He knew at once that this was the letter the old man had been waiting for: it must be from his daughter Miriam.

"Lakshmi Das!" called the postmaster, for such was the name of the clerk to whom Ali had given his money.

"Yes, sir?"

"This is for your old coachman Ali. Where is he now?"

"I will find out, sir."

The postmaster did not receive his own letter all that day.

He worried all night, getting up at three, went to sit in the office. "When Ali comes at four o'clock," he mused, "I will give him the letter myself."

For now the postmaster understood all Ali's heart, and his very soul. After spending but a single night in suspense, anxiously waiting for news of his daughter, his heart was brimming with sympathy for the poor old man who had spent his nights for the last five years in the same suspense. At the stroke of five he heard a soft knock on the door: he felt sure it was Ali. He rose quickly from his chair, his suffering father's heart recognizing another, and flung the door wide open.

"Come in, brother Ali," he cried, handing the letter to the meek old man, bent double with age, who was standing outside. Ali was leaning on a stick and the tears were wet on his face as they had been when the clerk left him. But his features had been hard then and now they were softened by lines of kindliness. He lifted his eyes and in them was a light so unearthly that the postmaster shrank in fear and astonishment.

Lakshmi Das had heard the postmaster's words as he came towards the office from another quarter. "Who was that, sir? Old Ali?" he asked. But the postmaster took no notice of him. He was staring with wide-open eyes at the doorway from which Ali had disappeared. Where could he have gone? At last he turned to Lakshmi Das. "Yes, I was speaking to Ali," he said.

"Old Ali is dead, sir. But give me his letter."

"What! But when? Are you sure, Lakshmi Das?"

"Yes, it is so," broke in a postman who had just arrived. "Ali died three months ago."

The postmaster was bewildered. Miriam's letter was still lying near the door; Ali's image was still before his eyes. He listened to Lakshmi Das's recital of the last interview, but he could still not doubt the reality of the knock on the door and the tears in Ali's eyes. He was perplexed. Had he really seen Ali? Had his imagination deceived him? Or had it perhaps been Lakshmi Das?

The daily routine began. The clerk read out the addresses – Police Commissioner, Superintendent, Librarian – and flung the letters deftly.

But the postmaster now watched them as though each contained a warm, beating heart. He no longer thought of them in terms of envelopes and postcards. He saw the essential, human worth of a letter.

That evening you might have seen Lakshmi Das and the postmaster walking with slow steps to Ali's grave. They laid the letter on it and turned back.

"Lakshmi Das, were you indeed the first to come to the office this morning?"

"Yes, sir, I was the first."

"Then how . . . No, I don't understand . . ."

"What, sir?"

"Oh, never mind," the postmaster said shortly. At the office he parted from Lakshmi Das and went in. The newly-waked father's heart in him was reproaching him for having failed to understand Ali's anxiety. Tortured by doubt and remorse, he sat down in the glow of the charcoal sigri to wait.

Translated by author

Dasi The Bridegroom

R. K. Narayan

R. K. Narayan, born in 1906, is one of India's most distinguished authors. He does not preach or moralize but observes closely and records the facts of life.

His name was Dasi. In all the Extension there was none like him – an uncouth fellow with a narrow tapering head, bulging eyes, and fat neck; below the neck he had an immense body, all muscle. God had not endowed him with very fluent speech. He gurgled and lisped like an infant. His age was a mystery. It might be anything between twenty and fifty. He lived in a house in the last street. It was a matter of perpetual speculation how he was related to the master of the house. Some persons said he was a younger brother, and some said he had been a foundling brought up by the gentleman. Whatever it was it was not a matter which could be cleared by Dasi himself – for, as I have already said, he could not even say how old he was. If you asked, he said a hundred one day and five on the next. In return for the food and protection he received, he served the family in his own way; he drew water from the well from dawn till midday, chopped wood, and dug the garden.

Dasi went out in the afternoon. When he stepped out scores of children followed him about shouting and jeering. Hawkers and passers-by stopped to crack a joke at his expense. There was particularly a group in a house nicknamed Mantapam. In the front porch of the house were gathered all day a good company of old men; persons who had done useful work in their time but who now found absolutely nothing to do at any part of the day. They were ever on the look out for some excitement or gossip. To them Dasi was a source of great joy. The moment Dasi was sighted they would shout, "Hey, fellow, have you fixed up a bride?" This question never failed to draw Dasi in, for he thought very deeply and earnestly of his marriage. When he came and squatted in their midst on the floor they would say, "The marriage season is closing, you must hurry up, my dear fellow."

"Yes, yes," Dasi would reply. "I am going to the priest. He has promised to settle it today."

"Today?"

"Yes, tonight I am going to be married. They said so."

"Who?"

"My uncle...."

"Who is your uncle?"

"My elder brother is my uncle. I am in his house and draw water from his well. See how my hand is . . . all the skin is gone. . . ." He would spread out his fingers and show his palms. They would feel his palms and say, "Hardened like wood! Poor fellow! This won't do, my dear fellow, you must quickly marry and put an end to all this. . . ." Dasi's eyes would brighten at this suggestion, and his lips would part in a happy smile showing an enormous front tooth. Everyone would laugh at it, and he, too, would sway and rock with laughter.

And then the question, "Where is your bride?"

"She is there . . . in Madras . . . in Madras. . . ."

"What is she like?"

"She has eyes like this," said Dasi, and drew a large circle in the air with his finger.

"What is the color of her skin?"

"Very, very white."

"Has she long hair?"

Dasi indicated an immense flow of tresses with his hand.

"Is she very good looking?"

"She is . . . yes, yes."

Dasi hid his face in his hand, looked at the group through a corner of his eye and said shyly, "Yes, yes, I also like her."

"Where have you the money to marry?"

"They have to give me three thousand rupees," replied Dasi.

"He means that his wages have accumulated," some one explained obligingly.

When he went home he was asked where he had been and he said, "My marriage." And then he went and sat down in the shed on his mat, his only possession in the world. He remained there brooding over his marriage till he was called in to dine, late in the night. He was the last to eat because he consumed an immense quantity of rice, and they thought it a risk to call him in before the others had eaten. After food he carried huge cauldrons of water and washed the kitchen and dining-hall floor. And then he went to his mat and slept till dawn, when he woke up and drew water from the well.

For years out of count this had been going on. Even his life had a tone and rhythm of its own. He never seemed to long for anything or interfere in anybody's business; never spoke to others except when spoken to; never so much as thought he was being joked at; he treated everyone seriously; when the Extension School children ran behind him jeering he never even showed he was aware of their presence; he had no doubt the strength of an ox, but he had also the forbearance of Mother Earth; nothing ever seemed to irritate him. . . . "

The little cottage in the third street which had remained vacant from time immemorial suddenly shed its "To Let" notice. Along with the newspaper and the letters, the train one morning brought a film star from Madras, called Bamini Bai – a young person all smiles, silk and powder. She took up her abode in the little cottage.

Very soon the Extension folk knew all about her. She was going to stay in Malgudi a considerable time training herself under a famous musician of the town. She had her old mother staying with her. The Extension folk had also a complete knowledge of her movements. She left home early in the morning, returned at midday, slept till three o'clock, went out on a walk along the Trunk Road at five o'clock, and so on.

At the *Mantapam* they told Dasi one day, "Dasi, your wife has arrived."

"Where?" asked Dasi. He became agitated, and swallowed and struggled to express all the anxiety and happiness he felt. The company assumed a very serious expression and said, "Do you know the house in the next street, the little house . . . ?"

"Yes, yes."

"She is there. Have you not seen her?"

Dasi hid his face in his hands, and went away. He went to the next street. It was about one o'clock in the afternoon. The film star was not to be seen. Dasi stood on the road looking at the house for some time. He returned to the *Mantapam.* They greeted him vociferously. "How do you like her?" Dasi replied, "My eyes did not see her, the door would not open."

"Try to look in through the window. You will see her."

"I will see through the window," said Dasi, and started out again.

"No, no, stop. It is no good. Listen to me. Will you do as I say?"

"Yes, yes."

"You see, she goes out every day at five o'clock. You will see her if you go to Trichy Road and wait."

Dasi's head was bowed in shyness. They goaded him on, and he went along to the Trunk Road and waited. He sat under a tree on the roadside. It was not even two o'clock, and he had to wait till nearly six. The sun beat down fully on his face. He sat leaning against a tree trunk and brooded. A few cars passed raising dust, bullock carts with jingling bells, and villagers were moving about the highway; but Dasi saw nothing and noticed nothing. He sat looking down the road. And after all she came along. Dasi's throat went dry at the sight of her. His temples throbbed, and sweat stood out on his brow. He had never seen anything like her in all his life. The vision of beauty and youth dazzled him. He was confused and bewildered. He sprang onto his feet and ran home at full speed. He lay down on his mat in the shed. He was so much absorbed in his thoughts that he wouldn't get up when they called him in to dinner. His master walked to the shed and shook him up. "What is the matter with you?" he asked.

"My marriage.... She is there. She is all right."

"Well, well. Go and eat and do your work, you fool," said his master.

Next afternoon Dasi was again at the Trunk Road. This became his daily habit. Every day his courage increased. At last came a day when he could stare at her. His face relaxed and his lips parted in a smile when she passed him, but that young lady had other thoughts to occupy her mind and did not notice him. He waited till she returned that way and tried to smile at her again, though it was nearly dark and she was looking away. He followed her, his face lit up with joy. 'She opened the gate of her cottage and walked in. He hesitated a moment, and followed her in. He stood under the electric lamp in the hall. The mother came out of the kitchen and asked Dasi, "Who are you?"

Dasi looked at her and smiled; at that the old lady was frightened. She cried, "Bama, who is this man in the hall?" Bamini Bai came out of her room. "Who are you?" she asked. Dasi melted at the sight of her. Even the little expression he was capable of left him. He blinked and gulped and looked suffocated. His eyes blazed forth love. His lips struggled to smile. With great difficulty he said, "Wife . . . wife, you are the wife. . . ."

"What are you saying?"

"You are my wife," he repeated, and moved nearer. She recoiled with horror, and struck him in the face. And then she and her mother set up such a cry that all the neighbors and passers-by rushed in. Somebody brought in a police Sub-Inspector. Dasi was marched off to the police station. The members of the *Mantapam* used their influence and had him released late in the night. He went home and lay on his mat. His body had received numerous blows from all sorts of people in the evening; but he hardly felt or remembered any of them. But his soul revolted against the memory of the slap he had received in the face. . . . When they called him in to eat, he refused to get up. His master went to him and commanded, "Go and eat, Dasi. You are bringing me disgrace, you fool. Don't go out of the house hereafter." Dasi refused to get up. He rolled himself in the mat and said. "Go, I don't eat." He turned and faced the wall.

On the following day Dasi had the misfortune to step out of his house just when the children of the Elementary School were streaming out at midday interval. They had heard all about the incident of the previous evening. They now surrounded him and cried, "Hey, bridegroom." He turned and looked at them; there were tears in his eyes. He made a gesture of despair and appealed to them: "Go, go, don't trouble me. . . . Go."

"Oh, the bridegroom is still crying; his wife beat him yesterday," said a boy. On hearing this, Dasi let out a roar, lifted the boy by his collar and hurled him into the crowd. He swung his arms about and knocked down people who tried to get near him. He rushed into the school and broke chairs and tables. He knocked down four teachers who tried to restrain him. He rushed out of the school and assaulted everyone he met. He crashed into the shops and threw things about. He leapt about like a panther from place to place; he passed through the streets of the Extension like a tornado. . . .

Gates were hurriedly shut and bolted. A group of persons tried to run behind Dasi, while a majority preferred to take cover. Soon the police were on the scene, and Dasi was finally overpowered.

He was kept that night in a police lock-up, and sent to the Mental Hospital next day. He was not very easy to manage at first. He was kept in a cell for some weeks. He begged the doctor one day to allow him to stand at the main gate and look down the road. The doctor promised this as a reward for good behavior. Dasi valued the reward so much that he did everything everyone suggested for a whole week. He was then sent (with a warder) to the main gate where he stood for a whole hour looking down the road for the coming of his bride.

On Learning to Be an Indian

Santha Rama Rau

Santha Rama Rau spent a good deal of her early life abroad, returning to India to become a writer.

My grandmother cannot speak English. I have never discovered whether this is from principle or simply because she has never tried, but she understands it perfectly. In England Mother had kept Premila and me familiar with Hindustani by speaking it to us sometimes when we were home for vacations, and by teaching us Indian songs. So during our first few weeks in Bombay we could both understand the language though we were still too out of practice to try speaking it. Consequently my grandmother and I spoke different languages to each other. But we got along very easily in spite of it.

I found after a few days that in her own indirect way she was trying to instill in me something of the traditional Hindu girl's attitude to the household, the rest of the family, and living in general. The servants were the first problem that came up. Whenever the telephone rang, one of the servants would run to answer it. They were unanimously terrified of the instrument and would hold the receiver well away from the ear and scream "Allo?"

Naturally unless the caller and the name of ther person who was being called were both very familiar to the servant, nothing was understood or accomplished. After watching this procedure for some time, I began to sprint for the telephone, too, whenever it rang. As long as I won it was all right, but occasionally I would reach it at the same time as the houseboy. The first time this happened he grasped the receiver and ignored my outstretched hand. I asked him please to let me answer the phone in future if I were in the house – this in very polite if halting

Hindustani. I used the formal form of "you" as I would have to any stranger.

Afterwards my grandmother called me into her room. In her own mysterious way she had overheard the conversation and wanted now to warn me against treating the servants in such a way again.

"They are not your equals, so do not treat them as such. It is not enough for the servants to be frightened of you; that fear must be founded on respect. This pandering to them is some unreasonable sentimentality you have picked up in the West. It embarrasses them as much as it irritates me. . . ."

She went on to explain that one could retain a feeling of equality (tinged all the same with condescension) for the cook, because he, after all, had to be a Brahmin – one of our own caste – as he handled the food. By all means we should give the servants medicines if they were sick, see that their children were well treated, visit their quarters and make sure that their rooms were kept clean, even give their children an education – which they would never get if it were left to their families – but we should always keep our social distance.

Then there was the matter of prayers in the mornings. My grandmother was always up by five o'clock and said her prayers, decorated the images in her shrine, and sang the hymns of the day at that time. She would light a little ceremonial fire, throw spices and something that smelled like incense on it; when the fire died she rubbed her fingers in the ash and smeared it on her forehead. This provided the white part of her caste mark for the rest of the day. The other women of the house were expected to join her, though there was no expressed compulsion. After a few days of this I decided that if I expected to be able to stay awake after nine at night I must stop keeping these hours.

One afternoon I told my grandmother that the prayers were meaningless to me except as a curiosity, that I could make no sense of the hymns, which were sung in Sanskrit (I'm pretty certain they were incomprehensible to her also), and that I felt

I was too old to be converted to Hinduism now.

She assured me briskly that even if I wanted to, I could not be reconverted to Hinduism, and that no such expectation had prompted her to suggest that I come to prayers with her. I had been born a Hindu, but since I had crossed water, eaten beef, neglected to wear my caste mark, and committed innumerable other offenses, I had lost my right to both my religion and my caste.

"But don't assume from that that you may marry anyone outside the Brahmin caste!" The real reason, it turned out, for this religious indoctrination had been to show me something of the values by which Indians live.

"Do you realize that you know nothing of a factor which is vital to the lives of most of your countrymen? Do you always want to see India through the eyes of a visitor? The real Indians are the villagers, the peasants. Poverty and the work on the land is so much a part of their daily living that they must have a tremendous, inclusive faith to make such living possible. If you want to understand these people, you must also understand something of Hinduism. It is the most rigid of beliefs, the most realistic of philosophies, and it determines for them everything from their food to their morals.

"We have been called pacifists," she continued, showing for the only time that I can remember a consciousness of the existence of contemporary politics, "but it is not ignorance that makes us so. We could be the most highly educated country in the world. We have all the prerequisites for intelligent 'political consciousness' – *if that were an end*. But I, for one, can only hope that the religion and philosophy of our people will secure them against civilization, and what you call 'progress.' Bless you, my child, progress is a convenient term for describing our journey from the great age of India."

If I had at the time been less scared of my grandmother, I would have argued with her about her attitude toward conditions in India, which I thought hopelessly reactionary. Concepts which had always seemed to me self-evident she ignored or nullified with her strange, kindly, patronizing attitude toward "those Indians less fortunate than ourselves." Equality of opportunity? Absurd!

"But I can see that you do not even know what I am talking about. Because we let politics pass us by, because we have evolved no way of writing down our music, because we do not preserve in a concrete form our art and our stories, the West considers that we have lost our culture. But it is in the oral traditions of the villages that the arts of India are really alive. The brief Western immortality of museums is pointless to people who have seen eternity in their earth. In comparison with this the people of the West are short-sighted, are they not?"

"I suppose so."

"And we are long-sighted – which is not the same as being far-sighted," she added.

I was growing impatient because I had invited a friend to tea, it was dangerously near tea time, and I had yet to change.

"Is it all right," I asked my grandmother casually, "if I have a friend to tea?" It was a very informal meal and Asha frequently had girls from her school to it, so I didn't think there would be any objections.

"Perfectly all right, my child, if she is a suitable friend."

"Well, it's a he. I should think he's suitable. He traveled over from South Africa with us. Mother liked him."

I have never seen anyone look as shocked as my grandmother did then.

"The more I see of you girls the more amazed I am at your mother for the extraordinary education she has given you, and above all for allowing such outrageous behavior from any girl in our family!"

"I don't think this concerns her at all," I said, surprised. "Because, she could scarcely have kept us in a vacuum during all those years in England – particularly when she was away so much of the time!"

"That is exactly what I told her. You should never have been taken to England. You should have been left here in our care."

"But we wanted –"

"Don't argue with me, my dear child. I will discuss this with your mother."

I turned to leave the room. "Well, shall I call him up and tell him not to come?"

"Of course you cannot do that. If you have invited him already, we are obliged to extend hospitality to him. But while I am the head of this house it will not happen again."

Upstairs I asked Mother what to do. I told her that my grandmother had not yet heard the whole story. I had promised John that I would have dinner with him. Mother looked at me despairingly. "Was it for this that I learned to be a diplomat's wife?"

"I don't see that I've done anything so awful."

"I suppose it never occurred to you that your grandmother never receives Englishmen in her house?"

"Why *would* it occur to me?" I asked.

"For obvious reasons. The stiuation being what it is in India, in her own inimitable way your grandmother makes a personal – or rather a social – issue of it."

"I thought she was supposed to be so detached from politics."

Then Mother began to think that the whole situation was funny. "But the really appalling thing is your dinner engagement with him! If you go out alone with him, and the family knows about it, you're as good as married to him."

"You mean I'm not supposed to be alone with any man until I decide I want to marry him?"

"I'm afraid that's right, as long as we stay in your grandmother's house."

"But *Mother*, doesn't that seem to you a little absurd?"

"Darling, I was never alone with your father until I was married to him."

"But *Mother* –"

"I know, I know, times are changing, *everybody* does it, but I'm sorry, dear, you'll have to break the dinner appointment."

"But *Mother* –"

"Let's not discuss it further, shall we?"

When John came we had tea in icy solitude on the front veranda. His first remark was, "You look pale. Do you feel all right?"

"I feel fine. I'm not allowed to wear make-up around here." I had had a brief argument with Mother about that, too.

"Never thought it would make so much difference."

"My grandmother doesn't approve of it."

"Damn right. Now you won't get lipstick all over the cups and the napkins."

As Mother came out to join us the curtains to the living room swung behind her, and I saw that the family was gathered there. I don't know how anything immoral could have gone on with the gardeners as an audience and on an open veranda, but I suppose they just wanted to make sure. I was thankful that John was facing out toward the garden.

He asked Mother where the family, of whom he had heard so much, were.

"Oh, they went out."

"*All* of them?"

"Of course," Mother said, as if it were the most natural thing.

"Oh."

"They went to the tennis tournament." When Mother says something in that carefully explanatory way, as if it were absurd that anyone shouldn't know, nobody can say, "What tournament?"

I took John out into the garden to tell him I couldn't dine with him that evening. I thought it would be best to tell him the whole story. I don't think he had the least idea what it all meant, for he just looked very hunted and said, "But you *don't* want to marry me, do you?"

This incident, when I looked back on it, brought into sharp contrast for me the astonishing changes that have taken place within fifty years in the ordinary girl's life in India. My grandmother was married when she was nine years old. When I heard that, I was profoundly shocked. Child marriage in books was one thing, but such a barbarous thing in my own family was quite another. Apparently I too had been influenced by the sensational inaccuracies that have been put out about India in books like Katherine Mayo's *Mother India*

When my grandmother says that she was married when she was nine, she means that a betrothal ceremony was performed between her and my grandfather. Perhaps "betrothal" indicates too weak a link, for she could not then have married any other man – even if my grandfather were to have died before the actual wedding ceremony. Her "husband's" family would have been obliged to clothe her and shelter her just as they would the widow of one of their sons. As soon as the betrothal was completed she went to live in her mother-in-law's home. She stayed there until her mother-in-law died and she, as the oldest woman in the house, became the head of the family.

Between the time when she first came to live at the house and the time that the real marriage ceremony took place, about seven years later, she was carefully chaperoned by some member of her "husband's" family on all occasions when she had to appear socially or in the presence of any men. This, Mother assures me, is the traditional method, at least in our caste .She took her place at once in the daily life of the home. A Hindu girl's duties in her mother-in-law's home are specific and exacting. Their purpose is to train the girl to be, as nearly as possible, the perfect wife and mother.

It is practically a tradition among Hindu women that their mother-in-law is always a monster of efficiency and demands equal competence from them. She insists that the young bride must give no order to a servant which she cannot perfectly carry out herself. Consequently the bride must learn to cook, sew, clean, bring up children (and there are always several in the house on whom she can practice), run the family life, advise those younger than herself, keep the accounts of the household, and keep a careful check on the finances of each individual member of the family. I'm sure every Hindu wife of that generation can tell stories about having had to cook meals for twenty-five people single-handed, or of having had to rip out a seam fifteen times because it was not sewn finely enough.

In those days, half a century ago, the joint-family system still dominated the social life of Hindus. My grandmother's mother-in-law, for instance, presided over her family, with her husband as a sort of consort. All their sons lived in the house with them, and as the boys married brought their wives to live in the family home. The daughters lived there until they were married and then they, like my grandmother, went to live in the homes of their mothers-in-law. The children of the sons were educated in the house by tutors until they were old enough to go abroad to college. My grandmother learned to read and write along with her nieces and nephews after she was married, but that was the limit of her education. Besides these close members of the family, various cousins, and great-uncles left over from another generation, lived in the same house. It was a joint family of the most conservative type.

Originally this social unit had grown out of the fact that India was almost entirely an agricultural country, and wealth was measured only in land. The sons of any land-owning family, therefore, were compelled to live together for economic reasons, and because the laws for property division were so sketchy. As the system took root and grew, somehow the women seem to have taken charge. Their province – and this is true to a wide extent even today – was the home and there they were dictators. The wife of the oldest man in the house held and dispensed all the money in the household. Anything that any member earned was given to her and she drew from each according to his capacity and gave to each according to his need. So although she had no legal rights, she could, if she wanted, have absolute control over the members of her own family.

By the time my grandmother, as the wife of the oldest son, came to be head of the household, the system was already breaking down. Our family moved from the south, which is our home, to Bombay. My grandmother found that her sons showed a regrettable tendency to wander off to what she considered the less civilized parts of the world. One of them, Shivan, even married a Viennese girl, beautiful – but a foreigner. Grandmother found that she had no control either over whom her sons married or over the education of her grandchildren. But to look at her and the way in which she lived you would never suspect that the conditions which made her standards valid were vanishing from India.

One of the minor forms which my grandmother's continued autocracy took was the examination of the mail received by anybody living in the house. Asha told me that she used to censor, and sometimes entirely remove, letters from people of whom she did not approve She did not know the people who wrote to me, and still had not gathered in her own way their respective life histories, so she would just question me closely about all my mail. From whom were the letters? Any of them from men? Where had I met them? Did my mother know their families? If the questions were not satisfactorily answered, she would say, "In my opinion you should not reply to that letter," or, "Surely a brief note will be sufficient answer."

To me even Mother's education – which seemed to her so progressive and enlightened – appeared incredibly narrow. Certainly she was not married at an appallingly early age – although her sisters were; she was given, on her own insistence and on the arguments of one of her brothers who was at an English university, a formal education at school and college. She had wanted to be a doctor and after endless arguments with her mother she was allowed to go to medical school in Madras. But unfortunately her mother heard that she was the only girl in her class and that every morning she would find notes on her desk from the men students – some expressing their view of women who broke the fine conventions of Indian womanhood by leaving their homes and entering a world of men, and some exclaiming poetically. "If I were Dante, you would be my Beatrice. . . . " She was taken out of the school immediately and continued, instead, more ladylike work in English literature in a women's college.

All the same, Mother defied two of the most rigid social conventions of the time before she was twenty-five. She earned a living by lecturing in English literature in a Madras college; and at twenty-five she was the first Kashmiri girl to marry outside her community. When we went back to Kashmir – more than twenty years after Mother's marriage – I met women who still would not receive Mother, and could scarcely be civil to her if they met her at somebody else's house, because of the shocking way in which she had broken their social rules when she was a girl. For at that time in India there was a prejudice not only against inter-caste marriages but against inter-community ones too. If your family or your ancestors came from Kashmir, your husband should come from there too.

Because Mother had to fight against the old standards, and because she was brought up to believe in them, she has an emotional understanding of them which my sister and I will never have. Brought up in Europe and educated in preparatory and public schools in England, we felt that the conventions were not only retrogressive and socially crippling to the country, but also a little ridiculous. We thought at the time that one needed the perspective of travel to see these things. But we were only flattering ourselves, for later we found many young Indians who had lived at home all their lives and had a far clearer picture of India's social problems and, moreover, were doing a great deal more toward solving them than we ever thought of doing.

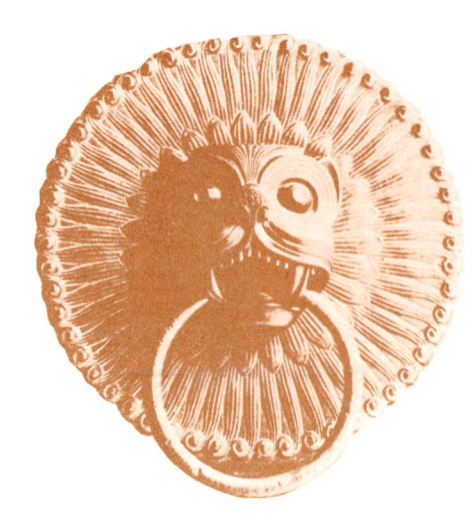

Further Reading

Contemporary Indian Short Stories: Series I. New Delhi: Sahitya Akademi, 1959

Contemporary Indian Short Stories: Series II. New Delhi: Sahitya Akademi, 1974

An Anthology of Contemporary Malaysian Literature. Malaysia: Anthony Blond with Rayirath (Raybooks) Publications, 1964

Ten Tales for Indian Students. London: Oxford University Press, 1931

The Mentor Book of Modern Asian Literature. London: The New English Library Limited, 1969

Modern Indian Short Stories. New Delhi: Arnold Heinemann Publishers, 1974

Fables and Stories. New Delhi: Indiana Publishers, 1974

Macdonell, A.A., *India's Past.* London: Oxford University Press, 1956

New Writing in India. Harmondsworth: Penguin, 1974

National Publicity Studios, New Zealand

an Information Service · Australian Information Service · National Publicity Studios, New Zealand · Australian Information Service

. Bell

A Glimpse of the South Pacific

Australia's first European settlement began in 1788, and by 1803 the first Australian literature was published. The literature consisted of odes commemorating the birthdays of the king and queen. For the next eighty years, Australian poets continued to see Australia through English eyes.

Gradually, Australian writers broke through the British traditions. In 1903, Joseph Furphy, in *Such Is Life*, firmly established the Australian novel with an Australian setting and a new narrative technique. Change came to poetry in the 1890's, as poets moved from bush ballads like "Waltzing Matilda" to combine narrative and lyrical forms that produced identifiable Australian poetry. The nineties also gave birth to Australia's short stories, many of which appeared in *The Bulletin*. The writers took a realistic approach, basing their short stories on local subject matter and personal experience.

Like Australians, New Zealanders moved away from Britain as a source of culture and inspiration, notably in the works on social issues by Jessie MacKay and W.P. Reeves. The depression of the 1930's caused New Zealanders to write more realistically about the harsher aspects of life in their own country. In addition, A. Curnow and others began translating Maori songs and basing their works on local history.

Before World War II, short story writers in Australia and New Zealand wrote in a simple, direct, and sentimental manner, intent upon depicting their countries in the raw. Emphasis has now shifted to revealing basic human concerns. Local settings and issues have become vehicles for universal themes.

Maori writers Witi Ihimaera and Patricia Grace blend Western short story tradition with Maori lore, customs, and idiom. The Maori and the Pacific Islanders express common concerns: the effects of Western culture, the problems encountered by communities in adjusting to change, and the relevance and importance of family relationships and traditions.

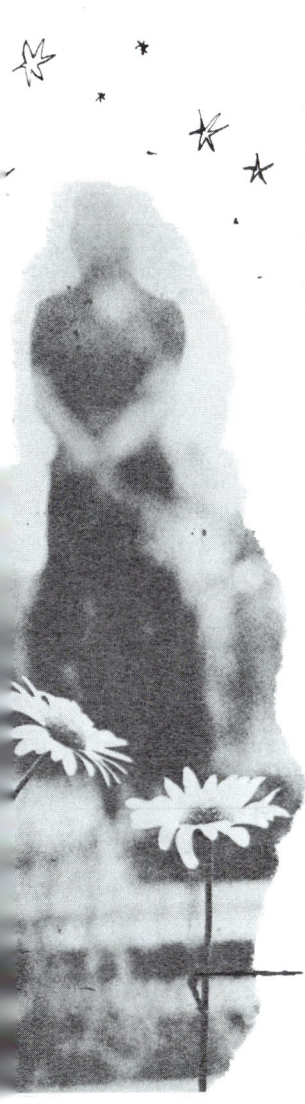

The literature of the South Pacific falls into two broad areas: the more established writings of Australia and New Zealand, and the emerging literary work of many of the smaller islands. In "The Man Who Caught the Wind" and "In the Beginning," early beliefs are described. "The Crookedest Raffle Ever Run" and "In Youth Is Pleasure" reflect the vital and imaginative personalities of Australians and New Zealanders. The ways of life of the island peoples are vividly shown in "To the Woman Selling Handicrafts outside Burns Philp's Doors" and "Seeing Life in a Suva Bus".

In the Beginning

Kenneth Bain

Kenneth Bain was born in New Zealand but has lived, with his partly Tongan wife, in Tonga and Fiji since about 1950. He was secretary to the government of Tonga and is now the British Commissioner in Suva, Fiji.

In the dim far-distant days of the past, Tongamatamoana was the great god of the heavens and his only daughter lived as one of the earthly creatures below. As the god's daughter grew to womanhood, she became as beautiful as any star in the universe; and to preserve her from earthly danger, Tongamatamoana took her away from the earth to the sky where she could enjoy his protection. So that the risk of earthly intrusion should be slight, the great god made to his house a hazardous pathway and few there were with knowledge of its beginning.

When her friends of the earth came to know that the girl had vanished, they searched in every village in every land. But they could find no trace of her. Then it was that the priests said that she had returned to the sky, since she was of the gods and not of worldly men. The young men of the village sought to find and traverse the road to the heavens to bring back the beautiful maiden they had lost. None succeeded; for all who made the attempt died on the way and did not return and no one could find the reason.

At last there were but two left who would make the attempt: the fishermen, Maui Kisikisi and his brother Maui 'Atalanga. Together they set out to face the wrath of the god and make their way to the girl's heavenly home. When they had found the place at which the path began, their way was easy until they passed Pulotu, where the spirits of the dead leave this world for the spirit world beyond. Soon, however, they were bewildered and lost and were unable to perceive which way to continue.

Maui 'Atalanga said, "Let us stay here awhile so that we shall find someone who will be able to tell us which way we should take; for I fear that if we do not do so, we may meet our death as have our brothers before us."

So Maui Kisikisi and Maui 'Atalanga waited by the side of the road and, as the day drew to its close, they saw in the distance the figure of a woman coming towards them. Observing that she was a goddess, the two brothers, though in great fear, resolved to speak to her. "O great one of the sky, is this the way which leads to the home of Tongamatamoana and his daughter?" they asked.

"Yes," the woman replied, "the road lies ahead."

"But how may we reach the heavens," they asked, "for we have heard that many have died on the way?"

"If you have good heart and take heed of what I tell you," said the goddess, "you will be safe and will find what you seek. If you do not, then you too will die and the daughter of Tongamatamoana will forever remain beyond the sight of earthly men."

"Pray tell us," they beseeched her, "and we shall obey."

"Then follow me," said the woman, "and do as I say."

So they started on their journey once more. After they had been walking for many hours and were growing cold and hungry, the woman turned to them and said:

"A short distance from this spot you will find the most succulent food set on the roadside. Since I can read what is in your minds and in your hearts, I know that you are nearly dead from hunger for you have not eaten for many hours. Should you touch or eat anything, you will die and your spirits will wander forever in the torment of the underworld below Pulotu. If you can resist the temptation to eat, you will live to continue your journey."

Presently the two brothers began to smell the aromas of roast pig, and fish of the sea and fowls of the air. As they turned a corner they saw, as she had promised, row upon row of choice delicacies set on banana leaves at the edge of the road. Exhausted from hunger and in great distress as they were, they determined to follow her instructions and began to go past the food. Then Maui 'Atalanga stopped and made move to taste it, his patience and strength at an end; but Maui Kisikisi put out his hand to his brother and together they went on their journey, their hunger unsatisfied.

In a while, they forgot their hunger and once again ahead of them they saw the goddess waiting and smiling at them.

"Well done," she said, "you have proved yourselves worthy to continue your quest."

When they had gone on a little further, the way suddenly narrowed into a hollow tunnel so tiny that they could not pass through it. "Do not take offence," said their companion, "if I strike you; for I must now change you from your human shape into something smaller."

With that, she hit them both on the head. At once they were changed into cats and so could pass through the tunnel. Then the path became still narrower. Once again the woman touched them on the head. They were changed into rats and so could continue. Although in great fear that they would never return to their earthly bodies, the two brothers took courage to continue their journey and were astonished to find the path becoming wide again. They themselves were no longer cats or rats, but men.

Soon they entered a village of fine houses, green grass and trees.

"You have done well," said their companion. "There is the house for which you are searching." And with that she left them and was not seen again.

Overjoyed at their good fortune, Maui Kisikisi and Maui 'Atalanga approached the house of Tongamatamoana and were greeted by the girl for whom they had come.

"You are welcome in my father's house," she said, "for the heavenly road is hard and narrow and many there are who have failed on the way."

When they had been given food and water, Maui Kisikisi explained that the second reason for their journey was to acquire a fish hook with the power to draw up land from the ocean; for they had heard that the great god Tongamatamoana was the possessor of such hooks.

"When my father comes back," said the girl, "you may tell him what you seek. He will invite you to examine his fish hooks and may even offer you whichever one you choose. I advise you to ignore the many fine hooks in his collection and to ask him for a small rusty hook which you will see together with the others. Even though it looks weak and old, it is this hook alone which has strength to do what you want."

Tongamatamoana returned to the house for his evening meal and the two brothers placed their request before him. They explained that the worldly place in which they lived was now too small for the many people who dwelt there and more land was needed. When the meal was over, the god and the brothers went to look at Tongamatamoana's collection of fish hooks. At once they saw that what his daughter had told them was true. There among many fine shining hooks was one which was rusted and dirty. Trusting the words of the girl, they asked the god if they might have it.

"Very well," said Tongamatamoana, "you shall have this hook, for I have heard of your courage in finding your way here and I believe you both to be brave and honest. Although it looks so poor, this is a sacred hook which is not to be given to ordinary men. Go now; and when you draw up your land from the bottomless depths of the ocean with this hook, you shall call it Tongatapu or sacred Tonga."

So Maui Kisikisi and Maui 'Atalanga returned to the earth and one day, as they fished in the waters of the ocean with the sacred hook granted to them by the great god of the sky, they pulled up the island of Tongatapu from the bottom of the sea. Then they went further and drew up Ha'apai and Vava'u and other smaller islands, all of which together they called Tonga after the god who had endowed the earth with this new and holy land.

And that is how the islands of Tonga arose from the ocean as part of the earth world.

At the River

Patricia Grace

Patricia Grace, the first Maori woman to publish a collection of short stories, was born in Wellington, in 1937, of the Ngati Raukawa tribe. After teaching at a number of country schools she returned to Wellington. Of her stories, she says: "My hope is that these stories show aspects of a way of life that is essentially Maori, and thus give some insight into what it is to be Maori."

Sad I wait, and see them come slow back from the river. The torches move slow.

To the tent to rest after they had gone to the river, and while asleep the dream came. A dream of death. He came to me in the dream, not sadly but smiling, with hand on heart and said, I go but do not weep. No weeping, it is my time.

Woke then and out into the night to watch for them with sadness on me, sadness from the dream. And waiting, there came a morepork[1] with soft wing beat and rested above my head. 'Go,' I said to the bird. 'He comes not with you tonight. He is well and strong. His time is not here.'

[1] morepork – New Zealand's native owl, whose night call sounds like "more pork"

But it cried, the morepork. Its call went out. Out and out until the tears were on my face. And now I wait and I see the torches come, they move slow back from the river. Slow and sad they move and I think of him.

Many times have we come to this place for eels. Every year we come at this time. Our children come and now our grandchildren, his and mine. This is the river for eels and this the time of year.

A long way we have travelled with our tents and food stores, our lamps and bedding and our big eel drums. Much work for us today preparing our camp. But now our camp is ready and they have gone with the torches down river to the best eel place. And this old lady stays behind with her old kerosene lamp and the camp fire dying, and the little ones sleeping in their beds. Too tired for the river tonight, too old for the work of catching eels. But not he. He is well and strong. No aching back or tired arms he. No bending, no sadness on him or thoughts of death like this old one.

His wish but not mine to come here this year. 'Too old,' I said to him. 'Let the young ones go. Stay back we two and tend our kumara[2] and corn.'

'This old body,' he said. 'It hungers for the taste of eel.'

'The drums will be full when they return,' I said. 'Let them bring the eels to us, as they would wish to do.'

'Ah no,' he said. 'Always these hands have fetched the food for the stomach. The eels taste sweeter when the body has worked in fetching.'

'Go then,' I said, and we prepared.

I think of him now as I await their return. 'My time is here,' he said in the dream,

[2] kumara – sweet potatoes

and now the bird calls out. And I think too of the young ones who spoke to him today in a new way, a way I did not like.

Before the night came they worked, all of them, to make their torches for the river. Long sticks of manuka,³ long and straight. Tins tied at the tops of the sticks, and in the tins rag soaked in oil. A good light they made as they left tonight for the river. Happy and singing they went with their torches. But I see the lights return now, dim. Dim and slow they come and sadly I await them.

And the young ones, they made their eel hooks. Straight sticks with strong hooks tied for catching eels. He smiled to see the eel hooks, the straight sticks with the strong hooks tied.

'Your hooks,' he said. 'They work for the hands?' But the young ones did not speak, instead bent heads to the work of tying hooks.

Then off, the young ones, to the hills for hare bait as the sun went down. Happy they went with the gun. Two shots went out and we awaited their return. The young ones, they came back laughing. Happy they came with the hare. 'Good bait this,' they said. 'Good bait and good hooks. Lots of eels for us tonight.'

But their nanny said to them, 'A hook is good for the eel but bad for the leg. Many will be there at the river tonight, your uncles, aunties, big cousins, your nanny too. Your hooks may take a leg in place of an eel. The old way, with the stick, and the bait tied is a safe way and a good way. You waste your time with hooks.'

But the young ones rolled on the ground. 'Ho Grandpa,' they called. 'You better watch your leg tonight. The hook might get your leg Grandpa.'

'And watch your hand Grandpa, the eel might get your hand.'

---

³ manuka – most common and abundant of old N.Z. shrubs, 12-15 ft. high. Known as the "tea-tree" as early settlers brewed its aromatic leaves.

'Bite your hand off Grandpa. You better watch out.'

Did not like their way of talking to their nanny but he has patience with the young.

'You'll see,' he said. 'You want to know how to get eels then you watch your Grandpa.'

They did not keep quiet, the young ones after that. Called out to him in a way I did not like, but he is patient.

'Ah Grandpa, that old way of yours is no good. That way is old like you Grandpa.'

'You might end up in the river with your old way of catching eels.'

Spoke sharply to them then in our own language.

'Not for you to speak in this manner. Not our way to speak like this. It is a new thing you are doing. It is a bad thing you have learned.'

No more talk from these two then, but laughing still, and he spoke up for them.

'They make their torches, the boys, and they make the hooks, and then they go to the hills for hare. They think of the river and the eels in the river, and then they punch each other and roll on the ground. Shout and laugh waiting for the night to come. The funny talk it means nothing.'

'Enough to shout and fight,' I said. 'Enough to roll on the ground and punch each other, but the talk needs to stay in the mouth.'

Put my head down then not pleased, and worked at my task of kneading the bread for morning.

Now I wait and stir the ashes round the oven while the morning bread cooks, and on the ashes I see my tears fall. The babies sleep behind me in the tent, and above me the bird cries.

Much to do after a night of eeling when the drum is full. From the fire we scrape away the dead ashes to put into the drum of eels. All night our eels stay there in the drum of ashes to make easier the task of scraping. Scrape off the ashes and with it comes the sticky eel slime. Cut the eels, and open them out then ready for smoking. The men collect green manuka for our smoke drum. Best wood this, to make a good smoke. Good and clear. All day our smoke house goes. Then wrap our smoked eel carefully and pack away before night comes and time for the river again.

But no eels for us this night. No scraping and smoking and packing this time. Tonight our camp comes down and we return. The dim lights come and they bring him back from the river. Slow they bring him.

Now I see two lights come near. The two have come to bring me sad news of him. But before them the bird came, and before the bird the dream – he in the dream with hand on heart.

And now they stand before me, the boys, heads down. By the dim torch light I see the tears on their faces, they do not speak.

'They bring your nanny back,' I say. 'Back from the river.' But they do not speak.

'Hear the morepork,' I say to them. 'It calls from the trees. Out and out it cries. They bring him back from the river, I see your tears.'

'We saw him standing by the river,' they say. 'Saw him bend, looking into the water, and then we saw him fall.'

They stand, the young ones in the dim torch light with tears on their faces, the tears fall. And now they come to me, kneeling by me, weeping.

'We spoke bad to him,' they say. 'They were bad things we said. Now he has fallen and we have said bad things to him.'

So I speak to them to comfort them. 'He came to me tonight with hand on heart. "Do not weep," he said. "It is my time." Not your words that made him fall. His hand was on his heart. Hear the morepork cry. His time is here.'

And now we weep together, this old lady and these two young ones by her. No weeping he said. But we will weep a little while for him and for ourselves. He was our strength.

We weep and they return. His children and mine return from the river bearing him. Sad they come in the dim light of torches. The young ones help me to my feet, weeping still, and I go towards them as they come.

And in my throat I feel a cry well up. Lonely it sounds across the night. Lonely it sounds, the cry that comes from in me.

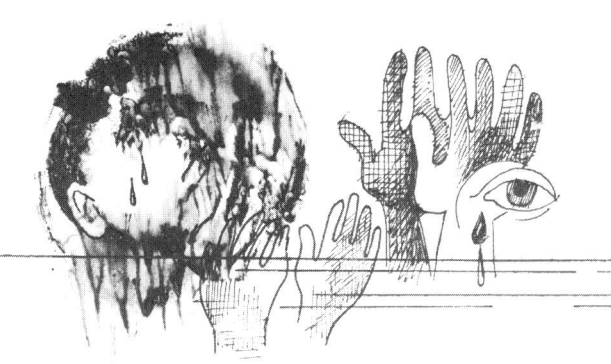

The Man Who Caught the Wind

Wolfe Fairbridge

Wolfe Fairbridge (1918-1950) was born in Perth but received his education in England. Returning home, he graduated in science from the University of Western Australia and became a specialist in marine biology. He was brilliant in everything he tried – sport, art, science, and writing – but died from a sudden attack of poliomyelitis. His *Collected Poems* was published in 1953.

Ngarloo,
Not yet free of the hands of women,
Tried to catch the wind. "When you are older,"
His mother said. "Ngarloo! Ngarloo, here now!
Catch the wind, here now! Here – " they cried, "catch her!"
Mocking him . . . "You cannot catch the wind," the old men said.

When the first warm days
Led summer into the ranges, Ngarloo –
The young man, tall as a high sugar-gum,
Adept in hunting, man of the tribe – saw
The wind playing at noon, high on a ridge,
In the flat-topped crest of an ironbark:
Pulling, playing, tossing the boughs. "It is
The wind!" they said: "Ngarloo, that is the wind!"
Then like the path of smoke he was
Over the stones, through the gum-boles, boulders,

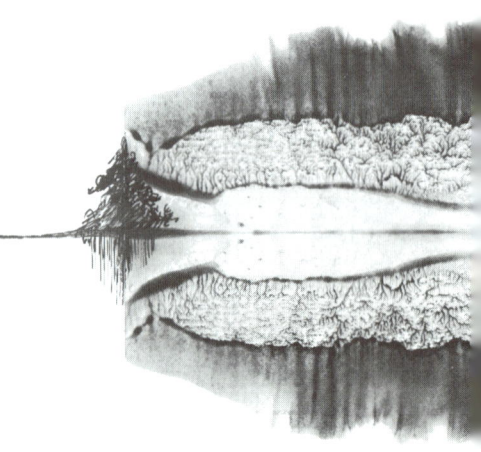

Leaping the tree ferns, up, where the wind led,
Onto the ridge; toehold and lean finger
Craning in groins of the bark; then the steep boughs.
While the wind played still, roistered and roared loud
In the leaves. And as he reached them, was gone.
And Ngarloo, aloft in the wing-travelled air,
Saw, as he clung, all the wide world rolling
Below him its long waves, grey, unchanging
And strong. And the treetops over them all
Silvered and stirred where the wind left playing.
Then his heart grew big with the size, and beat
On the blue hills, saying: "Now I have seen
The world . . ."

A Game of Cards

Witi Ihimaera

Witi Ihimaera was born in Gisborne, New Zealand, in 1944, and belongs to the sub-tribe Te Wanan A Kai, of the Maori nation. He began to work as a journalist in Wellington after graduating from university in 1971. Ihimaera's story shows the Maori's deep concern for his "whanau," or extended family.

The train pulled into the station. For a moment there was confusion: a voice blaring over the loudspeaker system, people getting off the train, the bustling and shoving of the crowd on the platform.

And there was Dad, waiting for me. We hugged each other. We hadn't seen each other for a long time. Then we kissed. But I could tell something was wrong.
– Your Nanny Miro, he said. She's very sick.

Nanny Miro . . . among all my nannies, she was the one I loved most. Everybody used to say I was her favourite mokopuna,[1] and that she loved me more than her own children who'd grown up and had kids of their own.

She lived down the road from us, right next to the meeting house in the big old homestead which everybody in the village called 'The Museum' because it housed the prized possessions of the whanau,[2] the village family. Because she was rich and had a lot of land, we all used to wonder why Nanny Miro didn't buy a newer, more modern house. But Nanny didn't want to move. She liked her own house just as it was.

---
[1] mokopuna – grandchild
[2] whanau – extended family

– Anyway, she used to say, what with all my haddit kids and their haddit kids and all this haddit whanau being broke all the time and coming to ask me for some money, how can I afford to buy a new house.

Nanny didn't really care about money though. Who needs it? she used to say. What you think I had all these kids for, ay? To look after me, I'm not dumb!

Then she would cackle to herself. But it wasn't true really, because her family would send all their kids to her place when they were broke and she looked after them! She liked her mokopunas, but not for too long. She'd ring up their parents and say:
– Hey! When you coming to pick up your hoha[3] kids! They're wrecking the place!

Yet, always, when they left, she would have a little weep, and give them some money. . . .

I used to like going to Nanny's place. For me it was a big treasure house, glistening with sports trophies and photographs, pieces of carvings and greenstone, and feather cloaks hanging from the walls.

Most times, a lot of women would be there playing cards with Nanny. Nanny loved all card games – five hundred, poker, canasta, pontoon, whist, euchre – you name it, she could play it.

The sitting room would be crowded with the kuias,[4] all puffing clouds of smoke, dressed in their old clothes, laughing and cackling and gossiping about who was pregnant – and relishing all the juicy bits too!

I liked sitting and watching them. Mrs Heta would always be there, and when it came to cards she was both Nanny's best friend and worst enemy. And the two of them were the biggest cheats I ever saw.

---

[3] hoha – wearisome
[4] kuias – old women

Mrs Heta would cough and reach for a hanky while slyly slipping a card from beneath her dress. And she was always reneging in five hundred! But her greatest asset was her eyes, which were big and googly. One eye would look straight ahead, while the other swivelled around, having a look at the cards in the hands of the women sitting next to her.
– Eeee! You cheat! Nanny would say. You just keep your eyes to yourself, Maka tiko bum!

Mrs Heta would look at Nanny as if she were offended. Then she would sniff and say:
– You the cheat yourself, Miro Mananui. I saw you sneaking that ace from the bottom of the pack.
– How do you know I got an ace Maka? Nanny would say. I know you! You dealt this hand, and you stuck that ace down there for yourself, you cheat! Well, ana![5] I got it now! So take that!

And she would slap down her hand.
– Sweet, ay? she would laugh. Good? Kapai[6] lalelale? And she would sometimes wiggle her hips, making her victory sweeter.
– Eeee! Miro! Mrs Heta would say. Well, I got a good hand too!

And she would slap her hand down and bellow with laughter.
– Take that!

And always, they would squabble. I often wondered how they ever remained friends. The names they called each other!

Sometimes, I would go and see Nanny and she would be all alone, playing patience. If there was nobody to play with her, she'd always play patience. And still she cheated! I'd see her hands fumbling across the cards, turning up a jack or

---

[5] ana – there
[6] kapai – good

queen she needed, and then she'd laugh and say:
– I'm too good for this game!

She used to try to teach me some of the games, but I wasn't very interested, and I didn't yell and shout at her like the women did. She liked the bickering.
– Aue . . . she would sigh. Then she'd look at me and begin dealing out the cards in the only game I ever knew how to play.

And we would yell snap! all the afternoon. . . .

Now, Nanny was sick.

I went to see her that afternoon after I'd dropped my suitcases at home. Nanny Tama, her husband, opened the door. We embraced and he began to weep on my shoulder.
– Your Nanny Miro, he whispered. She's . . . she's. . . .

He couldn't say the words. He motioned me to her bedroom.

Nanny Miro was lying in bed. And she was so old looking. Her face was very grey, and she looked like a tiny wrinkled doll in that big bed. She was so thin now, and seemed all bones.

I walked into the room. She was asleep. I sat down on the bed beside her, and looked at her lovingly.

Even when I was a child, she must have been old. But I'd never realised it. She must have been over seventy now. Why do people you love grow old so suddenly?

The room had a strange, antiseptic smell. Underneath the bed was a big chamber pot, yellow with urine . . . And the pillow was flecked with small spots of blood where she had been coughing.

I shook her gently.
– Nanny . . . Nanny, wake up.

She moaned. A long, hoarse sigh grew on her lips. Her eyelids fluttered, and she looked at me with blank eyes . . . and then tears began to roll down her cheeks.
– Don't cry, Nanny, I said. Don't cry. I'm here.

But she wouldn't stop.

So I sat beside her on the bed and she lifted her hands to me.
– Haere mai, mokopuna. Haere mai. Mmm, Mmm

And I bent within her arms and we pressed noses.

After a while, she calmed down. She seemed to be her own self.
– What a haddit mokopuna you are, she wept. It's only when I'm just about in my grave that you come to see me.
– I couldn't see you last time I was home, I explained. I was too busy.
– Yes, I know you fullas, she grumbled. It's only when I'm almost dead that you come for some money.
– I don't want your money, Nanny.
– What's wrong with my money! she said. Nothing's wrong with it! Don't you want any?
– Of course I do, I laughed. But I know you! I bet you lost it all on poker!

She giggled. Then she was my Nanny again. The Nanny I knew.

We talked for a long time. I told her about what I was doing in Wellington and all the neat girls who were after me.

– You teka!⁷ she giggled. Who'd want to have you!

And she showed me all her injection needles and pills and told me how she'd wanted to come home from the hospital, so they'd let her.
– You know why I wanted to come home? she asked. I didn't like all those strange nurses looking at my bum when they gave me those injections. I was so sick, mokopuna, I couldn't even go to the lav, and I'd rather wet my own bed not their neat bed. That's why I come home.

Afterwards, I played the piano for Nanny. She used to like *Me He Manurere* so I played it for her, and I could hear her quavering voice singing in her room.

Me he manurere aue....

When I finally left Nanny I told her I would come back in the morning.

But that night, Nanny Tama rang up.
– Your Nanny Miro, she's dying.

We all rushed to Nanny's house. It was already crowded. All the old women were there. Nanny was lying very still. Then she looked up and whispered to Mrs Heta:
– Maka ... Maka tiko bum ... I want a game of cards....

A pack of cards was found. The old ladies sat around the bed, playing. Everybody else decided to play cards too, to keep Nanny company. The men played poker in the kitchen and sitting room. The kids played snap in the other bedrooms. The house overflowed with card players, even onto the lawn outside Nanny's window, where she could see....

The women laid the cards out on the bed. They dealt the first hand. They cackled and joked with Nanny, trying not to cry. And Mrs Heta kept saying to Nanny:

---
⁷ teka – false

– Eee! You cheat Miro. You cheat! And she made her googly eye reach far over to see Nanny's cards.
– You think you can see, ay, Maka tiko bum? Nanny coughed. You think you're going to win this hand, ay? Well, take that!

She slammed down a full house.

The other women goggled at the cards. Mrs Heta looked at her own cards. Then she smiled through her tears and yelled:
– Eee! You cheat Miro! I got two aces in my hand already! Only four in the pack. So how come you got three aces in your hand?

Everybody laughed. Nanny and Mrs Heta started squabbling as they always did, pointing at each other and saying: You the cheat, not me! And Nanny Miro said: I saw you, Maka tiko bum, I saw you sneaking that card from under the blanket.

She began to laugh. Quietly. Her eyes streaming with tears.

And while she was laughing, she died.

Everybody was silent. Then Mrs Heta took the cards from Nanny's hands and kissed her.
– You the cheat, Miro, she whispered. You the cheat yourself. . . .

We buried Nanny on the hill with the rest of her family. During her tangi,[8] Mrs Heta played patience with Nanny, spreading the cards across the casket.

Later in the year, Mrs Heta, she died too. She was buried right next to Nanny, so that they could keep on playing cards. . . .

---

[8] tangi – a funeral ceremony, to mourn, weep

TRANSITIONAL

And I bet you they're still squabbling up there. . . .
– Eee! You cheat Miro . . .
– You the cheat, Maka tiko bum. You, you the cheat. . . .

The Crookest Raffle Ever Run...
As told by Billy Borker
in the Redfern Hotel

Frank Hardy

Born in Southern Cross in 1917, Frank Hardy left school at thirteen to work as a messenger, grocery clerk, farm and factory labourer, and black-and-white artist. He was tried for criminal libel upon the publication of his novel, *Power Without Glory*. A prolific writer of short stories, he recently won a contest for Australia's Talking Championship.

'Did I ever tell yer about the crookest raffle ever run in Australia?'

'No, but you told me about the only *fair dinkum*[1] one.'

'Ah, that's a different raffle all together. That's the one I ran at Dee Why during the depression.'

'You'd better have a drink.'

'Don't mind if I do. Well this here raffle I'm talking about was run in a place in Victoria called Benson's Valley. It was run by a fella called Trigger MacIntosh. Don't know how he got that nickname but I know he had thirteen kids. Little fella. Bald as a billiard ball. There was six raffles in the case, really.''

[1] fair dinkum – real, true

Six. You said there was only one.'

'Well, in a manner of speaking there was. Yer see, he raffled the same pumpkin six times in the same pub.'

'But people wouldn't buy a ticket in a raffle for a pumpkin surely.'

'Australians will buy a raffle ticket in anything. They got into the habit during the depression. Buying raffle tickets is like goin' to church or drinking beer, once you get into the habit. Anyway, this was a special pumpkin. The biggest pumpkin ever grown in the history of the world. It was so big it took six men six hours to dig it out of the ground.'

'But pumpkins don't grow under the ground.'

'I know that, but this one was so heavy it sunk into the ground till yer couldn't see it.'

'Yer don't say.'

'If yer don't believe me you can ask Trigger MacIntosh. He grew that pumpkin, brother. I'm tellin' yer: it took six men six hours to dig . . . '

'You told me that.'

'Yeh, but it took the same six men another six hours to roll it up six planks on to a six-ton truck to take it to the pub to be raffled.'

'And it was raffled six times . . . '

'Yes, but that's getting ahead of the story. Never get ahead of the story, that's what my father always told me. First, I must tell you how they came to grow this here pumpkin.'

'They. But you said this bloke grew it himself. What did you say his name was?'

'Trigger MacIntosh. Matter of fact, Trigger didn't grow this pumpkin at all. He owned it in partnership with another fella – name of Greenfingers Stratton. Old Greenfingers could grow a crop of show orchids on a concrete footpath, so my father reckoned. Well, one day Trigger said to Greenfingers: "I know where I can borra a block of land and start a market garden." Fancy mentioning a block of land, to old Greenfingers – always saying "if only I had a block of land, I'd grow somethin', I can tell yer." Funny how people never fulfil their ambitions. I knew a violinist once who wanted to be a League footballer . . . '

'You've told me about him. Have another drink and get on with your story . . . '

'Well, it turned out that Trigger had talked an old cocky[2] with more money than sense into lending him some land on the river bank. Very rich soil from the floods that happened every few years. A good magsman[3] was Trigger; would have made a fortune in Parliament, I can tell yer. Well, they decided to grow pumpkins for some reason, and Greenfingers went to work. Pretty soon pumpkin vines began to crawl all over the property across the creek, over some paddocks of lucerne, up the side of the cocky's house and down the road towards the pub. Well, anyhow, Trigger and Greenfingers waited for the pumpkins to bud but nothing happened until one day one solitary pumpkin began to grow right in the middle of the paddock. It grew so fast you could see it bulging. It became so heavy it began to sink into the ground. And eventually it took six men . . . '

'Yes, I know, six men, six hours to dig it out.'

'That's right, and the same six men another six hours to roll it up six planks on to

---

[2] cocky – landowner
[3] magsman – talker

a six-ton truck to take it down to the pub.'

'All right. Why didn't they sell the pumpkin or enter it in the Royal Show?'

'What? Made a lot more money rafflin' it six times – that's why! Anyway down to the pub they went with it. A'course, it wouldn't fit in the pub door, needless to say, so they left it on the truck outside. And Trigger put a sign on it: THE BIGGEST PUMPKIN EVER GREW – 6d. A TICKET. Bought six raffle books at the newsagent's with a hundred tickets in each . . . '

'Did they sell all the tickets?'

'For sure! In the pub. The pumpkin being so big and people being in the habit of buying raffle tickets, like I told yer. There was a crowd around the pumpkin all day outside the Royal Hotel and, during the afternoon, six blokes got on top of it and sat in the sun drinking beer. Just before closing time, the raffle was drawn.'

'Who won it?'

'Old Greenfingers himself, nacherally, seeing Trigger drew the ticket out of the kerosene tin he had for the purpose and seeing it was the crookest raffle ever run in Australia, as I said before.'

'You said the pumpkin was raffled six times.'

'And that's a fact. If you don't believe me you can ask Trigger MacIntosh . . . '

'And I suppose this bloke Greenfingers won it every time.'

'No, he only won it five times.'

'Well, who won it the other time? One of these days someone is going to kill you right in the middle of one of your stories.'

'Trouble with you is, you try to ruin a story by making me get ahead of myself. My father always said . . . '

'Yes, I know what he always said . . . Here's your beer.'

'Thanks. Well, now, to tell the story properly. Greenfingers Stratton won the first raffle on account of Trigger MacIntosh had a ticket with a secret mark on it. Anyway, the next Saturday they brought the pumpkin back to the pub again.'

'Be a bit awkward wouldn't it? Raffling the biggest pumpkin ever grew more than once.'

'Matterafact, they changed the sign to read "the second biggest pumpkin ever grew," sold 600 tickets again and old Greenfingers won it. The next Saturday, they raffled the third biggest pumpkin ever grew, and so on, until they arrived at the pub one Saturday morning with the sixth biggest pumpkin ever grew.

'You don't mean to say . . . '

'If you don't believe me, you can ask . . . '

'I believe you but thousands wouldn't. Go on; who won it the sixth time?'

'I'm coming to that. Needless to say, that there pumpkin was becoming a bit the worse for wear what with rolling it on and off the truck and people climbing up on to it to drink their beer. It was bruised and battered, so my father reckoned. Trigger MacIntosh said afterwards it seemed to have a face and usta snarl at him when he walked past it. Now for some reason certain people, wowsers[4] and the like, started to say the raffles wasn't fair dinkum.'

---

[4] wowser – a puritanical person, a "kill-joy," teetotaler

'You don't tell me.'

'It's a fact. There's no pleasin' some people Anyhow, my father reckoned that Danny O'Connell the publican said to Trigger: 'Listen, that there sixth biggest pumpkin that ever grew. I seem to have seen it somewhere before." "A simple case of mistaken identity," Trigger told him. He was as quick as a flash, was Trigger. Did I ever tell you about the time Trigger came in late at a concert in Melbourne?'

'No, I don't think you did. Just tell me about the sixth raffle. I'll settle for that.'

'But I got to tell yer how witty Trigger was to build up his character, as the saying goes. He's late for this here concert, and the singer on the stage stops warbling and says sarcastic like: "The gentleman with the bald head is late," Quick as a flash without thinking, Trigger answered him "You can go and get – for mine" Yer, he was witty all right, was old Trigger.'

'I can see that . . . '

'Anyhow, where was I? Ah, yes, up to where Danny O'Connell the publican had a shot at Trigger about the raffle. (You keep interruptin' me and I lose track.) O'Connell didn't like raffles bein' run in his pub on account his customers had only so much money to spend and he liked them to spend it on beer and bets with the SP bookie in the bar who O'Connell financed, see. So he says to Trigger, "Some of my customers are complaining. They say Greenfingers Stratton won your raffle five weeks in a row." Trigger had a good answer as usual. He said: "Old Greenfingers was always lucky." "Yeh," O'Connell replied, "and he's working with a very lucky partner too, if you ask me." "No one asked you, as it turns out," Trigger told him, "but at least we haven't watered that pumpkin and put a collar on it like you do with your beer." You couldn't beat old Trigger in an argument and that's for sure. Anyway, in spite of some bad publicity, they sold six books of tickets, Then, just when Trigger was going to draw Greenfingers' ticket out of the tin, Danny O'Connell said: "Just a minute, I'll draw the raffle this week." Well, you can imagine how Trigger felt. He loses all his capital, if someone wins that pumpkin off him. So he says: "I don't like no aspersions bein' cast on my character, but you can draw it, if you insist." And he was thinking fast. "You can draw it at five to six." '

'What difference did it make when he drew it?'

'A lot of difference. Trigger calls Greenfingers aside. "Here," he says, "here's six more raffle books. Go and lock yourself in the dunny and fill out every ticket in my name." '

'So old Trigger won the sixth raffle himself?'

'As a matter of fact, a bloke named Sniffy Connors won the raffle with the only ticket he ever bought in his life. Greenfingers got writer's cramp filling in 600 butts with his name. He had half of the tickets but, as luck would have it, O'Connell drew out the one Sniffy Connors bought.'

'And what did Sniffy do with the pumpkin? Eat it?'

'No, Sniffy was living in a tent at the time, so he blew a hole in the side of the pumpkin with a stick of gelignite and made a house out of it. Lived in it for six years with his wife and six kids . . . '

'You don't mean to say!'

'It's a fact. I could take you to the spot and show you the house except he got burnt out in the bushfires in 1936.'

'You win. Have another beer.'

'Not me. I'm busy today. Running a raffle. The biggest turkey ever bred in Australia. Two bob a time. How many tickets do you want?'

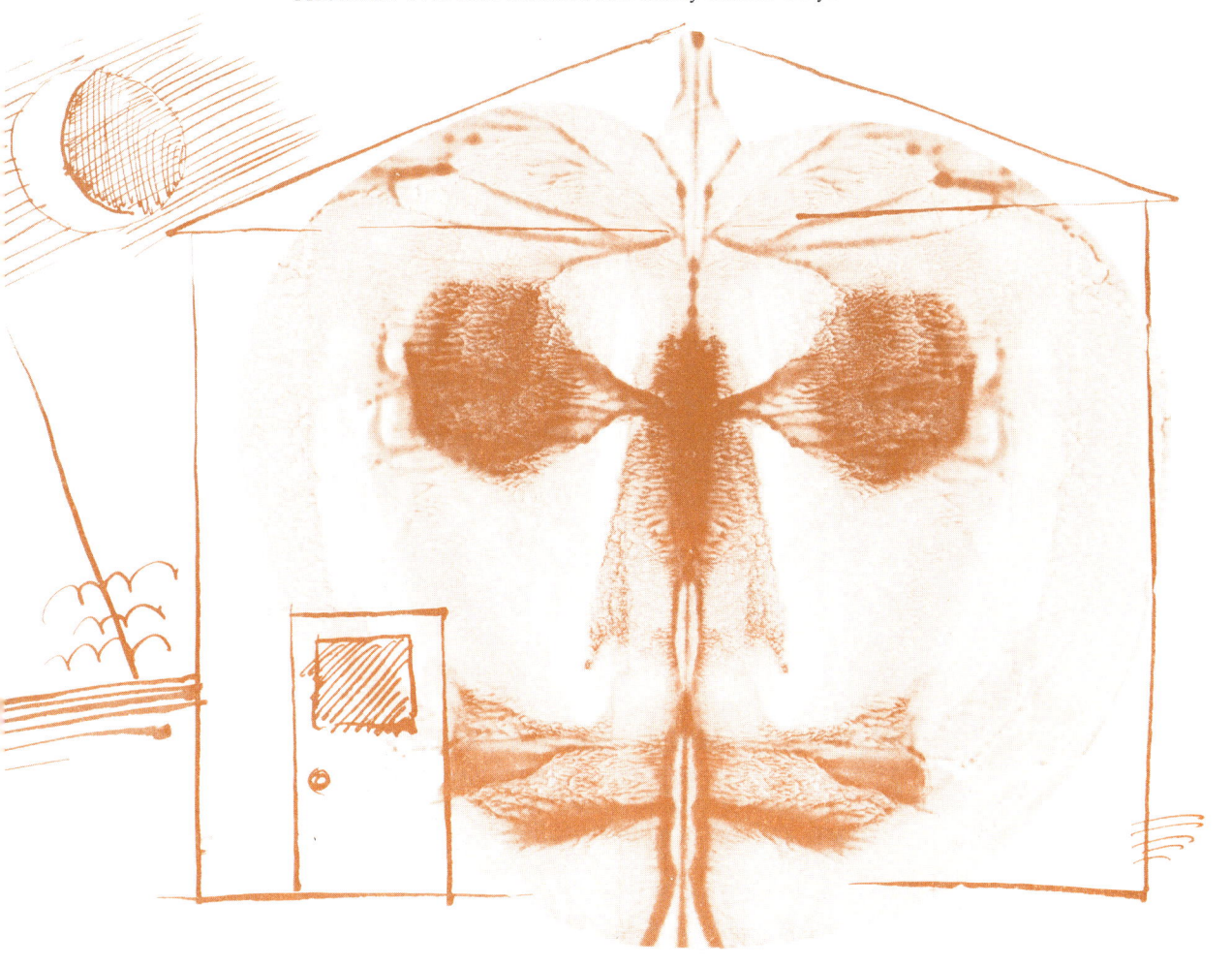

In Youth Is Pleasure

Maurice Duggan

Maurice Duggan (1922-1975) was born and lived in Auckland, New Zealand. He worked as an advertising executive and published several collections of short stories and children's books.

Hopkins had learned the translation by heart: with a pretence of difficulty intended to give his listeners the impression that he was translating at sight, he read slowly, filling the long pondering gaps of silence with a rush of words, and pausing again. He stood, huge and uncomfortable, at the edge of his desk and the book lay awkwardly in his hands. His eyes as he recited were fixed not on the lines of print but on the indifferent drawing which, as an aid to vocabulary and a key to the story below, headed the page. His voice, frequently mispronouncing, jerked sporadically forward like a fly trapped in a cobweb, faded a moment into silence and rose again with its suggestion of frenzy and tedium: it was not enough to hide his pretence.

– Stop, called Brother Mark. I say stop.

And as the recounting drone, telling its rote tale of sentry geese, choked like some stalled motor into silence the small, furtive, inattentive noises of the class died also. One by one the heads came up and one by one they swung about. Brother Mark and Hopkins were at it again: the play was on. As if above that other arena of spectacle and savagery the whole class leaned forward into the familiar drama which, because they were young, jaded them less in its familiarity, in its pattern too often rehearsed than, tiered in the hot imperial amphitheatre, it must have jaded those others.

Brother Mark stepped down into this almost tangible sense of expectation, rested a moment daintily poised on his dancer feet and began to sidle, to mince forward, threatening down the aisle. Hopkins, now with his mouth fixed as if in silent enunciation of his last word, raised his eyes slowly above the top of the breast-high book: like dancer or boxer, insolent and assured, smiling a very small smile that did not reveal his carious teeth, Brother Mark came on.

– We did not remember, he lightly mocked, so much of the scholar in you. He made a sly and bitterly amused appeal to the watching boys. I confess, he primly announced, I'd be put to it myself to do as nicely.

Hopkins blushed; the blood climbed over his face into his galleried ears. Brother Mark's eyes, winking and dancing in malicious delight, took him in from head to foot. Hopkins, under that stare, began to squirm: his socks with their striped turn-down of green and white had fallen over the tops of his heavy boots; his serge shorts, ending tightly above his grotesque knees, seemed about to split over his thighs – the tight cloth shone and bulged. Through the open neck of his shirt the hair could be seen, growing high up to the base of his neck, where it had been trimmed in an even line. His ears, dark with embarrassment, stood hugely out.

– Proceed, said Brother Mark. He rose on the balls of his feet and bending at the knee rocked forward. Proceed, he said.

Hopkins bent again, searching the meaningless page, searching his dumbed memory, pleading with his great slow tender eyes for the print to yield up, in some secret communication, its little mystery. His breathing in the quietened room came slow and heavy. Thirty heads and the eyes of Brother Mark watched and waited, and alone in the arena of that attention Hopkins felt ungainly and afraid. The palms of his hands began to sweat: the lines of print blurred under his eyes.

– Proceed, said Brother Mark. We are waiting.

The boys, feeling themselves enticed, conspirators and partners to this baiting game, shuffled and giggled: the sound rose abruptly and stilled. Brother Mark, frowning archly, placed himself at Hopkins' shoulder and peered down in enlightened contempt at the elementary page. His forefinger, precisely manicured, with a pale moon gleaming in the pale nail, poked forward and prodded with disdain at the point on the page where the reading had been interrupted: his eyes peered up, quizzical and sure, into the face of the boy who was a full head taller than himself.

– The soldier, Hopkins bellowed.

– *Of* the soldier, surely, Brother Mark cut softly in.

Of the soldier, wouldn't you agree? The soldier, do you see, possesses something. And Brother Mark's eyes examined a Hopkins bereft of all possession.

– Of the soldier, Hopkins parroted, staring down to where the finger rested elegantly on the page. Of the soldier, he muttered, and was silent.

– What? said Brother Mark. What of the soldier?

– I forget, Hopkins got out.

– Forget? Brother Mark exquisitely questioned. How forget? Isn't it all down there? The finger reared and fell. It isn't something to remember: come.

The page on which the finger lightly rapped trembled in the huge hands. The thirty heads watching from all sides offered neither assistance nor sympathy. Brother Mark raised his eyes and gazed about with an air of simulated wonder. His eyes looked out from under jet brows: he leaned forward. Hopkins, struck by that stale breath, drew back: the movement was slight but Brother Mark caught it.

– War, rapped Brother Mark. You see it?

– War, cried Hopkins, suddenly safe; and his doubled thumbs erectile and huge rose like twin horns on either side of the cupped book. War, he cried, and caught the thread and bolted on, bellowing through his flawless and cribbed translation, shouting in a meaningless rote while he watched the menacing finger retreat diagonally across the page.

– Enough, cried Brother Mark. Enough.

Once again the drone fell away: Hopkins' face, red and miserable, swung round.

– We think, said Brother Mark, you are not playing fair. We think, he menaced, that you are cheating.

– No, Brother, Hopkins said.

– No? said Brother Mark. Now it would seem that you are lying. Cheating and lying both. You would do well to think of your soul.

Hopkins was silent.

– Turn back, Brother Mark said. But without waiting he snatched the book, turned back half-a-dozen pages and thrust it back into the hands that were cupped still, the thumbs dejected, as though they had held it without interruption. Try that, Brother Mark said.

The class stirred again and settled: the summer sun shone into the room and the motes of dust, in inappropriate gaiety, danced before the green board chalked with sums. Through the silence a shout of laughter from a distant class-room mocked and died: Hopkins looked down.

– Regina, Hopkins read.

– Oh, in English, please, said Brother Mark.

– The queen, Hopkins said.

The silence tautened and drew out.

– Last week's lesson, said Brother Mark.

– The queen, Hopkins began again.

– The queen; the queen; shrilled Brother Mark. Get on. Get on. What queen: where? In irate and delightful fancy his eyes, as for that regal one, searched the room and his voice, whinnying in frenzy, rang out: Get on.

But he had shattered the conspiracy; the power relaxed. Faced with something that was not foreseeable or safe the boys' condoning interest flooded back so that once again there remained only that spectacle which, objective and judicious, they continued to watch.

Hopkins, challenged, could not meet it, could not keep up the inconsiderable pretence: the book sank slowly and the mournful face, no longer searching for that assistance once denied, swung slowly across those other glances which, meeting his, fell away or stared back imperious, curious and removed. Brother Mark stepped forward and a floorboard creaked and from a crack between the boards a small volcano of dust erupted among the bright motes, filtering still. The manicured hand reached forward, miming a gesture of plucking at something odious, and nipped, thumb and forefinger, into Hopkins' ear. Under its bite Hopkins shuffled forward with his eyes watering in pain; near the blackboard he was swung about until, clownish and wretchedly benign, he faced the facing class whose eyes like magnetised needles swung to that north, trembled, and stayed. The sun struck full on his great thighs; he was released. The book fell from his hand and at the noise the class shifted again, as if so small a detail brought to the tension some relief, let them off from whatever feelings – censure, sympathy, pleasure, condonation, pain, delight – isolate or complex, rose to their sense.

It was left to some other boy to read the passage: Brother Mark commanded the smallest. He came forward to the chosen place, so close to the body of Hopkins that he almost touched him and could smell the peculiar smell of sunwarmed cloth. Hopkins overtopped him: the smaller boy was set like something precious and human and compact within the mere animal mass of that greater bulk.

– Go on, Simpson, Brother Mark said.

Slowly and accurately, in a piping voice that as much as his size seemed to mock the ungainly Hopkins, Simpson read on. The very force of the authority which commanded him released him from blame, released him from any duty to contest it – as though being commanded by a force of grand compulsion should alter the relation between wrong and the doing of wrong. Simpson did not mock: he had been chosen to mock, and there lay all the difference; or so he consoled himself. There was no way out, no way other than to transfer that petty and womanish venom to his own head: he did not care for Hopkins enough for that – no one, it seemed, did care – and he was not brave enough, or foolhardy enough, to venture such a thing on its own account. Even among schoolboys, his actions seemed sturdily to proclaim, there is that sense of aptness; a natural prudence which suits itself to the occasion. This was not the first time Hopkins had been baited nor did anyone think it would be the last. They accepted all that happened as something which, determined beyond them, carried its own air of permanence and order.

The class grew restless under Simpson's unoffending voice: they stirred with the sound the watchers make when – as on the wall of the cave – the flickering pictures fail and the sense rises over them of how they are crammed, only human, into that sudden dark.

– Enough, called Brother Mark, consumed perhaps with a similar feeling. Go back to your place, Simpson.

Hopkins, doubled forward as though that paining hand nipped still at his ear, bent immobile in effigy of resignation and obscure despair, did not look beyond the heavy toes of his besmirched boots. He feared to find, in the eyes beyond, not the dispassion which he knew would be there, but sympathy which, even mistakenly, he knew he could not meet. He could not have sworn he was being truthful in so standing there; he knew for an instant that he had not done as much as he might have done, as much as, through all his fright, he could have done. Buried far down under his present despair was a bile of slow anger, a record of outrage. They were feelings, no more, but too much present for denial: they bore him along and yet kept him oafishly there, scapegoat to the class, because he had caught, like one glancing dance of light, the almost lost gleam of something there was not time – and never would be, perhaps – to examine. It underrode everything and was to him no more than suspected; and yet it was the reason he would have turned from sympathy: it had no presence and was not more than an ambience, a faint aura of something that, though obscure and lost, yet shone to his dozing mind with its suggestion of guilt and delight. He stayed bent forward and waited the next move: the little flame of anger burned up.

Brother Mark, gay again and smiling, regretting with light impatience that he had run the risk of losing face, of seeming even for an instant to have lost, stepped lightly up on to the teacher's dais.

– There is so little point, Hopkins, he smiled, in denying it. You mustn't think we are all fools. You cheated, you know; you cribbed and you lied to cover it up. That isn't, and he smiled again, the way a grown man is expected to behave.

Hopkins finding no relief but only a further threat in the light, reasonable voice, shuffled one foot over the dusty boards: under his tight shorts the muscles shifted.

– Admit it, Brother Mark lightly advised. Admit you were lying and cheating.

Hopkins' reply, hollow and averted, was lost.

– It is, and Brother Mark addressed the class, such a waste to put such a fellow to the classics. A convoy, do you see, must take its speed from the slowest ship: we all suffer through such a dunce.

Brother Mark's shepherding eye went out over his class and returned, light and contemptuous, to the dunce: his palms, turned theatrically upwards, rose as he shrugged and his eyebrows, arch and arched, comically indicated his despair. What could he do, he pleaded in eloquent silence, with such a dunce? How should he deal with such stupid deceit? His smooth voice prodded again at the slumbering bulk of Hopkins who protested no more than by moving his feet. A laugh skittered through the room.

– I am afraid, Hopkins, sympathised Brother Mark, that in our opinion you must be held unsuitable for any but the grosser tasks of this world. We are thirty-two in this room; and yours are the only boots with dung on them. Brother Mark, struck with this thought, paused, and then went on. Your parents would be ill advised to spend any more money on you. There must be country jobs you could do, surely? He sniffed fastidiously as if those blowing country smells were striking up from Hopkins' boots. There is nothing we can do, Brother Mark said, and his head struck forward and his eyes flared: nothing at all for such a massive dishonest lout.

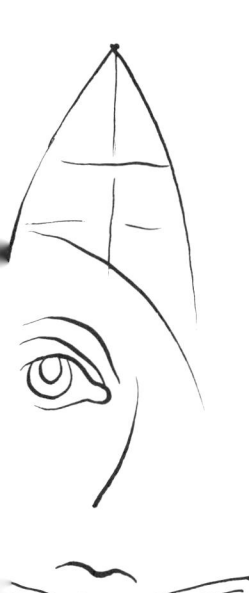

A small drop of saliva fell from his lips to the back of his wrist: with a gesture of amusing exaggeration Brother Mark drew forth his handkerchief and wiped it away. Not until he finished and raised his eyes did he see that he had gone too far. He had but a moment to compliment himself that he was a match for any overgrown boy before he retreated an involuntary step and came up against the edge of the reading stand: the handkerchief like some lax signal of premature surrender trailed from his hand. In silence and as one the thirty boys craned forward.

– There is no other way, the Brother Superior said. We will have to let him go.

– Without an explanation? Brother Ignatius asked.

– How, queried the Brother Superior, would you propose explaining? Or what?

– He had been baited, Brother Ignatius said. For a long time, by all accounts. You'll admit there's an end to turning the other cheek.

The Brother Superior smiled, almost with sadness.

– Not, he said, a Christian end. But that I blame him, don't think that.

– Has anything been said to Brother Mark?

– A reprimand, is that what you mean? the Brother Superior said. I have spoken to him. It isn't possible to change a man's nature.

– The man in question, Brother Ignatius said, might be reminded that it is, on the other hand, possible to lose his soul.

It drew no rebuke. They sat on either side of a table covered with green baize: a shaded lamp burned between them but left them both in shadow. Hopkins' school reports were spread before them. Brother Ignatius, much older, leaned back into his chair and through some trick of the light his cheekbones seemed to have fallen in and his eyes looked out from their ancient shadow.

– Brother Mark, the Brother Superior said, has, I think, learned a lesson. A painful one, in its way, he added.

– He has so many lessons to learn, Brother Ignatius said. There hardly seems time for them all. I hope it lasts, that's all.

– It's left its mark, the Brother Superior said, and frowned at the unintended pun. But why didn't the boy come to me before?

They looked with a common impulse towards the door; it too was covered in green baize: the Brother Superior had a fear of draughts.

– The sanctum sanctorum, Brother Ignatius mildly joked. He was afraid, I suppose. It wouldn't be an easy thing to do, especially for a boy like that: or for anyone. The place has an air.

– Yes. But it's curious, and the Brother Superior lightly touched the papers. He doesn't get marks in anything but botany and divinity.

– But? Brother Ignatius said. The world, surely?

– You know what I mean, the stern tones rebuked.

– It won't be easy to explain, Brother Ignatius said. What he did was both justified and wrong; right and wrong, so to say. It will seem like splitting hairs, to him.

– Oh wrong for discipline, wrong for the college, yes. But do you see a way of keeping him on? I'll confess I don't.

– Brother Mark might go, Brother Ignatius said.

– That's flippant, the Brother Superior said. You know that isn't possible. You're not being much help.

– It's not something I like, Brother Ignatius said.

– He's not stupid: the boy, I mean. But I quite see that there is something in his slowness that could be immensely irritating. Not that I'm making excuses, you know that. The whole thing is unpleasant. I've put him in the infirmary.

– Him? said Brother Ignatius. We're all turned about, surely?

– It's the only separate place. But what worries me is how best to go about things. He had no explanation, the Brother Superior said. Except to say he was sorry. And yet if I write to his parents and say that he isn't to blame and then in the same breath I say that I've expelled him, what will they think? What would anyone think? I can't hand them a dilemma like that; to say nothing of how it might reflect on us.

– Let him go, Brother Ignatius said, stirring. There's nothing else for it. Perhaps God and nature will know what to make of his good marks; perhaps he'll be taken in hand. There's nothing we can do: we aren't organised for such decisions. Right and wrong: it's splitting hairs. And yet, if we look for the evil, where are we then? Right in the mire, I'd say; uncomfortably close to home.

With great dignity the Brother Superior stood up: his impersonal eye roved over the walls of the room: he brought his unrelenting glance back to Brother Ignatius.

– And do you think, the Brother Superior said, that you have that thought entirely for your own?

Hopkins sat on the edge of one of the beds in the small two-bed infirmary. The other bed was empty and, on both, the white covers shone with a bleached purity. The room held nothing more: it had a faint smell of damp kapok and disinfectant and common soap. The window was open and the sun was going down: the clear window pane shimmered with light. The afternoon breeze tugged at the austere curtains and blew into the room the shouts of boys out on the playing fields, the sound of a motor-mower tracking over the summer grass, the smells of dust and summer, of hot bitumen and cooking food. Hopkins' face, patched with freckles and surmounted with a shapeless brush of pale hair, wore an expression of tiredness and gloom: his great spaniel eyes were closed but he was not asleep.

He knew what was coming: could anything be surer? He would be sent home, that was plain enough. His parents would be disappointed and grave but they would not punish him. Their aged faces rose to his mind: he felt himself as bent already under their perplexed and injured eyes, under their dumb reproach. They had sacrificed for him and he had let them down. From the world, those imagined eyes proclaimed, we would expect such things, but not from you. And in the over-furnished room hallowed to such occasions his mother would wait, with a tenderness that was more remorseless than blows, for the moment which would prise from him those assurances, those lies if need be, which would reaffirm her in her belief that he was, in spite of it all, a good boy yet at heart.

– I'm sorry Hoppy, Simpson said: and Hopkins, who had not heard him come, opened on him eyes framed still in a clown's sorrow and despair. I'm sorry, Simpson said, but what could I do?

The huge head shook and the hair trembled: Hopkins did not speak.

– I've scrounged a biscuit, Simpson said, and as to something hardly human offered the wholemeal square he had bartered for with a day-boy.

Hopkins took it: he broke it in half and put both halves in his mouth where they stuck a moment before he chewed and swallowed. Both boys were aware of a tension between them.

– Thank you, Hopkins said formally. He picked a crumb off the hairs on his chest and put it into his mouth.

– He's a bastard, Simpson said, loudly and with daring. Everyone knows that.

– It doesn't matter, Hopkins said.

– What will they do? Simpson said.

– Send me home, I suppose.

– Expel you, you mean? Simpson said; and put so bluntly it overcame them both. There was, after all, between them some bond and they looked at one another with an expression near to awe. They had touched on something; they had acknowledged between them that unspoken and even unconscious conspiracy that proclaimed, in the face of everything, their belief in a functioning standard: they were related in a conspiracy which, allowing for the absence of anything as definite as friendship, yet proclaimed, crudely and impermanently perhaps, their belief in some sort of justice. It was unadult, and perhaps between now and maturity they would forget it; but it was impelling and real.

– Will you go? Simpson asked. But he was not interested in the answer: he knew Hopkins would go; how could he do otherwise? No: what held him there was the feeling that something more was to be done. The precise moment for leaving had not come; and so, between them, Hopkins and he acted it out.

– I'll have to, Hopkins said.

– Won't your family make a stink?

– No, Hopkins said; they won't.

– Won't you even get a hiding? Simpson curiously asked.

– Not a real one, Hopkins said.

– I'll write you, if you like, Simpson said.

– If you want to. It doesn't matter.

– Are you mad at me? Simpson asked.

That was the point: they recognised it at once. Simpson hung, waiting for an answer. He wouldn't write; they both knew that. Simpson did not want Hopkins' friendship, and they would not be friends, but that Hopkins should know, should say, that under that force there was nothing else he could have done – that, to Simpson, was important.

Hopkins sat on: under the shouts that blew in, fainter now, through the open window, he stirred; he looked at the white beds; a bird chuckled in a tree. He wanted only to be on his own again and to have it all over, all done with. It had nothing to do with him for, even as they spoke, his sentence, he did not doubt, was being lightly decided behind the green baize door. What did they say? He squeezed his eyes shut as if in this way he might hear, but when he opened them again there was only Simpson waiting still, still to be satisfied. It was, Hopkins realised, out of his hands; it had always been so. Soon enough it would be his mother making a demand that in no way differed from this. He looked at Simpson gravely, lugubriously.

– Are you mad? Simpson said.

– I don't blame you, if that's what you mean, Hopkins said. Why should I? It hadn't anything to do with you. He stood up. Who has it to do with? he wondered to himself.

Simpson came round the edge of the bed. Across the white cover, and with all the solemn jesting of those who have found treaty, they touched hands.

– Anyway, Simpson said, it isn't much of a place. And he was gone.

Hopkins crossed the room, lumbering, and with his huge hands erased the impression of Simpson and himself from the white beds. He went to the window. The bird in the tree choked on a note and gave up, disgruntled. Two floors down the quadrangle lay, empty except for the Brother Superior walking towards the infirmary. Hopkins waited: the last of the sun shone like pale spears on the stones: the poplars shivered and stood up into the evening air: in puckish thanksgiving the bird found its song.

The Pink House in the Town

Albert Wendt

Albert Wendt was born in Western Samoa in 1939. After studying in New Zealand, Wendt returned to Western Samoa, where he became Principal of Samoa College. In 1974 he accepted an appointment at the University of the South Pacific. *Flying-Fox in a Freedom Tree*, a collection of stories which includes "The Pink House in Town," deals with the conflict between tradition and change.

My mother Lupe is dead. My father Tauilopepe is alive. He is now one of the richest in these little islands which the big god Tagaloaalagi threw down from the heavens into the Pacific Ocean to be used by him as stepping stones across the water, but which are now used by people, like my honourable father, as garbage-dumps, battle fields, altars of sacrifice and so on.

Like all the Tauilopepe men before me, I was born in Sapepe, and my *aiga*[1] is one of the main branches of the Sapepe Family who founded the village and district of Sapepe in long ago times. Sapepe is a long way from Apia, towards the west and, so legend tells, only a short way from the edge of the world. It is one of the biggest villages in Samoa, and it is cut off from other districts by low mountains to the east and west and the main mountain range behind it. Because of these mountains, Sapepe was separated from the rest of Samoa for hundreds of years, and so Sapepe had its own history and titles and customs different in many ways from the other districts. Things did not change very much. Life was slow until the *papalagi*[2] came and changed many things, including later people like my father.

---

[1] aiga: extended – family
[2] papalagi, palagi – person of European stock

. . . I get into the bus in my best clothes and sit beside Tauilopepe (Tauilo for short). I look out the bus window. Lupe, my mother, and my sisters are watching me. I look away from Lupe because I do not want to see her pain. The bus roars and off we go. I wave. My sisters call goodbye, waving to me. Lupe just stands there. I look back at her till the bus goes round the bend and I do not see her no more. Soon we pass the last *Fale*[3] in Sapepe and we are heading for the range eastwards to the morning sun.

The bus is full of people who laugh and talk like they are going to burn the town with their laughter. I feel hot and uncomfortable in my best clothes. Tauilo is talking with a man who has rotten teeth. Tauilo tells the man that he is going to Apia to take his son (me) to school there. The man says he wishes he had the money to send his son to a town school. Tauilo gives the man an American cigarette. They talk about the Bible and how God is good to men who work hard, and all that. It is Tauilo's usual talk. I fall asleep as we come over the range, thinking of my mother.

We get off the bus beside the Apia market and Tauilo smooths down his clothes and leads me towards my uncle Tautala's home just behind the picture theatre. The picture theatre looks like a big tin coffin.

'Now, you behave like a man,' Tauilo tells me. 'Tautala is a God-fearing man who does not want any silly nonsense. You understand?' I nod the head. 'You work hard at school. You only going to stay with Tautala until I get enough money to buy us a house here. You understand?' I nod the head again.

I have met Tautala many times before. He used to visit Sapepe to see Lupe who is his sister, but it is only an excuse to get from us some loads of *taro*[4] and bananas. Tautala is a short man who is nearly as fat as he is tall. Some of my aiga call him 'piggy' because that is what he looks like. He looks all the time like he is looking for a toilet. He always talks of palagi like they are his best friends. He works in a

---

[3] fale – Samoan house, round, without walls
[4] taro, talo – bulbous root, a dietary staple

government office where he gets $12 a month. Because he is a government worker with the white shirt and shorts and long socks and shoes, just like a palagi, most of the Sapepe people, including my father, are very impressed with him. Especially when he speaks English, which the Sapepe people do not understand. He is an educated man, Tauilo tells everyone. He is a palagi who does not know how to read, some of my aiga say.

I look at the neighbourhood as we walk to Tautala's house. The fale look like old men who are waiting to die. Some of them are made of banana boxes and rusty iron, and the area smells like a dead horse because of the toilets on the black stream flowing through it. The stream is called the 'Vaipe', my father tells me. (In English that means 'Dead Water'.)

We go over the small wooden bridge over the stream and I see some children playing under the breadfruit trees, and on the steps of a dirty-looking house there sit two women who have on the lipstick and coloured dresses. Tauilo sees them and he holds my hand and pulls me quickly through the neighbourhood, and I wonder why. Then we go through a high hibiscus hedge.

And there it is. Tautala's house. The pink house. It has two storeys and many windows of real glass. Next to the house is a fale with a sugar-cane patch behind it. All around the house and fale stands a high hibiscus hedge, just like a wall to protect something from thieves. At the far side, over the hedge and stream, is the police station and prison. Two boys and a girl are playing marbles in front of the house. They come running when they see us. One boy takes my suitcase. He is about my age but smaller. He leads us to the door.

I have never been in a palagi home before, so when I stand on the steps I feel like I am going to enter a temple or something. The smell of the house and the way it is so shiny scares me. Tauilo looks afraid too. Faafetai, Tautala's wife, comes and welcomes us inside. (My mother told me once that Faafetai runs Tautala's life.)

'Sit down,' Faafetai says, pointing at two wooden chairs.

'It is alright down here,' says Tauilo, sitting on the shiny floor. I sit down beside him. Faafetai sits on the chair facing us; she smiles.

Then Tauilo and her go through the Samoan oratory of welcome.

'How is your family?' she asks later.

Tauilo is lost for words. He is a nervous condition. 'They are well, thank you,' he says finally.

'Tautala will be home soon,' she says. She tries to smile as she looks at me and my suitcase.

'That is good. And how is he?'

'Working hard, very hard. Overtime all the time,' she says. I wonder what overtime is. 'He is so tired when he comes home that all he does is sleep.'

'Is he working on important government business?'

'Yes, all the time.'

'Did you hear that, Pepe?' Tauilo asks me. I nod the head. 'You get a good education and you will be like Tautala.' I nod again.

While they talk, I look around and sigh in wonder. There are photos of hundreds of people maybe, on the walls; smiling people, sad people, old people, ugly people, and one dead man covered with *ietoga*[5] with Faafetei weeping beside him. On one wall I see certificates like the ones on our Sapepe pastor's house. All the

---

[5] ietoga – fine mat

certificates belong to Tautala. I read one. It says that Tautala passed the standard four examinations.

'... I will take good care of Pepe,' I hear Faafetai say.

'Thank you. He is a good boy,' says Tauilo.

At the back of the room stands a table with chairs round it. I have never eaten on a table before so I look forward to it. On the other side is the biggest radio I have ever seen. It is so shiny I want to go and touch it. Faafetai's children giggle. The girl pokes her tongue at me. I hit her. She cries. Faafetai laughs but I know she does not mean it. Tauilo tells me not to do it again or else.

'I am sorry,' he says to Faafetai.

'It is alright,' she replies.

The boy, the one who took my suitcase, comes over and sits by me. 'What is your name, boy?' he asks. I do not answer. 'Have you got a palagi house like ours?' he asks. 'Bet you do not because you are poor.' He is the most childish kid I have ever met.

'Why you come to stay here?' his sister asks. 'Cause you are poor, that is why!' She is ugly bad.

My aiga in Sapepe teach me never to let common people insult me so I say to the children. 'Who you think you are?' They sit up. I repeat what I said but they are too stupid to know what I am talking about.

'You know how to play marbles?' the boy asks.

'That game is for kids,' I reply. 'You know how to spear fish?' I ask. The children get up, poke their tongues at me and leave, and I feel good because I am alone again.

I try to remember Sapepe and how if I were there now I would be out fishing with my friends, but here I am in the pink house with only the self for company.

Then Tautala enters, panting like he is drowning, with the starched palagi clothes and long white socks and brown shoes, with pencils and pens in his shirt pocket.

'Do not get up!' he greets Tauilo. They shake hands. 'Very hot day. And how is our family?' Tauilo makes the usual reply. Tautala sinks into the soft chair next to Faafetai and is wiping his face with a red handkerchief. 'Hot day. Oh!' He gets up and nearly runs out of the room to the back. I have the feeling he is going to the toilet.

'Hot, is it not? Hungry too,' he says when he returns, wiping his hands. Faafetai goes out to get the food ready. 'Been working all day adding up government money,' he says. Then he tells Tauilo, who is sitting like a lost boy on the floor, how Dave, his palagi boss, likes him because he can add up difficult sums of money and how Dave is going to promote him soon. He takes out a silver fountain pen and shows it to Tauilo. 'Dave gave that to me last week!' Tauilo looks at the pen and sighs in envy.

I get bored. I get up and leave the house. I sit on the bank of the stream and look at the jail on the other side. Smoke is rising from the prison *umu*[6] and two prisoners, in striped *lavalava*,[7] are fixing the food. A fat policeman comes and talks with them. They laugh behind the barbed-wire fence.

The stream is narrow at this point, and it has a steel pipe for a bridge across it to the prison. The stream is loaded with rubbish, and it stinks as I have said before. I pick up a rock and break my face in the water with it. The prisoners and the

---

[6] umu – stone oven
[7] lavalava – wrap-around, worn around the waist

policeman are talking still. I try to hear what they are saying but they are too far away. I bend my head into my hands on my knees and cry. Even when I think of all my friends in Sapepe I am still alone. There is only the black water and the stink.

'Boy!' someone calls. I look up scared. He is a giant prisoner with a bird tattoo on his chest. 'Why you cry?' he asks. 'You got no reason to cry, you not a prisoner!' he laughs. Then he is gone into the prison.

I return to the pink house.

The next morning Tauilo takes me to enrol in the government primary school. (Tautala is a graduate of this school.) In the afternoon my father gives me $2 before he leaves on the bus for Sapepe. I stand and hold the money. He waves at me from the bus window. Then the bus is off and I am alone in the market where there are so many people buying and selling. I start to shake. It is the first time I have been alone in the town. But when I see some kids eating ice-creams I run to the shop and buy one.

I whistle and run home past the police station, eating my ice-cream.

That night my ice-cream courage leaves me as I lie in the mosquito net. I pray to God, tell Him to look after me. I fall asleep saying I am going to be alright.

To the Woman Selling Handicrafts outside Burns Philp's Doors

(a word to the tourist)

Sano Malifa

Born and educated in western Samoa, Sano Malifa worked at a variety of jobs and began to write poetry in New Zealand between 1969 and 1974. After returning to Samoa, he journeyed to Hawaii and to Washington, where he is presently employed in a bookstore.

You have to walk slowly now:
these are treasures not to be missed –
stop, maybe, and inspect, feel the polished shell,
the turtleshell bracelet and the ring, unique.
The oyster sadness dusted clean
countless times a day just for your eye.
See the handbag! Such beautiful designs!
And those fingers weaving like spiders,
those arms sagging and frail can do wonders still –
watch the fingers alone – oh, how dexterous!
Unpolished dedication! See the stringing of
pearly shells. How lovely!

TRANSITIONAL

But you don't understand how they're stringing
their life beads outside these doors,
like corpses, the concrete mattress gathers
the cold and pumps it home.
But don't consider, inspect and make a bargain.
And you have to look a little above the collar bone
at the fleshy neck, blue veins, the wide jaw.
Remark! The high cheek bones,
the strong forehead, black hair locked or loose
and somehow stained at the edges,
those narrow-lidded brows and the brown
textures more like driftwood.
You look disappointed, surprised? Surely you
must have seen this face somewhere before,
perhaps in a museum: the Polynesian goddess,
a Gauguin's brown virgin, the Viking queen going drab,
all here now at your service, so be cheerful,
this is her in flesh and bone,
in rags and cheap stones.
Now you wonder why there isn't a better place,
a house, a counter, a few stools, something else, better.
Well knock wood, dear tourist, raise hell!
And if you have heart, ask around
because in all these years, I have never
heard the question raised;
in all these years, I've heard the desire
to breathe rich being smothered in the dust
outside these doors, these famous
Burns Philp's coffin doors.

But don't speak, dear tourist,
I didn't say a word.

Country Town

Judith Wright

Judith Wright is acclaimed as a poet both in Australia and in Europe. She was born in 1915 near Armidale, New South Wales, and was brought up on a sheep and cattle station. In addition to seven volumes of verse, she has published a family biography, tales for children, short stories, and critical articles. Much of her work tends to link the present with the past and reveal Australia's colorful and sometimes violent history.

This is no longer the landscape that they knew,
the sad green enemy country of their exile,
those branded men whose songs were of rebellion.
The nights were cold, shepherding; and the dingoes
bawling like banshees in the hills, the mist coming over
from eastward chilled them. Beside the fire in the hut
their pannikin of rum filled them with songs
that were their tears for Devonshire and Ireland
and chains and whips and soldiers. Or by day
a slope of grass with small sheep moving on it,
the sound of the creek talking, a glimpse of mountains,
looked like another country and wrenched the heart.
They are dead, the bearded men who sang of women
in another world (sweet Alice) and another world.

This is a landscape that the town creeps over;
a landscape safe with bitumen and banks.
The hostile hills are netted in with fences
and the roads lead to houses and the pictures.
Thunderbolt was killed by Constable Walker
long ago; the bones are buried, the story printed.

And yet in the night of the sleeping town, the voices:
This is not ours, not ours the flowering tree.
What is it we have lost and left behind?
Where do the roads lead? It is not where we expected.
The gold is mined and safe, and where is the profit?
The church is built, the bishop is ordained,
and this is where we live: where do we live?
And how shall we rebel? The chains are stronger.

Remember Thunderbolt, buried under the air-raid trenches.
Remember the bearded men singing of exile.
Remember the shepherds under their strange stars.

The Sunbather

John Thompson

John Thompson was born in Melbourne in 1907. After graduating from the University of Melbourne, he spent several years in England, but returned to join the Australian Broadcasting Commission in 1939. He has published a travel book and several volumes of poems.

I shield my face. My eyes are closed. I spin
With nearing sleep. I am dissolved within
Myself, and softened like a ripening fruit.
I swing in a red-hazy void, I sway
With tides of blind heat. From a far-off sphere,
Like scratchings on a pillow, voices I hear
And thundering waves and thuds of passing feet;

For there, out there beyond me, lads and girls
In dazzling colours and with gleaming skin
Through sands of gold and surfs of opal run;
They dive beneath the long green claw which curls
Above them; on the white comber they shoot
Shoreward; many in a slow spiral melt
Like me into oblivion under the sun.

CONTEMPORARY

Seeing Life in a Suva Bus

Lema Low

Lema Low is Fijian, first publishing in 1962.

Visitors to Fiji, expatriates and permanent residents, should not, under any circumstances, fail to enjoy the experience of riding in a local bus. Any route will suffice to give unforgettable memory, but the most exhilarating are the quick trips around Suva and environs.

There is no better way to see the city and surroundings, except by hiking (and that is a hazardous undertaking in Suva once you leave the region of footpaths).

The first essential is to catch the bus. The rest is reasonably simple. Timetables being rather vague, you can wait for half an hour, half a day, or walk straight on to a bus.

From dawn until 7.30 A.M. a joyrider should not try to get on a town-wards bus, because they're already crammed tight. Nine fifteen A.M. is a good time, as the last lingering civil servant has gone to his day's toil and the only passengers are harried housewives with shopping baskets, and budgets to balance. From 12.30 to 2 P.M. it's a bit of a rat-race, both ways; at 3.30 P.M. school-children are going home, and from 4.30 P.M. until midnight, especially on pay-days, you often have to run the gauntlet of beery breaths.

The driver is usually an Indian, courteous, and phlegmatically inured to any kind of passenger or cargo. He seldom gets temperamental. The space beside his seat is cluttered with taro, bananas, cabbage and shellfish. At each stop, he waits patiently while the disembarking passenger fumbles for his pennies and disentangles his cabbage from someone else's shellfish.

His radio blares programmes in Hindi, Fijian and English, providing an exciting accompaniment as the bus speeds along Suva's narrow streets.

You get a lovely view into a colourful garden. Another bus surges towards yours with no visible slackening of speed, and you close your eyes in fearful anticipation. There's no more than a sheet of paper between buses as they pass, but your driver never stops chewing gum. *You* must be nervy.

The bus passengers present a fascinating study: expressive faces, and mellow voices reflect their thoughts and emotions. You receive an impression of grace and relaxation. Two Indian men will start a conversation in their own language and finish it in perfect English.

There will be a Fijian chatting with a Chinese, a Tongan with a Gilbertese, a

Samoan with a Rotuman, a European with a Fijian – indicative of the surface amity in which the people live, although underneath there are dissensions which all are trying to solve.

The bus has an intoxicating perfume of coconut oil, hair pomade, face cream, soap and shoe polish, mingling with the fish, fruit and vegetables. The thought occurs to you that if this highly concentrated aroma could be bottled, it would cure anything.

The passengers are attired in a kaleidoscope of colour, and in all styles, ranging from sulus to saris. And the buses themselves, apparently not to be outdone, wear all sorts of intriguing insignia, such as leaping greyhounds, blooming water-lilies, jet aircraft, sleepy lagoons, hearts and arrows – and rude, scribbled remarks in several languages.

So – you pay your money and you take your choice. It's all the fun of the fair, costs only a few pence and will be an experience that you will long remember.

Suva Market

Sam Simpson

Sam Simpson is a Fijian author, first publishing in 1974.

At the centre of the city,
Suva boasts a Market
Its belly bursting obese.
A jostling throng,
A merry motley of people.

Pacific peasants, noble and humble,
Colourful as cocktail.
Bare feet, seared with clay
Fresh from the teitei.

SOUTH PACIFIC

I hear someone say,
Ya vica, sa vinaka.
Another, turbaned and toga
Boasts an eastern flavour to savour
Squatting like a yogi eating air.
Saris with a hue of blue and gold
Bodies blessed with bangles and with beads,
Odour of mystery and spices.

Fruit, root crops, vegetables
Fresh from tree, soil, garden
Mellow, blush and burden
With sap, syrup and starch
Ready for the housewife and kitchen.
Melody in tranquillity
Witness to Fiji's rich diversity.
It is here that east and west
Meet and fete with understanding.

Where Are These People Going?

Allain Jaria

Until 1968 Papua New Guineans were silent in the literary world. However, in 1968, after the publication of Albert Maori Kiki's autobiography, *Kiki: Ten Thousand Years in a Lifetime,* New Guinean students showed a sudden interest in telling their story. Their writing was simple and direct, having little concern for rhetoric. In 1972, Allain Jaria, a young man studying to be a priest, wrote "Where are these people going?" – a simple, unpretentious piece of writing about the problems in a changing society.

On Saturday afternoons Koki Market was always crowded. On this particular Saturday, Iosepa moved restlessly among the crowds rather than stand still. After a time he made his way from the centre of the busy market seaward to feel the refreshing saline breeze from the sea. Then he made towards the gravelled road intending to catch a bus but the bus, already full, wobbled past him. Now he would have to wait around for another bus. On second thought he abandoned the idea and walked back into the crowds.

The full heat of the day was upon him. The rows of market stalls seemed at the point of catching fire. Iosepa placed a hand through his unbuttoned shirt and felt the streaming sweat on his body. He again paced restlessly about, pausing now and then as if looking for something to buy, but really he was searching around to see if he could find some familiar faces. Earlier, he had already bought a few betelnuts.

He did not know how long he wandered about the market, but the sun was slanting to the west when Iosepa made his way back to the bus stop. It was cooler now. Five, ten, fifteen minutes passed and still no Kila Kila bus came along. Other people were waiting, too, some casually walking up and down, others just standing or sitting. Iosepa waited with them; what else could he do? He wanted to read something, a newspaper perhaps, but this was not customary. He had never seen anyone reading while waiting, ever. Somehow, sometime, somebody must start this – if someone did this then others would follow. At last the bus arrived and he dropped this line of thinking.

Leaving the bus on reaching his destination, he walked to his uncle's compound. The huts and dwellings were not built like a neat, permanent village, but sprawled untidily over the valley. They gave Iosepa the impression they would shift and move on their own at any minute. Entering his uncle's hut he sat on the floor. The only light in the room was from a lantern hanging from a nail in the timber wall.

"You are late again, Iosepa Aida Mona," warned his uncle, Mona Paulo. "When night is near we should all be safely in the compound. The town is no safe place for walking alone in the dark. . . . You hear that, don't you?"

Iosepa Aida Mona acknowledged his uncle's warning only by a slow movement of his head. He was tired after his wanderings about the market in the hot sun, and also because of waiting so long for the bus.

"Now tell me why you were late," Mona Paulo continued.

"I went to Koki Market to see if I could see some of our people," Iosepa replied. "As you know, Saturday is the best day when most of the people go out and can be seen." After a pause, he said, "I have not seen many of our people since my last holiday."

"It is not like a village where you can meet and talk to everybody," his uncle put in. "Here they are scattered all over the town, but I know where most of them live."

"Has this been your home since you came from our place?" Iosepa asked his uncle.

"No, I was at Brown River when I left home," Mona Paulo told his nephew. "I worked there for some time before coming to Konedobu, where Newtown now stands. It was there that I met your aunty. The huts were shifted from there to here. This is my third home and we do not know where we will be going next." After a short silence, "We just seem to be moving from place to place with no fixed village. It is hard going, isn't it son?" He continued gravely, "In these times it is the educated man who has the promising future. You must not leave school. You must learn everything before you come out of school."

"After your marriage, if I had been you," Iosepa said, "I would have gone back to the village. There you could have had a good home in a quiet and peaceful place."

"Sonny, I often think that way, too," Mona Paulo replied as he leaned against the wall. "I would like to take my family back home to the village where we could have a garden and a permanent home; where your cousins could grow up." He paused thoughtfully. "Gardening is always on my mind. We tried gardening at the back of Moresby town, but it didn't work." He went on with a change of voice. "In any case, more and more people are moving into town. I do not see why I should go back home. We think that the councillors and government officials are neglecting us instead of showing us how to make proper gardens and villages." He added sharply, "On some kind of modern planning basis."

"If our people think about what they are doing," commented Iosepa, "and where they are going, surely they will follow the right path." He continued thoughtfully. "People from all corners of the country come to Port Moresby to see and admire development. But so many radical changes make us confused. The Government and Missions do not seem able to face these radical changes. This capital town is centralized, and I hope will become the home, the museum of clan cultures in the future."

"Quite true," Mona Paulo answered. "Moresby is expanding and it will go on expanding. This is where we can find employment. There are no attractions in the village. What can we look forward to there?"

They had their supper, simple but enjoyable. The black coffee was good, hot and strong. It made Iosepa think that one always got some new strength from drinking black coffee.

After eating, Iosepa Aida Mona stretched out on the mattress and tried to fall asleep. But his mind was troubled and remained open in the dark. Problems were biting him like fleas, making him lie awake for a long time. After living several weeks with his uncle and his family, Iosepa had got used to their routine of life. Breakfast was sometimes uncertain, so was dinner.

Even with his two years of post-primary education, it was not easy for Iosepa to find a job in town during this vacation. He had gone around looking for a job continuously, but it seemed there were no job vacancies. He had to rely on his uncle's generosity for food and housing. Iosepa Aida Mona needed money to pay for his clothes, also his school fees. Besides, there were other little luxuries that a secondary student should have. No school fees meant that the school door would be closed against him. . . . And what if he failed. . . . ?

He knew his uncle could not help him very much, since the seven dollars and fifty cents a fortnight which his uncle earned, was not enough to support his family, let alone an extra mouth. Iosepa found it hard to sleep, and rolling over he opened his eyes. He saw his uncle was sitting quietly nearby.

"I thought you had gone to bed, uncle," he said.

"No," replied Mona Paulo. "I usually go to bed early during the week, but tomorrow is Sunday."

"How long have you been in this house?" Iosepa asked.

"That is a very interesting question. I'll roll some tobacco and smoke and tell you the story of this house," his uncle said.

Iosepa Aida Mona waited while his uncle gently rolled his smoke, lit it from the lantern, folded his legs in cross-fashion, then cleared his throat to speak.

"I occupied this hut two years ago, but it had been lived in before that. It was deserted when a woman died here. Some months after her death I asked your aunty if it would be all right to come and live here. One evening after work, we packed our belongings and moved into this compound. On the way I picked up a stone and held it in the palm of my hand. When we came within a stone's throw of this hut, I told your aunty and cousins to stand still. Then I threw the stone and it made a loud noise when it fell on the tin roof, and this frightened away the dead woman's spirit."

Iosepa watched his uncle intently and waited for him to go on. "In the stillness of the evening," he continued, "we could clearly hear the clanging of an empty pot, followed by the slamming of a door. I knew what the others were feeling."

" 'She is gone,' were my only words. I led the way into the house and the others followed very closely. That first night was very frightening. Some of the other people around were afraid to come to us, some told us we were looking for trouble, but their fears have now been conquered."

"Where do you think the woman's spirit has gone"? Iosepa asked eagerly.

"Who knows?" Mona Paulo said. "Maybe she has gone home; or she could still be around here. All we know is that she left this house on the very evening when I threw the stone."

Iosepa had been praised at school for his high marks on his knowledge of the subject of Christian religion. But now he could not express what was in his mind. Instead he dubiously asked a question.

"Do you think that people who die have another hidden life near us?"

"Why not?" replied his uncle. "Why do people at home renew death rituals when they gather the first fruits of the garden? We walk, we work, we plant with our ancestors – with the spirits. When the first fruit, the best produce of our garden is harvested, we assemble in the village to share with them."

"Is that the reason why you do not bury relatives in Port Moresby?"

"Yes, even though we have left our villages and clans behind, we do not like to bury our dead in strange ground," said Mona Paulo through curls of tobacco smoke.

"How did that stone frighten the spirit out of this house?"

"Because that stone had power."

"How?"

"Because I gave the power to the stone," Mona Paulo continued. "I have seen stones with the power to give abundant fruits to the gardens. And through the power of the stone has come money and fat pigs."

"Why don't you grow pigs in the garden?" asked Iosepa, smiling.

Both of them laughed.

"Well, you might convince a *white child* that pigs grow in the garden," Mona Paulo said, then continued seriously. "However, this was not planned at the beginning by Tsidib, our creator. Things must follow the order decided by Tsidib, our God."

He went on carefully. "There is a legend which says that once we could pluck the leg off a pig for meat at will. But the way to do it, in order to get the meat from the live pig, was not carried out in the right way by two people – a man and his sister of the same blood. They disobeyed the instruction and Tsidib became very angry and stopped them. The power was taken away from our people. In certain things, yes, we can do it because we have the spirit world behind us; in other things we cannot do it. This is the mystery of our life and existence. Sometimes we would like to preserve our very lives from perishing, but we cannot, because the power has not been given to us. Only Tsidib has it."

"If I died now where would I be?" Iosepa asked jokingly. "I think it would be very interesting for me to be around with you – and see how you express your views on death."

"And I think, son, you had better try to sleep now."

Iosepa Aida Mona rolled himself in his bed sheet but his mind wandered. Tomorrow he would be back on his way to school; this was his last night in his uncle's house.

He listened to the natural orchestra in his mind playing short, strange pieces. There were so many problems moving steadily in his mind like black fogs. Many of the boys with whom he had grown up were no longer in the village. They had scattered. The future backbone of the clan had been burnt; the embers blown away by the wind. With them went the village society which once was strong and intact. Where is the basic unity of the family to which the next generation will owe its existence? Where are we going to build the model of our present and future generations? No one any longer believes in the villages.

This vast, expanding town of Port Moresby, strung with great spreading slums and gardens that extend for miles around – will this be the future founder of family units, and the vestiges of clan cultures?" This is where the people are coming to. This is where they'll secure their very precious lives. And then, after that. . . .?

"Where are we going?" Deeper and deeper Iosepa sank into the mud of this thought, then, when he tried to rise to the top, he heard his uncle's words. "We walk, we work, we plant with our ancestors – with the spirits. Both the living and the dead share the first fruits of the garden."

Maybe after all, there is no difference and death is only after a visual absence of some people. It is only an accident; after all we live in a spirit world. We have vague glimpses of destination through dim mirrors. Where can we find another mirror that will present a true, vivid life? We know where we are going, but in a whizz-wazzy sort of way.

"Where are you going? Who is going to take your place after you have gone?" The village clan wanted him to get married; to hand on the heritage of the clan. If not, the clan would make him an outcast. Iosepa dreaded this.

Iosepa was totally confused. It was dark and gloomy and seemingly hopeless as he tried to linger upon some of the queer ideas that chained his mind. He listened to the orchestra and tried to fit his tune. In the midst of this he fell asleep.

Further Reading

Eri, V., *The Crocodile.* Middlesex, England: Penguin Books Ltd., 1970

Wendt, A., *Sons for the Return Home.* Auckland: Longman Paul Ltd., 1973

Ihimaera, W., *Tangi.* Toronto: Heinemann Educational Books Ltd., 1973

Beier, U., *The Night Warrior.* Melbourne: Jacaranda Press Ltd., 1972

Beier, U., *Words of Paradise.* Melbourne: Sun Books Ltd., 1972

Douglas, S., and Davis, B., *Best Australian Short Stories.* Victoria: Hawthorn, Lloyd O'Neil, 1971

Goodman, R., and Johnstone, G., *The Australians.* Sydney: Rigby, 1967

Sinclair, K., *History of New Zealand.* Harmondsworth: Penguin, 1959

Hart, R., and Reed, A.W., *Maori Legends.* Wellington Place: A.H. & A.W. Reed, 1972

Stead, C.K., *New Zealand Short Stories.* Wellington: Oxford University Press, 1966

LIST OF SELECTIONS

Abiku 203
Anancy 149
And This, At Last 235
At the River 316

Benefit Concert, The 22
Blackout 192
Broken Globe, The 130

Cabuliwalah 268
Calypsonian 173
Canadian Personality, The 98
Country Town 364
Crookest Raffle Ever Run, The 332
Cynddylan on a Tractor 51

Dasi The Bridegroom 288
Day of the Butterfly 117
Dead Men's Path 230
Death of an Outport 89
Depression Flashback 1937 85
Digging 45

Fight, The 34
Flame-Heart 151

Game of Cards, A 324
Gentlemen of the Jungle, The 226
Gitanjali 259

Good Old Uncle Albert 106
Grandfather 71

Highland Graveyard 41

In the Beginning 311
In Youth Is Pleasure 340

Jamaica Market 198
Jamaican Fragment 189

Lament for the Dorsets 82
Lancashire Winter 44
Letter, The 278

Man In Society 56
Man Who Caught the Wind, The 322
Man's a Man for A' That, A 39
Meditation on Man, A 249
Miracle 263
Mr. Portingale 73
My Heart Soars 67

New Life in Kyerefaso 217

On Learning to Be an Indian 295
Once upon a Time 246

Peasant, A   43
Penny in the Dust   75
Piano and Drums   243
Pink House in the Town, The   355
Pocomania   153
Poem for My Country   155

Rain Came, The   205

Seeing Life in a Suva Bus   367
Sensual City, The   111
Street Cries   277
Sunbather, The   366
Suva Market   369

Telephone Conversation   245
Titus, Hoyt, I.A.   157
T'Match   17
To Reach the Sea   52

What Is Our Aim   47
Where Are These People Going   371
Woman Selling Handicrafts
   outside Bruns Philp's Doors, To the   362

LIST OF AUTHORS

Achebe, Chinua 230

Bain, Kenneth 311
Bowering, George 71
Buckler, Ernest 75
Burns, Robert 39

Churchill, Winston S. 47
Connor, Tony 44

Davis, Rhys 22
Desbarats, Peter 111
Dhumektu 278
Dickens, Monica 52
Duggal, Kartar Singh 263
Duggan, Maurice 340

Fairbridge, Wolfe 322

George, Chief Dan 67
Grace, Patricia 316

Hardy, Frank 332
Heaney, Seamus 45
Hendricks, A. L. 189
Hutchison, Bruce 98

Ihimaera, Witi 324

Jaria, Allain 371

Kaunda, Kenneth 249
Kenyatta, Jomo 226
Kreisel, Henry 130

Low, Lema 367

Mais, Roger 192
Malifa, Sano 362
Maxwell-Hall, Agnes 198
Menzies, A.F. 85
Mowat, Farley 106
Munro, Alice 117
McCourt, Edward A. 73
McKay, Claude 151
McFarlane, Basil Clare 155

Naidu, Sarojini 277
Naipaul, V.S. 157
Nagenda, John 235
Narayan, R.K. 288

Ogot, Grace A. 205
Okara, G. 243, 246

Pittman, Al 89
Priestley, J.B. 17
Purdy, Alfred 82

Raine, Kathleen   41
Rau, Santha Rama   295

Salkey, Andrew   149
Selvon, Samuel   173
Sherlock, P.M.   153
Simpson, Sam   369
Snow, Charles P.   56
Soyinka, Wole   203, 245
Sutherland, Efua Theodora   217

Tagore, Rabindranath   259, 268
Thompson, John   366
Thomas, Dylan   34
Thomas, R.S.   43, 51

Wendt, Albert   355
Wright, Judith   364

Farley Mowat, "Good Old Uncle Albert," from NEVER CRY WOLF, by Farley Mowat, reprinted by permission of The Canadian Publishers, McClelland and Stewart Limited, Toronto.

Sarojini Naidu, "Street Cries," from THE SCEPTRED FLUTE, by Sarojini Naidu, published by William Heinemann Ltd. Reprinted by permission of William Heinemann Ltd.

V. S. Naipaul, "Titus Hoyt, I.A.," from MIGUEL STREET, by V. S. Naipaul, 1971. Reprinted by permission of Andre Deutsch Limited.

Gabriel Okara, "Once Upon a Time," from POEMS FROM BLACK AFRICA, edited by Langston Hughes, published by Indiana University Press. Reprinted by permission of Indiana University Press.

Al Pittman, "Death of an Outport." Reprinted by permission of the author.

J. B. Priestley, "T'Match," from ESSAYS OF FIVE DECADES, by J. B. Priestley, published by William Heinemann Ltd. Reprinted by permission of William Heinemann Ltd.

Al Purdy, "Lament for the Dorsets," from WILD GRAPE WINE, by Al Purdy, reprinted by permission of The Canadian Publishers, McClelland and Stewart Limited, Toronto.

Kathleen Raine, "Highland Graveyard," from THE HOLLOW HILL, copyright © 1965 by Kathleen Raine (Hamish Hamilton, London).

Santha Ramu Rau, "On Learning to be an Indian." Reprinted by permission of Harper & Row Publishers, India.

Sir Charles G. D. Roberts, "The Skater," from THE COLLECTED POEMS OF SIR CHARLES G. D. ROBERTS. Reprinted by permission of McGraw Hill Ryerson Limited.

Sam Selvon, "Calypsonian," reprinted by permission of the author.

Wole Soyinka, "Abiku," from IDANRE AND OTHER POEMS, by Wole Soyinka, published by Eyre Methuen. © Wole Soyinka, 1967.

Wole Soyinka, "Telephone Conversations," Reprinted by permission of African Universities Press.

Rabindranath Tagore, excerpts from GITANJALI, and "The Cabuliwallah," from A TAMGORE READER, by Rabindranath Tagore, published by Macmillan. Reprinted by permission of The Trustees of the Tagore Estate and Macmillan London and Basingstoke.

Dylan Thomas, "The Fight," from PORTRAIT OF THE ARTIST AS A YOUNG DOG, by Dylan Thomas, published by J. M. Dent & Sons. Reprinted by permission of J. M. Dent & Sons (Canada) Limited.

R. S. Thomas, "A Peasant," and "Cynddylan on a Tractor," from SELECTED POEMS, by R. S. Thomas, published by Hart-Davis MacGibbon/Granada Publishing Limited. Reprinted by permission of Granada Publishing Limited.

Albert Wendt, "The Pink House in the Town," from FLYING FOX IN A FREEDOM TREE, by Albert Wendt, published by Longman Paul (Pacific Paperbacks). Reprinted by permission of Longman Group Limited.

Judith Wright, "Country Town" from COLLECTED POEMS 1942-1970 by Judith Wright. Reprinted by permission of Angus & Robertson Publishers, Sydney.

While every effort has been made to trace the owners of copyrighted material and to make due acknowledgement, the publishers would be grateful for information enabling them to correct any omissions in future editions.